One True God

◆

ONE TRUE GOD

HISTORICAL CONSEQUENCES OF
MONOTHEISM

◆

RODNEY STARK

PRINCETON UNIVERSITY PRESS

PRINCETON AND OXFORD

Library of Congress Cataloging-in-Publication Data

Stark, Rodney.
One true God : historical consequences of monotheism / Rodney Stark.
p. cm.
Includes bibliographical references and index.
ISBN 0-691-08923-X (hardcover : alk. paper)
1. Monotheism. 2. God. I. Title.
BL221.S75 2001
291.1′4—dc21   2001021128

British Library Cataloging-in-Publication Data is available

This book has been composed in Sabon with Albertus MT LT Display

Printed on acid-free paper. ∞

www.pup.princeton.edu

Printed in the United States of America

1 3 5 7 9 10 8 6 4 2

Contents

◆

✦ Illustrations ✦

◆ Acknowledgments ◆

Books are written in solitude, but the scholarly life is not entirely solitary. I must especially acknowledge Roger Finke, Laurence Iannaccone, Patrick MacNamara, and Alan Miller for so frequently brightening my day. I thank the following for many years of friendship and advice: William Sims Bainbridge, Eileen Barker, James Beckford, David Bromley, Marion Goldman, Andrew Greeley, Jeffrey Hadden, Eva Hamberg, Phillip Hammond, Irving Hexham, Dean Hoge, Daniel Jackson, Benton Johnson, Graeme Lang, Armand Mauss, Gordon Melton, Mansoor Moaddel, Robert L. Montgomery, Karla Poewe, Thomas Robbins, Darren Sherkat, William Silverman, William Swatos, Melinda Wagner, Ruth Wallace, Michael Williams, and Bryan Wilson. I also thank some scholars of more recent association, including Christopher Bader, Ulrich Berner, Eli Berman, Sean Everton, Paul Froese, Anthony Gill, Rosemary Hopcroft, Lutz Kaelber, Julie Manville, Susan Pitchford, Mark Regnerus, Mareleyn Schneider, Christian Smith, Pino Luca Trombetta, James Wellman, and Robert Woodberry.

I am especially indebted to Jeffrey Burton Russell and to John Simpson, both of whom read the manuscript for the publisher and, having fully grasped what I was trying to accomplish, made some splendid suggestions.

Brigitta van Rheinberg, editor of history and religion at Princeton University Press, has been a constant source of enthusiastic support and inspired insights, for which I am very grateful. For the second time I have had the privilege of working with Princeton's Senior Editor Lauren Lepow, who brings taste and an amazing range of scholarship to every manuscript she touches.

February 14, 2001
Corrales, New Mexico

One True God

♦

Holy City. Jerusalem is crowded with sites regarded as sacred by each of the three great monotheisms. Here Jews pray at the Wailing Wall, all that remains of the Temple after its destruction by Romans in the year 70. Behind it rises the Dome of the Rock, sheltering the spot from which Muslims believe Muhammad ascended to heaven. Elsewhere in the city is the Church of the Holy Sepulchre, believed to cover the tomb where Jesus lay before the Resurrection.
© Annie Griffiths Belt/CORBIS.

The God of the universe is the God of history.
—Martin Buber

More than three thousand years ago, somewhere a group of people began to worship One God. Whether they were Jews, Persians, Egyptians, or someone else will probably never be known, but perhaps no other single innovation had so much impact on history. Consequently, while many wonderful books have made the last decade an exciting time for anyone interested in broad assessments of the past, I was prompted by their example to write a reminder that history is not shaped by "material" factors alone. Granted, germs, geography, printing, sailing ships, steel, and climate have mattered, but probably none of them so much as human ideas about the Gods.*

All of the great monotheisms propose that their God works through history, and I plan to show that, at least sociologically, they are quite right: that a great deal of history—triumphs as well as disasters—has been made on behalf of One True God. What could be more obvious? Well, one thing more obvious is that writing about the social effects of Gods just isn't done these days. It is widely assumed in scholarly circles that historical inquiries into such matters as the social consequences of monotheism are long outmoded and quite unsuitable. Of course, many who hold these views are the same ones who continue to express their certainty

---

* Being a traditionalist in matters of style, I decided it was appropriate to capitalize "God" when referring to the deity of one of the great monotheisms. This proved needlessly invidious, so I have capitalized "God" and "Gods" in all cases (but not "godlings"). I assume that Gods can be of either or no gender, and therefore I have not used the term "Goddess" except in several instances where I refer to a specifically female deity such as Isis.

1

that religion is rapidly dying out, while shielding their eyes and ears against the obvious signs of religious vigor all around them (Stark, 1999c). Invincible biases are regrettable, but there is a bright side to this one: It has afforded me the opportunity to reopen a subject that has been neglected for many decades during which a great deal of very important new material has been assembled and more powerful social scientific tools have been developed.

However, rather than just plunge into the tasks at hand, I thought it useful to offer a preliminary sketch of the chapters to come.

Chapter 1 is devoted to a theory of Gods. Why do humans care about Gods at all? What sorts of Gods have the greatest appeal? Why will people accept an exclusive relationship with One God, rather than pursue blessings from a pantheon of specialized Gods? Why has each of the great monotheisms taught not only that the One God is surrounded by a vast supporting cast, but that there exist very powerful evil supernatural beings? In short, what really constitutes monotheism?

Building on this theoretical base, Chapter 2 explores the missionizing imperative. Many faiths spread, but only monotheisms are able to sustain organized efforts by the rank and file to convert others. How has this shaped history? Why did Buddhism die out in India, its land of origin? What was the impact of Jewish missionizing on the Greco-Roman world? Why did medieval efforts to Christianize northern Europe fail? Did Islam really convert most of the people of the Middle East and North Africa in only a few years, or was this an illusion? How did images of God enter into the resumption of Christian world missionizing in the nineteenth century, and do they explain why some denominations have dropped out of the mission enterprise? And what about Hindu missions to the West?

Chapter 3 shifts the focus from conversion to repression. When and why does monotheism generate bloody and brutal conflicts? Having constructed a model to predict when monotheisms will attack or tolerate other faiths, I then apply it to the sudden outburst of fatal attacks on Jews that began in 1096, not only in Christian Europe but also in Islamic societies. I further assess why vigorous efforts by the Church and the State in this era to prevent attacks on Jews were successful in most of Europe but failed in the towns and cities along both sides of the Rhine River. I also seek the reasons for the "rediscovery" of heresy that occurred in Europe at precisely the same time.

If commitment to One True God makes groups militant in their efforts to overcome competing faiths, it makes them equally militant to retain their faith when they are a minority. Thus Chapter 4 attempts to explain how the Jewish diaspora was possible. How were the Jews so often able to withstand all efforts to convert them? Why, on many occasions, did entire Jewish communities commit suicide rather than convert? Here it proves especially useful to explore circumstances in which Jewish communities did assimilate (as in China) or did so to a substantial extent. The chapter concludes with an extended survey of Jewish assimilation in the United States.

Finally, Chapter 5 demonstrates how the potential for conflict can be muffled, even among militant monotheisms, by public norms of civility. Here the emphasis will be on the American experience with religious pluralism.

This is the first of a projected two volumes on the social consequences of monotheism. Both will be very historical, but this volume will be more purely historical, and the second will pay greater attention to slightly more cultural matters such as science, witchcraft, and the Reformation. Both volumes span sociology, history, and comparative religion. Assuming that few readers will be specialists in all three areas, I have written for nonspecialists. An additional reason for my doing so is that I believe writing for the general reader results in better scholarship. Jargon mainly deludes its users into thinking they have said something—if I can't say something in clear prose, I assume it's because I don't understand it.

It is appropriate here that I confess I am not a historian by trade, and no part of this book is based on original historical research. For example, I did not comb medieval manuscripts to demonstrate that Christian missionizing broke down in the fourth century, leaving much of Europe un-Christianized. Instead, I had the pleasure of learning this by reading the work of historians such as Marc Bloch, Jean Delumeau, Alexander Murray, Keith Thomas, and many others. As in that instance, I have depended on the best histo-

3

rians to educate me about any particular historical topic, and I have usually concurred with their interpretations. My contribution consists of assembling these historical pieces into a more comprehensive structure as a test of original sociological theories, which, in turn, are meant to illuminate the history.

It also seems appropriate for me to acknowledge that until very recently, nearly all social scientists who studied religion did so from antireligious motives and premised their work on atheism—and many still do (Stark, 1999; Stark and Finke, 2000). This was evident as far back as when Thomas Hobbes, one of the celebrated "founders" of social science, dismissed all religion as "credulity," "ignorance," and "lies," and Gods as "creatures of . . . fancy" ([1651] 1956, 1:98). A century later, David Hume echoed Hobbes, dismissing all miracles as limited to "ignorant and barbarous nations" ([1748] 1962:123). During the nineteenth century antireligious social science was rampant. August Comte coined the word "sociology" to identify a new field that would replace religious "hallucinations" as the guide to morals ([1830] 1896, 2:554). Then, Ludwig von Feuerbach "discovered" that humans create Gods in their own image ([1841] 1957), while Karl Marx and Friedrich Engels found God in the economy, busy sanctifying "wage slavery" ([1844] 1964). At the start of the twentieth century, the famous French sociologist Emile Durkheim taught that the fundamental reality is that society itself is always the true object of religious worship: "god . . . can be nothing else than [society] itself, personified and represented to the imagination" (1915:206). Next came Sigmund Freud, who explained on *one page* of his celebrated psychoanalytic exposé of faith, *The Future of an Illusion*, that religion is an "illusion," a "sweet—or bittersweet—poison," a "neurosis," an "intoxicant," and "childishness to be overcome" ([1927] 1961:88). Even more recently, no reviewer as much as flinched when, on the first page of his book *Mystical Experience*, Ben-Ami Scharfstein (1973:1) revealed that "mysticism is . . . a name for the paranoid darkness in which unbalanced people stumble so confidently," and went on to identify the supernatural as a "fairy tale" (ibid.:45). In similar fashion, Oxford's distinguished Bryan Wilson (1975:81) identified "supernaturalist thinking" as an "indulgence." And from Louvain, Lilliane Voyé and Karel Dobbelaere (1994:95) recently announced that "the successful removal by science of all kinds of anthropomorphisms from our thinking dooms the concept of 'God as a person.' "

Our having access only to the human side of religion does not justify the assumption that religion is but illusion and that the Gods are imaginary products of "wish fulfillment." It is entirely impossible for science to discover the existence or nonexistence of Gods. Therefore, atheistic *and* theistic assumptions are equally unscientific, and work based on either is equally deficient. One is, of course, entitled to one's private convictions, but it is important to try to minimize their impact on one's scientific work. The appropriate *scientific* assumption, and the one I have made every effort to observe, is *agnostic*: scientifically speaking, we do not know and cannot know whether, for example, the Qur'ān was spoken to Muhammad by an angel or merely by his own inner voices. And, scientifically speaking, it doesn't matter! Our only access is to the human side of religious phenomena, and we can examine this with the standard tools of social science, *without* assuming either the real or the illusory nature of religion. The result will be better science, since both the atheistic and the theistic assumptions are faith-driven and often less than responsive to evidence. I suspect this was the point Max Weber had in mind when, after writing that he was "absolutely unmusical religiously," he added, "But a thorough self-examination has told me that I am neither antireligious *nor irreligious*" (his emphasis, in Swatos, 1998:548).*

Finally, even if they abide by the agnostic assumption, social scientists are unlikely to grasp the human side of phenomena for which they have no empathy. While it obviously isn't necessary that social scientists who want to understand religion be religious, it is necessary that they be able to sufficiently suspend their disbelief so as to gain some sense of the phenomenology of faith and worship. Even Emile Durkheim seems eventually to have accepted this. In remarks made to a meeting of "free thinkers" in 1914, he ex-

---

* The phrase about being "unmusical religiously" is often quoted, but only once have I ever encountered his next sentence.

pressed it this way: "[W]hat I ask of the free thinker is that he should confront religion in the same mental state as the believer . . . [H]e who does not bring to the study of religion a sort of religious sentiment cannot speak about it! He is like a blind man trying to talk about color" ([1915] 1995:xvii). This was not Durkheim's view when he was young, nor was it mine. But, just as Durkheim came to a more mature outlook, so have I.

It is in this spirit that I invite you to examine some of the direct consequences of monotheism on our common history.

Father of the Gods. This artistic re-creation of the Temple of Zeus shows how the giant statue of the God, seated on his throne, overwhelmed those who came to worship. However, the Greeks did not believe this statue to be Zeus himself but merely his representation. © Christel Gerstenberg/CORBIS.

. 1 .

God's *Nature*: A Theory of Gods

And God said unto Moses, I AM THAT I AM.
—Exod. 3:14

All religions involve conceptions of the supernatural. Most people in all societies believe that there is *something* that somehow is above, beyond, over, or otherwise superior to the natural world. But, beyond this vague generalization, there is unending conflict about what the supernatural is like, and intense disputes concerning what it does, if anything.

Notice that I have not suggested that all religions are based on belief in supernatural *beings*. They are not. Nor are all systems of beliefs about the supernatural properly termed religions. Some such systems are merely magic, not religion, and within magic the supernatural is little more than an exotic property of various inanimate objects, symbols, incantations, or rites. Moreover, magic fails to provide any general account of existence, which all religions do (Stark, 1965c, 1999a; Stark and Bainbridge, 1985; [1987] 1996). But even among religions there is immense variation in conceptions of the supernatural.

In some religions the supernatural is conceived of as an omnipresent *essence* or principle governing all life, but as impersonal, remote, and definitely not a being. The Tao is an example. Is it merely a philosophical principle? Is it the origin of heaven and earth? Nonexistent? Always existent? Unnameable? The name that can be named? Of yin or yang? To each, the answer is yes, according to the *Lao-tzu*. Which is why the Tao is best described as an essence. However, religions based on essences are not found only in the East. Many Western intellectuals, including some theo-

9

logians and bishops, have reduced their conception of "God" to an essence as impersonal as Immanuel Kant's (*1724–1804*),* of which he wrote: "God is not a being outside me, but merely a thought in me . . . God must be represented not as substance outside me, but as the highest moral principle in me" ([ca. 1800] 1929:373–74).

Although many scholars of comparative religion are content to do so, it strikes me as inappropriate to identify supernatural essences as Gods. I am comfortable with the claim that Taoism, for example, is a *religion*, but it seems unwise to identify the Tao as a God. Indeed, for centuries sophisticated devotees of Buddhism, Taoism, and Confucianism have claimed that theirs are *Godless* religions. I agree. But it must also be noted that Godless religions are unable to gather a mass following, always being limited in their appeal to small, intellectual elites. The reasons are obvious. Neither the Tao nor Kant's "thought" nor any other divine essence is a suitable exchange partner, as it takes no notice of the individual or, indeed, of anything. Because divine essences can do nothing on behalf of humans—provide no benefits or blessings—they are not the object of sacrifices, supplications, or worship. Rather, divine essences inspire only meditation and ritual—often accompanied by an abundance of magic.

At a minimum, the term "God" ought to refer to *beings*. Hence: *Gods* are *conscious supernatural beings*. If further justification of this definition of God is needed, throughout this volume I will demonstrate that, in terms of social consequences, there is no more profound religious difference than that between faiths involving divine beings and those limited to divine essences.

Indeed, because only divine beings *do* anything, religions are also distinguished as to whether they are "revealed" or "natural." That is, some religions derive from truths "discerned within the natural order," whereas revealed religion "comes from a source other than

* During the course of the book we will meander over more than three thousand years of history, all of the major continents, and many subjects. Because I sometimes got confused about who was when, it seemed appropriate to ease the burden on readers by providing the dates for every significant person mentioned in the text who lived and did his or her primary work before 1930. Dates will be placed at the first substantial reference to the person, not at the first mention if it is only incidental.

that of the human recipient, usually God" (Bowker, 1997:814). Consequently, there is an immense difference in the *authority* attributed to various systems of religious doctrine: On what grounds are they regarded as true? The authority of Buddhist doctrines, for example, rests on human wisdom, often stated in terms of what a particular master concluded about what it all means. But in the Torah we read, "The Lord said to Moses." Or, a further example, Chuang Tzu (*ca. 369–286* B.C.E.)* taught what he had intuited about the Tao, while Muhammad (*570?–632*) taught what he had been told.

Moreover, from the sociological point of view, Godless religions are of far less significance than might be assumed given the immense amount of attention paid to their scriptures by scholars of comparative religion. Although Godless religions are attributed to major societies such as China and Japan, as already noted only tiny elites within these societies have ever actually pursued them in their pure form (Ch'en, 1964; Lester, 1993; Parrinder, 1983; Smart, 1984). In imperial China, the forms of Taoism, Buddhism, and Confucianism practiced in various monasteries and among court philosophers and other such intellectuals were Godless, but most people associated an abundant pantheon of divine beings with the Taoist, Buddhist, and Confucian ideals. Indeed, even when backed by imperial power, attempts by Chinese philosophers to exclude all Gods from Taoism failed to withstand the existential concerns of the general public. According to Geoffrey Parrinder (1983:337): "Whatever the official religion taught, people still sought for personal relationships with gods and spirits of a personal and individual kind. And belief in such deities . . . provided for the religious needs which the philosophers and the official religions had bypassed." The same is true of Buddhism. Buddha (*563–483* B.C.E.) himself rejected the existence of supernatural beings, but popular

---

* It has become conventional to use B.C.E. (Before the Common Era) rather than B.C. (Before Christ), on grounds that the latter is too "parochial." I have willingly adopted the new usage, although it needs to be recognized that *all* calendars are parochial in this sense, and the current year is thousands of years later on the Chinese and Jewish calendars than on the Western calendar, and six centuries earlier on the Muslim calendar. I have not used any designation for years in the "Common Era" on grounds that it can be assumed that all years not identified as B.C.E. belong to the era that was once designated as A.D.

Buddhism sustains an impressive array of Gods (Smart, 1984). For a sociologist, then, the Godless forms of Taoism, Buddhism, or Confucianism are of very limited interest, for they exist primarily as *writings*, not as human activities. Indeed, to say that the religion of imperial China was Godless is equivalent to saying that the religion of the United States is Unitarianism. However, even though popular Chinese religion abounds in Gods, do not suppose that they much resemble Allah or Jehovah. Instead, these Chinese Gods and godlings are of very limited power, scope, and virtue (Shahar and Weller, 1996).

By now it should be clear that this chapter is *not* an exercise in comparative religion. While I have read sufficiently in that literature and will cite and quote it often, my real interest is not sacred writings, and I am not at all concerned to create categories that respect all of the nuances and ambiguities in the various conceptions of Gods to be found in history and around the world. No! My goal is to construct a *theory of Gods* that is *sociologically useful*. I wish to identify aspects of the *human images* of God that have differential social results. Consequently, the remainder of this chapter will examine primary aspects of Gods and of exchange relationships between Gods and humans. I will pursue this line of theorizing until I have arrived at conclusions from which each of the subsequent chapters can proceed. Unlike the other chapters, there will be a minimum of historical content here, as I instead pursue relatively abstract theoretical principles.

Supernatural Exchange Relations

Why do humans even care about remote beings inhabiting an unseen world? My answer is utilitarian: Because the supernatural is the only plausible source of many benefits we greatly desire. To say this is *not* to say that Gods are the product of "wishful thinking" (Guthrie, 1996:413). Although I may have seemed to do so in some of my early work, I need not and do not address the question of whether Gods exist. Indeed, one may stipulate the existence of Gods and still ask why humans would care about them, in which

Buddhist Polytheism. Only monks and intellectuals have been able to sustain the Godless religion proposed by Buddah. The popular form of Buddhism includes many Gods, as can be seen in the many deities represented on this altar in a Buddhist temple in Singapore. © Earl & Nazima Kowall/CORBIS.

case my answer would remain the same: People care about Gods because, if they exist, they are potential exchange partners possessed of immense resources. Furthermore, untold billions of people are certain that Gods do exist, precisely because they believe they have experienced long and satisfying exchange relations with them.

I have written at length on the implications of exchange relations between humans and the divine (Stark, 1965a, 1996a, 1999a; Stark and Bainbridge, 1980, [1987] 1996; Stark and Finke, 2000). I will summarize and reorient that theorizing here.

My starting point involves human rationality and reason. We are conscious beings having intentions and desires. We want things. Let's call them "rewards." There also are things we don't want, or want as little of as possible. Let's call them "costs." In pursuit of rewards, we attempt to make rational (i.e., effective and efficient) choices—limited, of course, by our information, by the available options, and by our understanding of what's involved. In addition, of course, our choices are determined by our tastes, which are, in turn, greatly shaped by culture and socialization. Provision must also be made for character—laziness often influences our choices, and impulsiveness may short-circuit our calculations.

Despite the complaints by postmodernists and other opponents of reason, there is nothing radical or new about the assumption that human behavior generally makes sense and is, therefore, relatively predictable. From the moment our earliest ancestors achieved consciousness, this has been the assumption that all humans make about others, withdrawing it only in clear cases of madness. Were our behavior substantially irrational, not only would all of social science be invalid, but social life would be impossible—if the behavior of others were utterly unpredictable, we could not interact. Fortunately, within the suggested boundaries, humans generally act in reasonable ways—*at least as they see it*. This qualifying clause reminds us that, as James Coleman (1990:18) put it, "much of what is ordinarily described as nonrational or irrational is merely so because observers have not discovered the point of view of the actor, from which the action *is* rational."

Obviously, the capacity to act in reasonable ways rests on the ability to reason. Indeed, having memory and intelligence, humans will attempt to formulate explanations about how the world works, and how they can satisfy their needs and desires. By *explanations* I mean *conceptual simplifications or models of reality that often provide plans designed to guide action.*

Because explanations help humans maximize rewards and minimize costs, in and of themselves explanations constitute rewards and will be sought, valued, and retained by humans. Among the many kinds of explanations humans will acquire and value are those concerning the supernatural. These may be identified as *religion*, which I define as consisting of *explanations of the meaning of existence based on supernatural assumptions and including statements about the nature of the supernatural.*

That is, religion tells us the meaning of life (if any) and what the supernatural is like, whether essences or beings, and if the latter, about their character and concerns. Because Gods are conscious beings, they are potential exchange partners because all beings are assumed to want something for which they might be induced to give something valuable. Indeed, the core of Godly religious doctrines consists of explanations about what Gods want and what one must do to earn their blessings. This aspect of religious thought is known as *theology* and consists of *explanations that justify and specify the terms of exchange with Gods,* based on reasoning about *revelations*, which are *communications* believed to come from Gods.

Put another way, theology is the result of *applying reason to revelation* in order to expand understanding of divine concerns and desires, and to increase the range of applications to which that understanding may be applied. This definition is entirely traditional. In *Summa Theologiae* (pt. 1, q. 1, a. 1), Thomas Aquinas (*ca. 1225–1274*) referred to theology as "doctrine about God according to divine revelation," and Karl Rahner (1975:1687) stated the authoritative contemporary Catholic view: "Theology is the *science* of faith. It is the conscious and methodical explanation and explication of the divine revelation." A classic example of such reasoning is the evolution of an elaborate theology concerning Mary despite how little is actually said about her in the New Testament (Pelikan, 1996).

Because divine essences are incapable of exchanges, they may present mysteries, but they pose no tactical questions and thus prompt no effort to discover terms of exchange. Of course, the sacred books of Godless religions also tell us about the divine, but the sacred books of Godly religions claim to report what the divine has to tell us. Eisai (*1141–1215*), the first Zen master, taught what he had *intuited* about the supernatural realm; Joseph Smith (*1805–1844*), the first Mormon, taught what had been *revealed* to him. As Avery Dulles (1992:3) put it: "Judaism, Christianity, and Islam . . . profess to derive their fundamental vision not from mere human speculation, which would be tentative and uncertain, but from God's own testimony—that is to say, from a historically given divine revelation." Indeed, the authority of the Mishnah rests on the Jewish belief that revelations are granted to scholars through their close study of the Torah.

It is important to see that this definition does not reduce theology (or religion) merely to a set of commandments or divine demands. Terms of exchange with God provide the foundation for religious thought, but there will be an extensive collection of ideas, principles, myths, symbols, images, and other elements of religious culture built upon this base. Within the context of clarifying what God wants, theology explains the fundamental meaning of life: how we got here and where we are going.

The crucial aspect of theology is that it consists of a structure of doctrine created by reasoning upon the meaning of knowledge gained from direct communication with a God. That is, Godly religions assume that divine beings not only have desires they wish humans to fulfill, but that they communicate them. Hence theology begins from revelations and consists of trying to reason out the full meaning and implications of divine desires.

It is true, of course, that Godless religions also provide statements concerning the meaning of life, or the lack thereof. But, as noted, these statements constitute *wisdom*, not theology. They originate in introspection and meditation, not through revelation and reasoning. Indeed, religious wisdom tends to place a premium on mystery and to withhold full enlightenment from all but the few. By comparison, theology seeks clarity, and while that often is not achieved, obscurity of expression tends to be seen as the result of human limitations, not as a virtue. In the ideal theology, all doctrines would be absolutely clear and so utterly reasonable as to compel belief. In future work I will pursue this aspect of theology to challenge the notion that there is any intellectual incompatibility between religion and science. Indeed, I will argue that the long heritage of rational Christian theology was the basis for the Scientific Revolution and the rise of the West.

If theology, in effect, tells us what God wants, it is equally important that we understand the other side of this exchange relationship: what do people want from God? To answer, we must acknowledge the most fundamental aspect of the human predicament, namely, that rewards are always in *limited supply*, and some are *entirely unavailable*—at least they are not available here and now through conventional means. The supply of fame and fortune is limited. For someone with a permanent disability or a terminal illness, good health is unavailable. No one possesses the secret of eternal life. In response, humans tend to seek alternative means to overcome limited supplies or complete unavailability. The most common of these involve explanations about how the rewards may be obtained by *recourse to the supernatural*. These involve three general forms: *magic, miracles,* and *otherworldly rewards*.

My attempts to define magic have gone through several versions, but two criteria are adequate to distinguish it from religion: magic lacks a general perspective on existence, and it is not an appeal to the Gods. Rather, magic deals in *impersonal* supernatural forces, often in the belief that such forces are *inherent properties* of particular objects or words—especially written or spoken formulas and incantations (Stark, 1999a; Stark and Finke, 2000).

Since this book is about Gods, magic will be of little interest. Miracles and otherworldly rewards come only from Gods and so are of central concern here.

17

Miracles

Humans approach the Gods for two sorts of rewards: those to be gained in the indefinite future and those to be gained here and now. The latter are miracles: *desirable effects believed not to have been possible except for the intervention of Gods in worldly matters.*

Miracles vary from the quite limited (a specific person's recovery from cancer or survival of a seemingly fatal event) to the immense (the parting of the Red Sea or the sinking of the Chinese invasion fleet by a "divine wind" during its voyage to Japan). All of the major Godly religions accept miracles, but they also regard them as problematic. For example, as they offered prayers for victory, priests of Roman temples did not assure the results of an impending battle. They merely sought the support of their Gods, fully acknowledging that the Gods retain their autonomy and freely choose whether or not to grant a request. Modern-day pregame prayers take the same form—indeed, athletes seldom ask for victory per se. It is assumed that, in deciding to grant a miracle, Gods must consider larger plans or concerns. Many faiths also teach that Gods consider the motives and moral worthiness of the beneficiaries of requested miracles as well as possible unanticipated consequences of their request for the supplicants. Thus the saying "God answers all prayers, but often the answer is no." In this way, even those religious explanations involving worldly rewards are relatively immune to disproof. Nevertheless, things thought to be miracles happen in *this* world. And when something is perceived as a miracle, that greatly reinforces confidence in the entire religious system.

Otherworldly Rewards

The truly immense rewards sought from Gods are to be realized only later and elsewhere. *Otherworldly rewards* are those that are to be obtained from Gods in a *nonempirical (usually posthumous) context.*

Unlike the case of miracles, it is impossible or at least extremely difficult to know whether otherworldly rewards are forthcoming as promised. While that aspect attaches some degree of risk to such rewards, this can be offset by several other crucial features of otherworldly rewards. First of all, nondelivery cannot be observed. Second, otherworldly rewards typically are of far greater magnitude than are miracles. Recovery from cancer is rather minor compared with everlasting life. But perhaps the most significant aspect of otherworldly rewards is that the realization of these rewards is postponed (often until after death). Consequently, in pursuit of otherworldly rewards, humans will accept an *extended exchange relationship* with Gods. That is, humans will make periodic payments over a substantial length of time, often until death.

This is a major factor allowing Godly religions to generate the long-term levels of commitment necessary to sustain strong religious organizations. In contrast, since magic deals in very tangible, this-worldly, relatively immediate rewards, magicians cannot involve their clients in extended exchange relations, which is why, as Emile Durkheim accurately noted, "There is no Church of magic . . . The magician has a clientele and not a church" (1915:44). The same limit applies to Godless religions as well as to those Godly religions having *many* Gods. Godless religions sustain no exchange relations, and hence there can be no Church of Tao, although there are Taoist temples and monasteries, just as there are guilds of magicians (see Chapter 2). Polytheistic religions sustain only short-term exchanges, as humans seek specific and quite immediate benefits from the Gods and spread their risks by shopping around and patronizing multiple "suppliers" (Iannaccone, 1995; Stark and Finke, 2000). Thus Egyptian polytheism generated many temples—each with a clientele—but no Church of Egypt, or even a Church of Osiris. Nor could there be a Church of Rome until Christianity supplanted pagan pluralism.

Images of God

Whether or not people find the prospects of miracles and otherworldly rewards to be plausible depends greatly on what they believe about their source. Consider prayer. Only to the extent that

Divine Cafeteria. In the Temple of Five Hundred Gods, located in Canton, China (until it was destroyed during the Cultural Revolution), suppliants placed a burning incense stick in the porcelain container in front of each God whose aid they sought—often invoking several Gods at the same time.
© Underwood & Underwood/CORBIS.

the hearer is conscious does prayer represent rational exchange behavior, as distinct from superstitious utterances and activities directed toward blind fate such as the use of prayer wheels or gamblers' litanies to luck. The act of prayer postulates a "hearer"—someone or something "out" or "up" there. *Consciousness* is thus the minimal aspect of a divine being as a prayer partner. Moreover, the perceived efficacy of prayer or of any other efforts to exchange with divinity is determined by various other characteristics attributed to this divine consciousness.

The first of these is *rationality.* Humans will prefer Gods who tend to function in a logical, goal-oriented manner. Nothing is to be done with or about irrational beings; they cannot even be propitiated. If the Gods truly are crazy, then religion is futile. But if the

Gods are rational, then there is an immense range of possibilities. However, even among Gods conceived of as conscious, rational beings, these possibilities are contingent on other characteristics, such as whether they are *responsive*.

As strange as it may strike people raised in Judao-Christian or Islamic cultures, Gods may not be responsive. Most of the Greeks and Romans believed that their Gods *could* hear their pleas, but that they mostly didn't listen and didn't care. Aristotle taught that the Gods were incapable of real concern for humans—lust, jealousy, and anger, yes, but never affection. Such Gods may require propitiation, and it may be possible to sometimes bargain with them for favors. But they are not to be counted on, and it is quite uncertain that it is wise even to attract their attention, for if they speak, they may or may not be truthful.

I selected "responsive" as the most appropriate term to sum up many similar attributes ascribed to Gods, including "personal" (as contrasted with impersonal), "loving," "merciful," "close," "accessible," all of which can be summed up as the belief that "there is somebody up there who cares." The Nuer often refer to their God as their father and themselves as "'*gaatku*,' thy children," using these terms not literally but to indicate a relationship that involves "the sense of care and protection parents give to a child," and they commonly acknowledge God's care with the remark "God is present" (Evans-Pritchard, 1956:8–9). This same sense of divine responsiveness is found in the orthodox conception of God presented by Judaism, Christianity, and Islam. Such a God makes an extremely attractive exchange partner who can be counted on to maximize human benefits.

In addition to being rational and responsive, Gods will be preferred as exchange partners to the extent that they are *dependable*. Undependable Gods are legion. There is a huge anthropological literature on "trickster" Gods and spirits (Evans-Pritchard, 1967; Hynes and Doty, 1993; Radin, 1956). Trickster Gods are unusually frequent in the religions of Native North Americans but are common around the world. In Dahomey people never know what to expect from "the lecherous, mischievous, but sometimes humanly helpful god Legba" (Norbeck, 1961:79) while Japanese Shintō includes the misbehaving Susa-no-o, who is "divine yet subject to the most infantile of human passions" (Ellwood, 1993:142). Gladys Reichard (1950) reported that the Navaho distinguish their Gods according to their dependability in giving help.

As conceived of by the ancient Greeks, most of their Gods were quite undependable, being capricious and amoral. Sometimes they kept their word, and sometimes they provided humans with very valuable rewards. But sometimes they lied, and they often did humans great harm for very petty reasons. As William Foxwell Albright (1957:265) put it, "the Olympian deities of Greece [were] charming poetic figures [but] unedifying examples." It may have been worthwhile to periodically offer such Gods a sacrificial animal or two (especially since the donors feasted on the offering after the ceremony), but they were not worth more.

Gods can be thought of as responsive and dependable and still be of very limited significance, depending on the diversity of their powers and the range of their influence—their *scope*. Having more diverse powers, a God of weather is of greater scope than a God of wind or a God of rain. A God who controls weather everywhere is of greater scope than a God who controls weather only in a small tribal territory. At one extreme are the minor Gods and godlings that abound in preliterate societies or on the periphery of pantheons, and at the other extreme is the omnipotent God of the Jewish-Christian-Islamic tradition.

Gods of greater scope can provide far more valuable rewards and therefore can require more in return. Indeed, only Gods of great scope offer rewards so valuable as to justify a demand for an *exclusive* exchange relationship, wherein humans may exchange only with one specific God (and approved divine subordinates such as angels). Not only must Jews, Christians, Muslims, and members of several other Godly faiths engage in long-term relationships with the divine, they must do so with only one God.

Having identified the reason why humans will prefer Gods of infinite scope, and why they will accept exclusive exchange relations with such Gods, we have arrived at the threshold of monotheism.

Rain God. This is Tlaloc. Centuries ago he was believed to
control the rain in the area around Veracruz, Mexico.
© Danny Lehman/CORBIS.

Dimensions of Monotheism

Many scholars have noted the tendency for religions to evolve in
the direction of monotheism (Albright, 1957; Bellah, 1964; Caird,
1899; Frazer, 1927; Spencer, 1893; Swanson, 1960; Tylor, [1871]
1958). The fundamental principle is this: "As societies become
older, larger, and more cosmopolitan they will tend to worship
fewer Gods of greater scope" (Stark and Bainbridge, [1987]
1996:86).

As with all propositions concerning social evolution, this is a general tendency only. Some quite simple societies believe in few Gods of great scope (and even in a High God), and some quite advanced societies believe in many Gods of small scope, as did the Greeks and Romans. But the generalization holds. Nevertheless, this trend toward Gods of greater scope very seldom results in limiting belief to only *one* supernatural entity. *Absolute* monotheism is very rare. According to Herbert Spencer (*1820–1903*), "Only by unitarians of the advanced type, and by those who are called theists, is a pure monotheism accepted" (1893:748). In none of the great monotheisms—Judaism, Christianity, Islam—is there only one supernatural entity. In each, God is surrounded with "a cloud of beings" (Swanson, 1960:55). As Spencer pointed out:

> Another fact to be noted respecting the evolution of monotheisms out of polytheisms . . . is that they do not become complete; or at least do not maintain their purity . . . [for example] the Hebrew religion, nominally monotheistic, retained a large infusion of polytheism. Archangels exercising powers in respect to their respective spheres, and capable even of rebellion, [a]re practically demi-gods . . . [Christian] trinitarian[ism] is partially polytheistic . . . Nay, even belief in a devil, conceived as an independent supernatural being, implies surviving polytheism. (1893:747–48).

Spencer's mention of a devil acknowledges that there is a clear distinction among the various supernatural beings within the great monotheisms between those regarded as good and those who are evil. Therein lies the limiting principle of monotheism.

In practice, absolute monotheism is possible *only* when the supernatural is conceived of as an essence. If there is only one supernatural *being*, such a God would of necessity be *irrational* and *perverse*; one God of infinite scope must be responsible for *everything*, evil as well as good, and thus must be dangerously capricious, shifting intentions unpredictably and without reason. Within the confines of absolute monotheism, the only alternative to such a fearsome God is a divine essence that is responsible for *nothing*, being utterly remote from human concerns. But such nonbeings have little to offer most people and never supplant supernatural beings, except among small elites.

This necessarily limits monotheism since, in order for a divine being to be rational and benign, it is necessary for the religious system to postulate the existence of other, if far lesser, beings. That is, *evil* supernatural forces (such as Satan) are essential to the most rational conception of divinity. Hence monotheistic religions typically distinguish between good and evil supernatural beings, the good ones being those who intend to allow humans to profit from their exchanges, and the evil ones being those who intend to inflict coercive exchanges or deceptions on humans resulting in losses for human exchange partners. Thus Judaism, Christianity, and Islam are *dualistic* monotheisms—each teaches that, in addition to the existence of a supreme divine being, *there also exists at least one evil, if less powerful, supernatural being.* As Jeffrey Burton Russell (1977:32) put it, "Dualism posits two opposite powers of good and evil, attributing evil to the will of a malign spirit." The principle of dualism reflects the necessity that we either conceive of a single divine essence—one that is above the question of good or evil by virtue of being remote from any exchanges with humans (the Tao)—or admit the existence of more than one supernatural being.

However, entirely symmetrical dualism is rare and tends to be limited to good and evil essences. When Gods are conceived of as beings, the good ones are typically seen as having greater power, and the ultimate victory of good in the conflict between good and evil is assumed. Indeed, in the major dualistic monotheisms, evil is not accorded full Godhood—Yahweh, Jehovah, and Allah merely tolerate lesser evil beings.*

I do not mean to suggest that this portrait of the Gods is the product of conscious human "creation." No one sat down and decided, Let's believe in a supreme God, surround him/her with some subordinate beings, and postulate an inferior evil being on whom we can blame evil. Rather, this view tends to evolve over time be-

---

* Purists may object to my identifying the Christian deity as Jehovah on grounds that this is merely a poor rendering of Yahweh (YHWH), just as some will object to Yahweh, or indeed to using "G-d's" name at all. But these names have enjoyed an extensive common usage, and, more important, everyone knows the intended referent.

cause it is the most reasonable and satisfying conclusion from the available religious culture.[1] Thus the rise of Judaic monotheism probably did not involve a sharp break with or rejection of the past. Rather, the early monotheists "chose not to reject but to affirm the traditions of the past as expressions of true reality that previously had only been perceived darkly in limited human terms" (Thompson, 1996:116). The evolution of Yahweh, as revealed in the Ugaritic texts as well as the Old Testament, seems to have begun with a four-tiered pantheon. "Yahweh" emerged as the supreme God from among the Gods on the highest tier, "Satan" from the disobedient Gods of the third level, and the "angels" from the servant Gods or messengers of the lowest tier (Handy, 1996). To the extent that one wants to see this process of evolution as human handiwork, it might best be equated with editing on behalf of an increasingly plausible theology.

In any case, there is an immense theological literature on the problem of evil and considerable agreement that associating evil with subordinate supernatural beings is an attractive solution. Implicit in much of this writing (and explicit in some of it) is the observation that within dualistic monotheism, *God underwrites the moral order.*

It seems inevitable that if Gods of great scope are regarded as good and in opposition to evil, their commitment to good will extend to human behavior—hence doctrines concerning sin and divine judgment. Elsewhere I have demonstrated that it is very unusual for religion to be linked to morality in polytheistic societies, and that this link is lacking where the supernatural is conceived of as an essence (Stark, in press). However, the belief that Gods are concerned with morality is especially appealing because it depicts the Gods as concerned with the fate of the individual and supportive of the efforts of each to achieve a secure and rewarding existence. Albright (1957:265) put it well: "For the average worshipper, however, it is very essential that his god be a divinity who can sympathize with his human feelings and emotions . . . it was precisely the anthropomorphism of Yahweh which was essential to the initial success of Israel's religion."

As with other aspects of culture, these features of monotheism do not simply appear. They are the result of the progressive formulation and refinement of ideas. In my judgment, the Old Testament provides us with an illuminating record of this process. As mentioned, Hebrew monotheism evolved gradually following the Exodus. Hence early passages in Genesis do not proclaim an Only God. Indeed, even the First Commandment does not deny the existence of other Gods but only demands that Yahweh be acknowledged as their superior—"thou shalt have no other Gods before me." Judging from the Old Testament, it was only slowly that the existence of other Gods was denied.[2]

In fact, the rise of monotheism often does not result in its adherents' defining all other Gods as false but merely in their demoting them to supernatural creatures subordinate to the Supreme Being, the One God. It is common knowledge that as Christianity spread to northern and western Europe, many pagan Gods were redefined as saints; thus their local patronage could continue within a safely orthodox context. Spencer (1893:748) makes the same point concerning Islam. Indeed, Sir Edward Tylor (*1832–1917*) noted that "[b]eings who in Christian or Moslem theology would be called angels, saints, or demons, would under the same definitions be called deities in polytheistic settings" ([1871] 1958:417).

However, if the God who spoke to Moses from a burning bush was *the* God, his status as a *good* God was not yet certain. He is depicted as fierce, frightening, and extremely dangerous. Thus having lost patience with wickedness, Yahweh declared that he "was sorry that he had made humankind," and announced his intention to "blot out from the earth the human beings I have created—people together with animals and creeping things and birds of the air" (Gen. 6:6–7). Thence the Flood. In early days Yahweh also appears to be unpredictable and arbitrary. For example, he struck people dead on what seem to be unreasonable grounds—as in the case of Moses' nephews Nadab and Abihu, whom God burned to death because they mistakenly lit their censers from "unholy fire." It is reported that Moses chided God for some of these actions, and in at least some scriptural passages it is suggested that God repented.

In any event, it has often been noticed that by the end of the Old Testament, God seems very different—far more understanding, forgiving, and humane. Many Christian and Jewish theologians object to any interpretation suggesting that God changed. Thus John Calvin (*1509–1564*) asserted that God is unchangeable and hence above all repentance. But, Calvin continued, God's repentance, like God's anger, is *imputed to* God by humans on the basis of their own human experience, as this better enables them to understand God ([1559] 1989, bk. 1, chap. 13).

Whatever the theological status of Calvin's interpretation, it entirely suffices for social science, which is fully served by analysis of changes in the *human images* of God, and nothing more needs to be assumed. What the Old Testament reveals is the evolution of Hebrew images of God from a moody and touchy "Holy Terror" into a virtuous Supreme Being. And, as noted above, this evolution is in tandem with the emergence of a clear conception of a powerful, though ultimately subordinate, Evil Being (Pagels, 1995; Russell, 1977).

There is no need to pursue the implications of dualistic monotheism further here, since they are central to the remainder of the book. Suffice it to note that people tend to prefer a God meeting all of the aspects noted above to an impersonal essence or "higher power." They will also prefer few Gods of great scope to pantheons teeming with small divinities. The former have greater intellectual and emotional appeal; moreover, the greater the scope of the Gods, the greater the commitment they are able to generate, culminating in the extraordinary power of dualistic monotheism to inspire prodigious undertakings, to maximize the capacity of religions to mobilize human action.

Conclusion

Let me assure readers that this is my *theory* of Gods, not my belief about the nature of God. As to the true nature of God, I plead ignorance. As for the theory, its worth can be assessed only by results. Is it consistent with the facts, and does it reveal connections and processes not previously noticed or thought unimportant? In short, does it help us to better understand social processes, and does it illuminate history? We shall see.

Notes

1. Nor am I prepared to deny that this evolution reflects progressive human discovery of the truth.

2. I am aware that there is controversy concerning the actual order in which the parts of the Old Testament were written, but I am comfortable with the assumption that the Pentateuch is rather earlier than the books of various prophets.

Pharaoh Amenhotep IV. The enigmatic ruler of Egypt (1365 to 1347 B.C.E.) who embraced monotheism and then changed his name to Akhenaten. © Richard T. Nowitz/CORBIS.

· 2 ·

God's *Chosen*: Monotheism and Mission

Praise the Lord, all you nations! Extol him, all you peoples.
—Psalm 117

The origins of monotheism are buried along the misty frontiers of history. One of the earliest known instances occurred in Egypt where, more than a thousand years before the birth of Jesus, Pharaoh Amenhoptep IV proclaimed *Aten* to be the One God (Albright, 1957; Aldred, 1988; James, 1960; Redford, 1984; Rohl, 1995). A hymn attributed to the pharaoh himself begins, O living Aten, creator of life! The hymn continues:

> O Sole God, beside whom there is none!
> You made the earth as you wished, you alone.
> All peoples, herds, and flocks;
> All upon earth that walk upon legs,
> All on high that fly on wings.
> You set every man in his place,
> You supply their needs;
> Everyone has his food,
> His lifetime is counted.
> Their tongues differ in speech,
> Their characters likewise;
> Their skins are distinct,
> For you distinguished the peoples.
>
> . . . .
>
> For you made them for yourself . . .
> Lord of all lands . . .
> You are in my heart.
> (Lichtheim, 1976:96–99)

31

Aten was long thought to have been the first fully developed image of God as a conscious, responsive being of unlimited power and scope—a God who created everything and continued to look after every aspect of life, everywhere. This led many, including Sigmund Freud (*1856–1939*), to propose that this was the true origin of Hebrew monotheism, learned during their bondage in Egypt ([1939] 1957). However, this seems very unlikely because it is now accepted that the Israelites did not fully embrace true monotheism until many centuries after the Exodus, and because their monotheism seems to have emerged from a pantheon that has been traced to Persian sources, not to Egypt (Edelman, 1996; Niehr, 1996; Thompson, 1996, 1992). Just where true monotheism first arose remains unknown.

The quest for the origins of monotheism is a fascinating scholarly undertaking, but the sociological importance of monotheism resides in its consequences. The lesson I wish to draw from this episode in ancient Egyptian history concerns the extraordinary capacities of monotheism to *unite* and to *divide*.

Upon embracing Aten as the One God, Pharaoh Amenhoptep changed his name to Akhenaten[1] (the glorious spirit of Aten) and initiated worship of the solar disk as Aten's visible aspect. This alone would not have unsettled religious life in Egypt, since the Sun was already worshiped as Re and an abundance of solar temples existed throughout the kingdom, side by side with temples devoted to at least thirty other major divinities. But, unlike Re, Aten wasn't one of the Gods; he was the *One* God. As such he required *exclusive* worship. So, in addition to building many splendid new temples to Aten, Akhenaten withdrew funding from the other temples and denounced worship of "false" Gods. Overnight, the Egyptians, including the thousands of priests serving other temples, were expected to be monotheists. This was rather more than unsettling—it was an attempted revolution imposed from above and quite lacking in popular support. A semblance of monotheism endured, at least in public, for the remaining ten years that Akhenaten ruled, only because of the unquestioned sovereignty of the pharaoh. But upon Akhenaten's death Egyptians rebelled against the new religion. Akhenaten's son Tutankhamen briefly succeeded him as pharaoh and was in turn succeeded by his vizier Aye, who then restored the traditional religions. Almost immediately, all temples of Aten were destroyed or rededicated to other Gods; Akhenaten's name was systematically removed from all monuments and, insofar as possible, from history. The rediscovery of Akhenaten is an impressive example of archaeological craft (Aldred, 1988; Redford, 1984).

Monotheism and Mission

The rise and fall of Aten worship illustrates the central themes of the next three chapters: the ability of monotheism to unite and mobilize humans on behalf of great undertakings, and to also plunge them into bitter and often bloody conflict. These are, of course, aspects of the same phenomenon as seen from within a group or from outside. In this chapter I will be mainly concerned with the view from within—with seeing how monotheism unites people and prompts them to seek to convert others to their God. Chapter 3 is devoted to how monotheism inspires bitter religious conflicts, although aspects of conflict cannot be entirely excluded from this chapter because the two are so intimately linked. Then, Chapter 4 combines both the internal and external effects of monotheism as it explores the capacity of monotheistic groups to stand fast against persecution as well as resist temptations to assimilate.

Stripped to basics, social science addresses two questions about groups: What holds them together? What divides them? What is it that causes some set of people to constitute a group toward which they feel a strong a sense of solidarity—mutual feelings of common identity, purpose, and concerns? Conversely, what is it that causes groups to see themselves as pitted against one another—as strangers and enemies? Group solidarity is sustained primarily by a common culture—language, traditions, religion, history. These same factors serve as boundaries that set groups apart. The extent to which religion enters into either solidarity or conflict appears to be in direct proportion to the *scope* of the Gods involved. The extraordinary episode of ancient Egyptian history involving Aten reveals that implicit in conceptions of One God is the concept of One *True* God—which provides a potent basis for intense solidarity and for equally intense conflict.

If there is only One God, this necessitates an *exclusive* exchange relationship, there being no logical alternatives. Thus Akhenaten did not merely ask that everyone *also* worship Aten, but that they worship Aten alone. It is illogical to deal with a flock of specialized Gods if there is One God of unlimited scope and capacity. An exclusive relationship with One God is also an *extended* relationship— usually lifelong. No longer are humans able to go "God shopping" or to pit one God against another. This results in extremely strong organizations possessed of immense resources, consistent with a God of unlimited power and concern. Therein lies the key to the durable and vigorous religious institutions found in Judaism, Christianity, Islam, and, to a somewhat lesser extent, Hinduism.

The One God referred to as Yahweh, Jehovah, or Allah commands lifelong, exclusive obedience in return for rewards "beyond price." No running off to Baal if response to one's requests is not immediately forthcoming. Instead, one is asked to sacrifice and demonstrate steadfastness in the face of earthly trials—indeed, martyrdom is revered as reflecting unusual character, not irrationality. Such expectations about commitment can be justified only if they involve exchange relations with a God capable of keeping track—of noting virtue in the personal account of individuals. If, as I have demonstrated elsewhere (Stark, in press), no one hesitates to cheat because of faith in an *essence*, obviously such flimsy conceptions of God cannot inspire anyone to face lions. Neither the Tao nor the "ground of our being" warrants significant sacrifice, let alone martyrdom. Akhenaten did not really worship the Sun— Aten was not an *essence* but was conceived of as a fully conscious and concerned *being*. As will be seen, divine essences are able to inspire monastic movements and schools of philosophy but not mass followings. Indeed, even within faiths presumably based on essences, such as Buddhism or Taoism, their appeal to the general public is focused on the collection of supernatural beings that have been attached to these traditions. Even so, there is a world of difference between the ability to attract a clientele, as the Gods of polytheisms do, and the capacity to inspire intense, lifelong dedication and sacrifice on the part of the general public. That capacity is limited to dualistic monotheisms.

When we examine history, we find no massive mobilizations on behalf of *the Gods*. Polytheistic societies are capable of prodigies of effort including those of conquest. But the armies of Rome, imperial China, or ancient Egypt did not march on behalf of divine will—unlike the armies of Islam or those enlisted by popes for Crusades to the Holy Land. Granted, many Christian crusaders and Islamic conquerors also had nonreligious motives, and some may even have been irreligious. But, lacking the powerful religious justification of doing God's Will, these *events* would not have taken place. Only One True God can generate great undertakings out of primarily religious motivations, and chief among these is the desire, indeed the duty, to spread knowledge of the One True God: *the duty to missionize is inherent in dualistic monotheism.*

Later in the chapter I will refine the definition of missions, but for now it is sufficient to think of it in biblical terms: *Go therefore and make disciples of all nations, baptizing them in the name of the Father and of the Son and of the Holy Spirit, and teaching them to obey everything that I have commanded you* (Matt. 28:19–20).

Rather than focus here on the potential for conflict that lurks within directives to missionize, in this chapter I wish to stress the admirable aspects of missions. Imagine a society's discovering a vaccine against a deadly disease that has been ravaging its people and continues to ravage people in neighboring societies, where the cause of the disease is incorrectly attributed to improper diet. What would be the judgment on such a society if it withheld its vaccine on the grounds that it would be ethnocentric to try to instruct members of another culture that their medical ideas are incorrect, and to induce them to adopt the effective treatment? If one accepts that one has the good fortune to be in possession of the true religion and thereby has access to the most valuable possible rewards, is one not similarly obligated to spread this blessing to those less fortunate? I see no flaw in this parallel—other than the objection that the religious claims may not be true, which objection misses the phenomenology of obligation.

35

The remainder of the chapter explores the historical record of missions in terms of the theory developed in Chapter 1. In part, these explorations are intended as empirical tests of the theory, and in part they will show how the theory draws attention to little-noticed aspects of some well-known events. Indeed, to properly set the stage, I will begin with matters that have been given virtually no explicit attention. First, how do polytheistic faiths spread? Second, how do religions based on divine essences spread? Answers to these questions provide useful comparisons for examinations of the spread of monotheisms. In that connection, I examine missions in Judaism, in early Christianity, and in the rise of Islam. I then offer an extended analysis of the modern era of Christian world missions, showing that variations in their image of God determine when and which Christian bodies participate. I conclude with a brief account of Hindu missions, a subject so neglected that it has often been claimed that Hinduism is not a missionizing faith.

The Diffusion of Polytheistic Faiths

Anthropologists agree that diffusion[2] holds the key to the origins of most culture within any society. As Ralph Linton (1936:324) explained:

> the number of successful inventions within . . . any one society . . . is always small. If every human group had been left to climb upward by its own unaided efforts, progress would have been so slow that it is doubtful whether any society by now would have advanced beyond the level of the Old Stone Age. The comparatively rapid growth of human culture as a whole has been due to the ability of all societies to borrow elements from other cultures . . . This . . . is known as *diffusion*.

Oddly enough, anthropologists have mostly been content to label the spread of culture across societies as diffusion without attempting to identify or analyze specific mechanisms or social pathways through which diffusion occurs. Nevertheless, five primary channels of diffusion seem apparent: conquest, exchanges of women, trade, migration, and travel.

Simple Societies

Among simple societies, conquest, trade (barter), and exchanges of women probably are the most common pathways of diffusion. Often, one group has conquered another and in the process acquired additional Gods or rites. Conversely, conquerors have often spread their Gods as they spread their rule. In addition, even the most primitive groups usually engage in barter with their neighbors, as the possession of seashells by groups far inland demonstrates. Exchange of females also is common, even among the most primitive groups. Recent studies of DNA indicate that, over the millennia, women have been far more geographically mobile than men, having often been exchanged between groups as wives or concubines or kidnapped for similar purposes (Seielstad, Minch, and Cavalli-Sforza, 1998). It can be assumed that sometimes women transmitted new Gods to their new masters or in-laws.

In any event, the fact of the extensive diffusion of religious culture seems obvious in the immense similarities that exist in the beliefs, myths, rites, and taboos found not only among neighboring societies but worldwide. Documenting these "universals" of religious culture has always been a primary activity of comparative religionists, exemplified by Sir James Frazer's *(1854–1941) The Golden Bough* ([1890] 1922). Perhaps the most important motivation for works such as Frazer's has been to reveal that the central features of Christian faith and practice are no more than instances of a "generic religion," typical of "backward" people everywhere, and long predating Christianity (Stark, 1999b). As Thomas Whittaker (1911:3) pointed out, "the critical attitude of anthropologists" is their determination to reveal that even "the most distinctive [Christian rituals] are transformations of worldwide savage or barbaric rites." Thus Frazer compiled an enormous set of examples in order to argue that tales of crucifixion and resurrection are standards of world mythology, and he dwelt at length on myths of Gods or princes who died upon or next to a sacred tree—the "golden bough." All is said to be generic, occurring again and again. Hence in addition to "identifying" many myths as concerning crucifixion and/or resurrection, Frazer frequently cited such "similarities" as those equating various forms of ritual cannibalism with the Christian practice of communion, and those showing that the Christ story is but one of many in which a God impregnates a human female. The goal, often openly stated, has been to demonstrate that all modern religions are but survivals of more primitive and credulous cultures, and equally invalid. "Each refutes each" has been a common refrain in one branch of comparative religion for more than three centuries (Allen, 1996; Stark, 1999b).

No sooner had everyone accepted this claim, that the monotheistic religions had evolved from barbaric beginnings, than the evidence let them down. Andrew Lang (*1844–1912*), famous for his work in folklore and for his translations of the *Odyssey* and the *Iliad,* surveyed the most recent and reliable ethnographic accounts of religion in the most primitive societies and concluded that many of these tribes believed in High Gods of the kind associated with monotheism. *The Making of Religion* (1898) should have been a bolt from the blue. Not only was the author famous, but, being a distinguished student of Tylor, he also had the appropriate credentials. Nevertheless, his conclusion doomed his book to obscurity for a generation: since a substantial number of the most primitive societies believe in one High God, monotheism cannot always be the end product of a linear evolutionary process. Indeed, Lang argued, it is equally plausible that primitive forms of animism and ghost worship represent *degeneration* from earlier, purer forms of religion.

Even though Lang offered substantially more evidence favoring his position in two subsequent books (1899, 1901), his work was very carefully ignored in the leading anthropology journals, either going entirely unmentioned or dispatched with very brief notices of publication—a German notice called it an "unexpected theory" and pronounced that it "has been received with due mistrust" (quoted in Schmidt, 1931:174). Lang (1899:14) himself wrote, "I must expect to be thought importunate, tedious, a fellow of one idea, and that idea wrong. To resent this would show great want of humour, and a plentiful lack of knowledge of human nature."

Eventually Lang was vindicated, although posthumously. In 1924, in a lecture to the Jewish Historical Society of England, the distinguished American anthropologist Paul Radin remarked that Lang's "insight has been abundantly corroborated . . . That many primitive peoples have a belief in a Supreme Creator no one today seriously denies" (1924:21). Radin's admission reflected a general reaction against the rather mechanical model of social evolution, wherein societies inevitably pass through a set of common stages, as proposed by the previous generation of social scientists (including Tylor and Spencer). But Radin dismissed, as without "the slightest justification," Lang's conclusion that the animistic and ghost-ridden religions most commonly found in primitive societies could have occurred by degeneration from higher forms. Radin's dismissal was not surprising since by then anthropologists had been made fully aware of the theological possibilities inherent in Lang's position.

One leading anthropologist did not reject Lang's work when it first appeared. Father Wilhelm Schmidt (*1868–1954*) at the University of Vienna was inspired by Lang's book not only to reconsider the evidence but to think seriously about what it could mean. Schmidt (1931:262) asked himself, What if "the Supreme Being of the primitive culture is really the god of monotheism?" His answer required twelve volumes, *Der Ursprung der Gottesidee* (1912–1955), and a summary volume was published in English (1931). This enormous output, and Schmidt's extraordinary mastery of ethnography, made his conclusion impossible to ignore, and even some of the most militant atheists among his opponents have willingly acknowledged the scholarly merit of his work—Anthony F. C. Wallace (1966:12) found in it "a refreshing objective quality." In opposition to the conventional anthropological wisdom that the many similarities among religions show all religions to be nothing but "just-so" stories of obvious human invention, Schmidt proposed that the striking similarities found in religions around the world exist because they derive from a "universal revelation" dating to earliest times. That is, at the dawn of humanity all religions were alike! Everyone knew God. Thus it is the *variations* from one religion to another that reveal the insertion of human inventions, of misunderstanding, and of faulty transmission across the generations (an additional source of variation being, of course, subsequent revelations). In this way, Schmidt showed how snugly the anthropological literature fits within the Genesis account of the Creation and the Fall. It is a brilliant counterpoint, massively documented. And although Schmidt's work is based on the theistic assumption, his conclusion is no more faith-driven than that of his opponents, all of whom based their work on the atheistic assumption (Stark, 1999b).

Neither Lang nor Schmidt fully equated the High Gods of primitive societies with Yahweh, Jehovah, or Allah. Nor did they argue that religion and morality were necessarily linked in these societies—as, indeed, often they are not. Typically, the High God of a primitive group is acknowledged as the Creator of all things but is also seen as remote and unresponsive. Thus, although it remains significant that such a God is acknowledged in some quite unsophisticated groups, fully developed dualistic monotheism is very uncommon and does seem to appear only in a more complex cultural context. Keep in mind, however, that the ancient Hebrews were far from being the most advanced society of their day. Why them? That remains one of the greatest of all historical questions—and one rather unlikely ever to be fully answered.

To return to the main point: religious culture obviously diffused far and wide across even the least sophisticated societies. And the primary pathways probably were conquest and exchange of females, and to a lesser degree trade, since this often involves very little direct contact. Aside from these modes, there is little traffic among simple societies. But as societies become larger and more culturally complex, migration and travel become major pathways of cultural diffusion.

Classical Times

There was far more travel in classical times than most people now realize. A grave inscription in Phrygia attests that a local merchant had made seventy-two trips to Rome—a one-way journey of more than a thousand miles (*Inscriptiones Graecae ad Res Romanas Pertinentes* 4.841). As Wayne Meeks (1983:17) put it, "the people of the Roman Empire traveled more extensively and easily than any . . . would again until the nineteenth century." Much of this frequent travel involved trade, and this, in turn, often led to the establishment of local enclaves of foreign traders. Although seldom intentionally, religion was often one of the "goods" transmitted back and forth by these trading communities, if for no other reason than that the traders typically brought their Gods with them and established local temples, as appropriate. Since these traders interacted with locals, the opportunity existed for their Gods to spread. Moreover, being exposed to the local Gods, traders often took them back to their homeland. The result was not merely the spread of Gods but their recombination and amalgamation.

In his *History*, the Greek historian Herodotus (*ca. 484–425* B.C.E.) paid extensive attention to comparing Gods and rituals and to tracing how they might have spread, based on his personal observations of about fifty different societies. For example:

> I will never believe that the rites [of Dionysus] in Egypt and those in Greece can resemble each other by coincidence . . . The names of nearly all the gods came from Egypt to Greece . . . but the making of the Hermes statues with the phallus erect, *that* they did not learn from the Egyptians but from the Pelasgians, and it was the Athenians first of all the Greeks who took over this practice, and from the Athenians, all the rest. ([Ca. 450 B.C.E.] 1987:152–53)

As this process continued, the Gods proliferated in classical societies. It is difficult to say how many different cults eventually flourished in the major Greco-Roman cities. Ramsay MacMullen noted that in most cities there were fifteen or twenty *major* Gods "atop

41

a mass" of others (1981:7). But whatever the total, it was large and the mix very complex.

There is considerable controversy over just how the Gods of Rome became so numerous and diverse. Everyone agrees that as the dominion of Rome spread, Gods from the new territories found their way back to Rome, as well as to other major trade and population centers. And everyone agrees that these new faiths were spread by migrants—by traders, sailors, and slaves, and by soldiers returning from long tours of duty in foreign lands. But there is disagreement about what happened next. Franz Cumont ([1911] 1956) stressed successful recruitment as the basis for the new cults, such as that of Isis. Jules Toutain (in MacMullen, 1981:116) denied this, claiming that Isis worship remained "an exotic cult, taking no root in provincial soil"—and MacMullen agreed. From examination of collections of inscriptions, he (1981:116) concluded that "we can explain what favor the cult did enjoy by supposing it to have been passed on within families, whose members moved about, rather than communicated to new recruits."

On the other hand, MacMullen (1981:188) does agree that the cults of Jupiter of Doliche and of Mithraism grew and spread "entirely through conversions." I find it difficult to quite see how faith could be so solidly ancestral in origin as to preclude widespread acceptance of Isis, but that these ties should fail in comparable instances.

Far more important, however, is Arthur Darby Nock's (1933:12–15) caution that the modern notion of conversion does not represent the phenomenology involved in the acceptance of new Gods in Greco-Roman times. Rather, these Gods "were as a rule supplements rather than alternatives" and consequently were easily accepted (and easily dropped). Nock argued further that "[g]enuine conversion to paganism will appear in our inquiry only when Christianity had become so powerful that its rival was, so to speak, made an entity by opposition and contrast." That is, there really was no self-conscious community of pagans until they were so designated by Christians for their collective failure to embrace the One True God. Also in keeping with Nock's insight, not only did people not convert to pagan Gods, these Gods were not trans-

Isis Goes West. The Goddess Isis originated in Egypt, and her popularity eventually spread throughout the Greco-Roman world. The diffusion of Isis worship was accompanied by a considerable change in appearance. The statue on the left is of Egyptian origin (© Gianni Dagli Orti/CORBIS); the one on the right is Roman (© Araldo de Luca/CORBIS).

mitted by persons dedicated to spreading belief in a God. That is, new Gods were adopted on the basis of opportunity and example, not because of missionizing. Thus in the third century B.C.E. when Isis and Serapis spread from Egypt to the major Greco-Roman cities, they were brought by travelers and immigrants who erected and patronized local shrines or temples to them. Granted, the establishment of new Gods often involved the importation of priests, but they came only to conduct temple ceremonies, not as missionaries seeking new followers—although, of course, they usually welcomed newcomers. Missions directed toward mass conversion seem beyond such Gods. Indeed, even when paganism was collaps-

43

ing under the pressure of Christian missionizing, Greco-Roman polytheism was unable to generate countermissionaries.

At this point, many students of comparative religion will want to cite the spread of Buddhism from India to China and on to Japan as a glaring counterexample. But it isn't.

Essences and Monastic Movements

No God of the Egyptian, Roman, or Greek pantheons was able to generate the exclusive commitment of the general public, but all of them did enlist a priesthood. And while most priests no doubt acknowledged the authenticity of other Gods, they often made a lifelong and apparently exclusive commitment to their particular God. The appropriate comparison here is with magic. Durkheim (1915:44) correctly recognized that "[t]here is no church of magic." By this he meant that no "lasting bonds" can be maintained between "the magician and the individuals who consult him." Instead, "[t]he magician has a clientele and not a church, and it is very possible that his clients have no other relations between each other, or even know each other; even the relations they have with him are generally accidental and transient; they are just like those of a sick man with his physician." However, like physicians, magicians tend to form guilds with fellow practitioners, and to pursue a specific and relatively consistent set of magical teachings and techniques. And, like magicians, the priests of a particular God within a polytheistic culture also are unable to sustain a church, in Durkheim's sense of that term, but even more so than most magicians they are united in a guild—a priesthood of those dedicated to a specific God. In that sense they resemble monotheists; it is in this way that Gods of relatively limited scope can generate quite intense levels of individual commitment. This kind and quality of commitment does not develop in the general public, which continues to patronize many Gods. Rather, it is limited to specialists of the sort Max Weber ([1922] 1993:162) referred to as "religious virtuosi," who devote themselves fully to the pursuit of religious fulfillment, and who tend to set themselves apart. It is

not only the great monotheistic faiths or the Gods of polytheism that are able to inspire religious virtuosi. This capacity is also
present in religions wherein the supernatural is conceived of as
an essence—Weber made specific mention of Buddhist monks. In
fact, that is probably why some scholars call such essences Gods—
because of their capacity to serve as the focal point of monastic
movements.

It was as a monastic movement that Buddhism first gained its
success in India and subsequently established itself in China and
Japan (Ch'en, 1964; Collins, 1998; Dutt, 1962; Earhart, 1984,
1993; Lamotte, 1988; Lester, 1993; Parrinder, 1983; Smart, 1984;
Zürcher, [1959] 1972).

Siddhartha Gautama (563–483 B.C.E.), known to history as Buddha, was himself a member of a wandering group of ascetics, and
after his enlightenment he formed his own monastic order. At first
they too wandered, and only later did they adopt a settled lifestyle,
establishing an elaborate system of large monasteries. As noted in
Chapter 1, Buddha denied the existence of divine *beings* (although
he did report a series of confrontations with the evil Mānra); hence
his teachings are often identified as a philosophy rather than a religion. But even philosophies often inspire a contemplative life of
meditation and pursuit of enlightenment. Indeed, as Randall Collins (1998:272) explained:

> At core, Buddhism is an intellectual's religion . . . [consisting of] a
> hierarchy of meditators.
>
> As practitioners of a monastic religion, devoted to withdrawing
> from the world, its monks were not preachers or administrators of
> sacraments to lay congregations. This ideal of Buddhist monasticism
> often slipped away into practices of making a livelihood from preach-
> ing, ritualism, or magical display. But the core form, the organization
> of world-withdrawing meditators, gave Buddhism its central identity.
> Detached from family life and practical concerns, focusing on the
> analysis of inner experience, viewing even the . . . gods and ritualism
> of religion as parts of the world of illusion to be transcended, the
> Buddhist monk might be regarded as living a life of philosophy to its
> extreme.

While orthodox Buddhism did make some provision for lay involvement, anything less than full-time monkhood was considered an absolute barrier to enlightenment. Needless to say, Buddhism was not a mass movement, but it did have considerable impact on the public—in order to devote themselves to a life of meditation, Buddhist monks needed economic support as well as political license. The major initial basis of support for Buddhists came from public patronage of them in the role of Holy Men—as organized, highly visible counterparts to the familiar shamans and magicians. As Buddhist monks began to circulate in their distinctive dress, living entirely on charity, and prepared to teach the principles of their faith, the people of India soon came to believe them to be "possessed of special powers . . . that the very presence of a monk would subdue forces of misfortune and disease" (Lester, 1993:866–67). An additional advantage enjoyed by Buddhist monks, at least in the early period when they were getting established, is that they were overwhelmingly from privileged backgrounds. Not only was Buddha himself a former prince—of the first sixty men he admitted to his new priesthood, at least fifty-five were "of prominent families" (ibid.:867). As these monks interacted with the public, their class was apparent, and therefore their self-denial was all the more impressive. In contrast, traditional shamans and magicians were of quite undistinguished origins.

Public patronage of Buddhist monks and of their shrines soon made the monasteries powerful and extremely wealthy—accumulating large landholdings, just as Christian monasteries did in medieval Europe (a comparison I will pursue in the discussion of early Christian missions). But the public veneration of Buddhist monks as Holy Men did not lead to any decline in the centrality of supernatural beings in the religious life of the people—in that sense they steadfastly refused to become Buddhists! To the contrary, public commitment to supernatural beings led to the "corruption" of orthodox Buddhism by associating an amazing array of Gods and godlings with the Buddhist tradition, as practiced. As Father Schmidt (1931:2) put it, "everywhere that it [Buddhism] has become a popular religion, it has included . . . innumerable personal deities, brought in by a thousand back doors." Indeed, even though classical Buddhism rejects divine beings, its proponents have "never felt it necessary to deny popular religion," as Ninian Smart (1984:182) pointed out. Rather, "the gods, spirits, and demons that people the world of the ordinary folk in the lands to which Buddhism has come . . . are not rejected."

Thus it is vital to distinguish the *orthodox* or *elite* Buddhism from *popular* Buddhism. True to its founder's rejection of supernatural beings, elite Buddhism has maintained its "Godlessness." In contrast, popular Buddhism long ago erected and began to venerate, and even pray to, large statues of Buddha himself (Gombrich, 1971). Also, from earliest days, the bodhisattvas, a kind of Buddhist saint to whom one might appeal for all sorts of aid, have been included in the popular pantheon. Even so, the Buddhist pantheon never managed to become an exclusive faith—the people continued to recognize many other Gods and spirits, just as they continued to patronize local shamans and magicians. Then, beginning in about the fifth century, when confronted with a reinvigorated Hinduism's supernatural beings of immense power and scope, both popular and elite Buddhism *failed in India*! By the seventh century, Chinese Buddhist monks who visited India discovered that most of the monasteries were uninhabited, the temples were deteriorating, and there were few Buddhists to be found—"[l]ay devotionalism [having been] easily absorbed into Hinduism" (Lester, 1993:883). The last gasp came in the eleventh century when Muslim invaders of northern India destroyed the few remaining monasteries and dispersed the monks. By 1200, "Buddhism ha[d] disappeared altogether from India" (Parinder, 1983:286).

Meanwhile, of course, Buddhism had diffused to the East. However, just as had been the case in India, this did not involve the conversion of the masses to worship an essence. And here too Buddhism originated as monasticism. Indeed, according to Eric Zürcher ([1959] 1972:1), in China "Buddhism has always remained a doctrine of monks." The move eastward began with the founding of monasteries along the busy trade route from India and to China. By about the first century, Buddhist monks appeared in China. At first they attracted few novices and little notice, but then, in the third century, the fall of the Han dynasty precipitated a period of "travail and disunity" (Ch'en, 1964:57) that caused widespread suffering and misery. As Parrinder (1983:285) observed:

> The unsettled condition in China . . . was such that people were in a receptive mood for the coming of a new religion. Even though upper-class Confucian scholars might view it with contempt, many of the Chinese masses were prepared to welcome a new teaching, especially its message of celestial *bodhisattvas* to whom appeal might be made for help and salvation from the ills and sorrows of this life.

That is, aside from intensification of a need for religious compensation in bad times, conditions in China provided an opportunity because of the insistent Godlessness of Confucianism. For, by this time, the elite and popular forms of Buddhism were sufficiently mixed to be traveling companions, offering different aspects according to taste. Thus the orthodox Buddhist message, that suffering is intrinsic to karma and to be escaped through enlightenment, proved especially attractive to Chinese elites—Zürcher ([1959] 1972:4–6) referred to the dominant form of Chinese Buddhism as "gentry Buddhism" based on "the formation of a wholly new type of Chinese intellectual *élite*, consisting of cultured monks." By the start of the seventh century China was finally reunited and pacified by the T'ang dynasty, whose emperors professed Buddhism. But while the court pursued the orthodox form of Buddhism, which acknowledged no divine beings, popular Chinese Buddhism depended on "a bewildering array of deities" (Bowker, 1997:173). Keep in mind Nock's observation that new Gods enter polytheistic cultures not as replacements but as additions. Popular Buddhism did not ask the Chinese to change Gods but supplemented their current supply. This made it easy to become, in some sense, a Buddhist, but equally easy to cease to be one. Moreover, aside from the monks, virtually no one was exclusively Buddhist.

By the ninth century, Buddhism had lost much of its initial momentum in China and was forced to find a niche alongside Taoism and Confucianism. Accommodation was accomplished only after a great deal of conflict and several waves of anti-Buddhist persecution, led by Confucian or Taoist state officials. In response, during

Monumental Failure. Buddhism began in India and from there swept over most of Asia. However, it eventually died out in India when confronted with the vigorous Gods of a renewed Hinduism. By the thirteenth century India's many Buddhist monasteries were empty ruins, like this one in the Ladakh region.
© Craig Lovell/CORBIS.

periods of increased Buddhist influence on the state, there were several eras of anti-Taoist policies. Ultimately, none of these three religions could mobilize sufficient political support to win out. It must be recognized that these were conflicts over wealth and power, not over religious truth. The Buddhist monasteries, for example, amassed great wealth and large landholdings, thus motivating confiscations by the state. Moreover, each of these three religious traditions has endured in China because none has a *religious* basis for overwhelming the others. Unlike Hinduism, all three began as "Godless" philosophies and were "corrupted" by popular demand for supernatural entities—albeit of large number and small scope. Thus Taoism and Confucianism lacked a God of the kind needed to supplant Buddhism as Hinduism had done in India.

Buddhist penetration of Japan followed precisely the same fundamental pattern, except that since it entered from China it was regarded as "the religion of a superior civilization" (Lester,

1993:884). Monks arrived in about the sixth century, and their philosophical ideas had particular appeal for the elite (Earhart, 1993:1087); before the century was out, the emperor himself professed Buddhism in addition to Shintoism. Indeed, popular Buddhism had much in common with Shintoism in terms of a large pantheon of small Gods, and soon the two sets were amalgamated, although the traditions themselves have remained distinctive. Japanese Buddhism has been reinvigorated periodically by schisms and sect formation (Collins, 1998; Earhardt, 1993, 1984).

To sum up: Buddhism traveled as a monastic movement that attracted intellectuals. As for the public at large, elite Buddhism gave an aura of profundity and legitimacy to the "add-on" collection of small Gods included in popular Buddhism. But Buddhism had no elements of a mass movement to save the world. I turn now to such missions.

On Missions

Devotees of particular Gods within a pantheon may recommend their favorite to others, but in the expectation only that others may benefit from this option, not that they will convert. Recall Nock's admonition that it is inappropriate to use the word "conversion" within a polytheistic setting. To take up with new Gods does not require that one abandon one's old Gods any more than enjoying a new soda requires one to cease drinking others, let alone that one must condemn other sodas. The term "conversion" is best reserved for matters of more serious commitment. Hence to *convert* is *to newly form an exclusive commitment to a God.*[3]

As Nock knew, conversions happen only with Gods having the qualities needed to inspire and sustain such commitments. And it is people who believe in One True God who will undertake missions.

Missions are *sustained efforts to convert the rank and file.* Successful missions are not the work of specialized missionaries, if for no other reason than the fact that conversion is not primarily a response to religious teachings. People may be quite willing to try *another* God because it is said to have certain interesting powers, but this is not how they decide to commit their fate exclusively into the hands of One God. Conversions are based on social networks, on bonds of trust and intimacy between those who believe and those who come to accept their beliefs. Converts are made through direct, person-to-person influences—people adopt a new faith as a matter of aligning their religiousness with that of their friends, relatives, and associates who have preceded them into the faith (Lofland and Stark, 1965; Snow and Phillips, 1980; Snow and Machalek, 1983; Stark, 1996a; Stark and Bainbridge, 1980, 1985, [1987] 1996; Stark and Finke, 2000).

It follows that conversion of the masses will occur only when the rank and file of any religious persuasion feel impelled to spread their faith—when they believe it is their duty to God to proselytize. This does not mean that there will be no full-time missionaries, or that initial efforts to convert a group or society will not be made by missionaries. Often, the initial contacts must be made by missionaries. But their efforts to convert a lay following will require that they first develop close interpersonal relationships with some members of the group to be missionized and through them gain access to local social networks. Moreover, once these initial attachments have been made, the primary "carriers" of the new faith are no longer missionaries but the rank and file, with missionaries now limited to playing roles as advisers, educators, or supervisors. For example, Mormonism arrived in Latin America via American missionaries. It took a generation for the missionaries to slowly gather a local nucleus, after which conversion began to spread rapidly through local social networks (Stark, 1998b).

Thus even if one defines Buddhist monks as missionaries, their efforts in China did not constitute a mission, as they made no effort to convert the rank and file. In contrast, ill-conceived though it was, Akhenaten and his followers did engage in a mission. They seem not to have possessed much in the way of rank-and-file supporters, but their aim was to *force everyone to convert* to Aten. As will be seen, coercion can stifle dissent, but it seldom produces heartfelt conversions. Where Akhenaten failed, Moses did not.

CHAPTER 2

Missions of the Jews

As everyone knows, the Old Testament teaches that Israel is God's Chosen People, and that this may have been the first significant instance of monotheism. It is well known, too, that Judaism possessed immense durability in the face of various episodes of captivity and persecution and was also able to retain the loyalty of its adherents through generations of living in foreign enclaves—the Jewish "diaspora" predated the first Roman emperor by centuries. What is far less known, and sometimes denied,[4] is that the Judaism of this era was a missionizing faith—probably the "first great missionary religion" (Moore, 1927, 1:324). There are four main bases for this claim. First, Jewish doctrines set the goal of saving the entire world. Second, both Jewish and Roman writers testify to extensive, and often very successful, Jewish proselytism, especially in the Greco-Roman diaspora. Third, estimated growth rates of Jewish populations, especially in the diaspora, strongly support the assumption of high rates of conversion. Finally, early Christian writers frequently reported large numbers of converts to Judaism. It is worth summarizing this evidence, not merely to establish that the ancient Jews did missionize, but for insights into how missionizing faiths work (Bamberger, 1939; Baron, all volumes; Cohen, 1992, 1990, 1987; Derwacter, 1930; Feldman, 1993; Gager, 1983; Georgi, 1986; Goodman, 1994; Grant, 1973; Harnack, [1908] 1962; Leon, [1960] 1995; McKnight, 1991; Moore, 1927–1930; Parkes, [1934] 1961; Schäfer, 1997; Smallwood, 1981).

Despite Shaye J. D. Cohen's (1987:58) remark that "the motives of the [Jewish] mission to the gentiles are obscure," monotheists really have little choice but to missionize. One can hardly condemn everyone else's religion as false and their Gods as imaginary and yet withhold access to true religion and the opportunity to worship the real God. Of course, elite-based initiation religions, such as some gnostic groups, do withhold access, but no mass monotheistic movements can. And, in fact, while Scripture identifies the Jews as the Chosen People, it also reveals Yahweh's intention to extend that opportunity to the world, as Isa. 49:6 makes clear: "I will give you as a light to the nations, that my salvation may reach to the end of the earth." And later in Isaiah (66:18–19), God reveals his plan to "gather all nations and tongues" and to send missions "to the coastlands far away that have not heard of my fame or seen my glory; and they shall declare my glory among the nations." Or Psalm 117: "Praise the LORD, all you nations! Extol him, all you peoples!" These and similar passages inspired Rabbi Eleazar ben Pedat (*ca. ?–279*) to argue that "God sent Israel into Exile among the nations only for the purpose of acquiring converts" (in Grant, 1973:61).

The Book of Judith (14:10) reports the conversion of an Ammonite general to the "God of Israel," and Ruth offers a poignant story of conversion: "[Y]our people will be my people, and your God my God" (1:16), for, as Moses told the multitude assembled at Mount Sinai, the Lord's covenant was "not only with you who stand here today before the Lord our God, but also with those who are not here with us today" (Deut. 29:14–15). Rabbinical writers have long interpreted this to mean future converts, and include it among those passages of Scripture used to justify the conclusion that "converts are dearer to God than born Jews" (Bamberger, 1939:153). Resh Lakish (*ca. 200–274*) put it thus: "The proselyte who converts is dearer than Israel were when they stood before Mount Sinai. Why? Because had they not seen the thunders and the lightning and the mountains quaking and the sound of the horns, they would not have accepted the Torah. But this one [a proselyte], who saw none of these things came, surrendered himself to the Holy One and accepted upon himself the Kingdom of Heaven. Could any be dearer than he?" (in Bamberger, 1939:155).

First-century Jewish writers reported that, in keeping with this theological imperative, there were missions to the gentiles. Thus Josephus noted the widespread impact of Judaism on the general culture of the diaspora: "[T]he multitude of mankind itself have had a great inclination for a long time to follow our religious observances; for there is not any city of the Grecians, nor any of the barbarians, nor any nation whatsoever, whither our custom of resting on the seventh day hath not come, and by which our fasts and lighting up the lamps, and many of our prohibitions as to food, are not observed" (*Against Apion* 2.40). Indeed, although many gentiles converted, many others in this era adopted Jewish religious customs, frequented the synagogues, and expressed their faith in One God but did not fully convert, being unwilling to adopt Jewish ethnicity (including adult circumcision). These people were known as "God-fearers," and their frequent mention in early Christian sources (see Acts) is also indicative of the successful mission efforts by diasporan Jews (Stark, 1996a).

Josephus also reported that during the second and first centuries B.C.E., following victories by Maccabean armies, the Jews imposed their religion upon the vanquished (*The Antiquities of the Jews* 13.15.4, also 11.3). His claims are confirmed by Strabo and Ptolemy (Cohen, 1990; Feldman, 1993). Similarly, in Esther 9:17 it is reported that, fearing Jewish militance, "many peoples of the country professed to be Jews." Granted, such events seem to have been uncommon, but so were periods of Jewish expansionism and military power. The fact that forced conversions took place at all reveals a sense of mission lacking elsewhere at this time. Although pagan conquerors often butchered or enslaved their defeated enemies, they did not demand conversion—it being a concept incongruous with polytheism.

Philo (*ca. 20* B.C.E.–50), the famous Alexandrian Jewish theologian, wrote at length about converts and missions to the gentiles. He reported that many converts left Egypt as part of the Exodus (*On the Life of Moses* 1.27.147). Like Josephus, he described the widespread observance of Jewish religious customs (ibid. 2.4.20–24). He also often mentioned specific converts and praised their zeal. But of particular importance is Philo's report that synagogue services were *public*, that everyone was welcome and that it was common for Jews to invite gentiles to attend (*The Special Laws* 2.15.62–63). This was confirmed by Josephus (*The Jewish War* 7.44): "All the time they were attracting to their worship a great number of Greeks, making them virtually members of their own community." The attendance of Greek gentiles was facilitated by the fact that the language of the synagogue in the diaspora was Greek, not Hebrew,[5] and thus was comprehensible to everyone in Hellenistic regions and to all educated Romans (who more commonly spoke Greek than Latin). Indeed, Dieter Georgi (1986:89) has proposed that mission was the primary basis for synagogue sermons: "[T]hen one can understand why the synagogue service was open towards pagans and why the latter felt they were directly addressed, for the continuing dialogue with paganism was then at the heart of synagogue worship, in form as well as in content."

Greek and Roman writers often mentioned the success of Jewish mission efforts. Dio Cassius (*ca. 163–235*) reported that the Jews "were converting many of the natives [Romans] to their ways" (*History 57.18.5a*). He made this comment to explain why in about 40 B.C.E. Emperor Tiberius ordered the Jews expelled from Rome, a claim supported by Josephus, Tacitus, and Suetonius (Smallwood, 1981). This was neither the first nor the last time Jews were expelled from Rome. They were expelled again in the reign of Claudius, and two earlier edicts of expulsion survive, one citing the Jews for introducing "their own rites to the Romans," the other noting their efforts to "infect Roman morals" (in Smallwood, 1981:129). This led to frequent complaints such as that of Seneca (*3 B.C.E.–65*), about the popularity of Judaism—"the customs of this accursed race have gained such influence that they are now received throughout all the world. The vanquished have given their laws to their victors" (quoted by St. Augustine, *City of God* 6.11). As to the expulsion of the Jews from Rome in the year 19, E. Mary Smallwood (1981:208) explained that "the Jews in Rome, together with the more ardent of their gentile converts, were driven from their homes . . . because their proselytizing activities had reached dimensions at which they were regarded as a menace to Roman order."

Since Rome was filled with temples, and new Gods were hardly a novelty, why all the upset about Judaism? Because Yahweh was offered not as an addition to the pantheon but as requiring its renunciation. It was for the crime of "atheism" that Jews (and the Christians after them) were condemned. Tacitus (*ca. 55–117*) wrote of "[p]roselytes to Jewry" that "the very first lesson they learn is to despise the gods" (*The Histories* 5.5). Indeed, the Romans seem to have been especially hostile toward converts, for unlike those born into Judaism, converts were traitors to their own heritage. Dio Cassius reported that several very high-ranking Romans, including a cousin of Emperor Domitian, were executed for having converted—"the charge against them was atheism, a charge on which many others who were drifting into Jewish ways were condemned, some to death and others to the confiscation of their property" (*History* 67.14.1–3).

In addition to textual evidence, the arithmetic of demography testifies to substantial conversion. Adolf von Harnack (*1851– 1930*) pioneered this line of analysis, as he did so many others. Based on the most plausible estimates of the size and rate of growth of the Jewish populations in various parts of the diaspora and in Palestine, Harnack ([1908] 1962:8) calculated that

> it is utterly impossible to explain the large total of Jews in the Diaspora by the mere fact of the fertility of Jewish families. We must assume, I imagine, that a very large number of pagans . . . trooped over to Yahweh . . . Now if Judaism was actually so vigorous throughout the empire as to embrace about seven per cent. of the total population [of the empire] under Augustus, one begins to realize its great influence and social importance. And in order to comprehend the . . . [rise] of Christianity, it is quite essential to understand that the religion under whose "shadow" it made its way out into the world, not merely contained elements of vital significance but had expanded till it embraced a considerable proportion of the world's population.[6]

More recent estimates of the size of the Jewish population substantially exceed Harnack's, thereby increasing the strength of his conclusions (Georgi, 1986).

Finally, many early Christian sources report vigorous Jewish mission efforts, note the large numbers of converts and near converts (God-fearers) in attendance at the synagogues, and often portray the Jews as serious competitors to Christian missions. In Matt. 23:15, Jesus is quoted as saying that "scribes and Pharisees" will "cross sea and land to make a single convert." Acts 2:5 notes the existence of "devout Jews from every nation under heaven" and notes that among "visitors from Rome" to Jerusalem are "both Jews and proselytes" (converts to Judaism). Acts 13:43 tells us,

"When the meeting of the synagogue [in Antioch] broke up, many Jews and devout converts to Judaism followed Paul and Barnabus, who spoke to them and urged them to continue in the grace of God."

Before concluding this section, I must deal with several credible arguments that have recently been made against there having been any substantial rates of conversion to Judaism in antiquity. The first of these is based on genetic evidence. In response to an early draft of this chapter, Eli Berman suggested that genetic diseases afflicting Jews almost exclusively demonstrate that very little conversion to Judaism could have taken place. The claim that Jews have long constituted a relatively closed genetic pool is further strengthened by the very recent discovery of a characteristic genetic "signature" found only in the DNA sequences of the Y chromosomes of some Jewish men. Around 5 percent of all Jewish men (both Ashkenazi and Sephardic) have this signature, and about 50 percent of those claiming to be *cohanim*—the priestly "class" descended from Aaron—have it (Skorecki et al., 1997; Thomas et al., 1998). Calculations dating the original mutation that produced the DNA signature (based on its spread through the generations) suggest that it occurred nearly three thousand years ago, which could be interpreted as showing that Jews have taken in very few outsiders since that time. Then came an astonishing discovery (Wade, 1999).

Anthropologists have long known that the Lemba—a Bantu-speaking tribe living in southern Africa—claim to be Jewish. They practice circumcision, do not eat pork, and observe the Sabbath. Their traditions tell of their having come south from a city called Senna in Ethiopia following a flood that destroyed their homes. However, given the long history of misguided, false, or occult claims concerning "Lost Tribes of Israel," these traditions were dismissed as mythical. That began to change when, ten years ago, Tudor Parfitt, director of the Center for Jewish Studies at the School of Oriental and African Studies in London, discovered the existence of a ruined city in Ethiopia that was once called Senna and was destroyed by a flood about a thousand years ago (Kaplan, Parfitt, and Semi, 1995; Parfitt and Semi, 1999). Still, Parfitt's find-

ings were given little credence until the sensational announce-
ment by Oxford's David Goldstein in 1999 that Lemba men possess the Jewish genetic signature as frequently as do other Jewish
populations! Moreover, more than 50 percent of the members
of the Lemba's hereditary priestly clan have it, indicating that they
too are *cohanim*. Given that the Lemba are otherwise physically
indistinguishable from other black Africans, it is evident that a substantial amount of conversion is compatible with the genetics of
Judaism.

A second attempt to minimize the mission orientation of Jews
in the Greco-Roman diaspora is based on the inability of several
scholars to identify "professional Jewish missionaries" (Goodman,
1994; Cohen, 1992). Cohen (1992:16) claimed that none of the
"priests of the temple" or "rabbis of the Mishnah and Talmud,
none of them, as far as is known, organized missions to the Gentiles." Cohen then quotes Salo Baron (1952, 1:173), who was also
bothered by this observation and met it by arguing that "[a]lthough
there were not professional missionaries," the evidence of substantial conversion requires us to assume that "[t]here must have been
Jews among the itinerant preachers and rhetoricians who voyaged
from city to city." Cohen is correct to dismiss "must have been"
statements as evidence. But he misses the main point as completely
as Baron did, when he cites (ibid.:17) the absence of professional
missionaries as a telling point against "the standard scholarly
view" that ancient Judaism was a mission religion.

Mission religions may or may not employ professional missionaries. What makes a religion a mission religion is the involvement
of rank-and-file members in proselytizing their family, friends,
neighbors, and associates.[7] As Max Weber wrote in the first sentence of the section titled "Proselytism in the Diaspora" of his classic *Ancient Judaism* ([1917–1919] 1952:418), "Jewish [prosely-
tism], like early Christian of post-apostolic times, advanced
through voluntary and private endeavor, not through official authorities." An example can be found in Josephus (*Antiquities of
the Jews* 20.2.3), who reported that "a certain Jewish merchant,
whose name was Ananias, got amongst the women that belonged
to the king [of Adiabene], and taught them to worship God ac-

cording to the Jewish religion," which led to the conversion of the king and the entire royal family. This account notes that, in addition to Ananias, two other Jews were involved in proselytizing the royal family, and there is no hint that either of them was a professional missionary either. Rather, the appropriate modern parallel is with efforts by individual evangelical Protestants to witness to those around them.

Of course, not all religions will spread equally well through social networks. Clearly, monotheism enjoys an immense advantage in this regard. And Max Weber clearly knew why. Writing about the success of Jewish proselytism ([1917–1919] 1952:420), he identified the appeal of Judaism as twofold: "the purity of the ethic and the power of the conception of God." Yahweh was presented as a conscious, responsive, good, morally concerned being of unlimited power and scope.

And then Paul asked, *Is God the God of the Jews only? Is he not the God of the Gentiles also? Yes, of the Gentiles also, since God is one . . .* (Rom. 3:29).

Early Christian Missions

The first mission efforts by the early Christians followed a pattern already well defined by generations of Jewish proselytism. Being themselves Jews, and regarding theirs as a legitimately Jewish movement, the first Christians did nothing innovative by seeking converts beyond the ethnic boundaries of Judaism. The only thing novel about Paul's proposals concerning the mission to the gentiles was that converts could become Christians without first becoming Jews. Therein lay the decisive difference. What Christianity offered the world was monotheism stripped of ethnic encumbrances. People of all nations could embrace the One True God while remaining people of all nations.

It is necessary to examine early Christian missions apart from their later mission efforts because soon after the conversion of Constantine there came more than a millennium during which Christians no longer sustained missions, their efforts subsiding into little more than the spread of monastic movements and the baptism of kings. Indeed, far more can be learned from the demise and subsequent rebirth of Christian missions than from the obvious fact that initially Christians set out to save the world.

Weren't Paul and Barnabus, and the other apostles who left Palestine to seek converts throughout the empire, professional missionaries? Yes. But unlike Buddhist monks, their aim was not to recruit other full-time devotees but to enlist the masses to an exclusive and extended commitment. From very early on it is clear that the apostles saw their role not as a settled clergy but as advisers to a network of local congregations that were run by and recruited by local, part-time amateurs. Nor can the early Christians be confused with initiation cults based on arcane wisdom, like some of the so-called gnostic groups (Williams, 1996). Like the synagogues, Christian gatherings were open, except for brief times of intense persecution, which were far rarer and usually far less intense than has been believed (Frend, 1965, 1984). Indeed, we know so much of what went on in early days because the apostles were not secretive, nor did they settle down to run a local mission somewhere. Instead, they traveled from congregation to congregation and wrote letters to offer advice, theological clarification, and moral exhortation to the scattered groups.

The most plausible curve of the first three centuries of Christian growth is entirely consistent with conversion's having occurred as a network phenomenon, the faith's having spread through ties of family and friendship (Stark, 1996a). The movement began with perhaps no more than a thousand converts in the year 40; three centuries later more than half of the population of the empire (perhaps as many as thirty-three million people) had become Christians. This result can be attributed to the work of missionaries *only* if we recognize a universal mission on the part of all believers. I have pursued this matter at great length in my book on the rise of Christianity (1996a).

Then, just as the wave of Christian growth was reaching tidal proportions, along came Constantine. Very soon thereafter the Christian mission subsided.

The Collapse of Christian Missions

For far too long, historians have accepted the claim that the conversion of Emperor Constantine (*ca. 285–337*) caused the triumph of Christianity. In fact, Constantine's conversion was, in part, the response of a politically astute man to what was soon to be an accomplished fact—the exponential wave of Christian growth had gathered immense height and weight by the time Constantine contended for the throne (Drake, 2000; Stark, 1996a). However, despite a century of ill-founded skepticism (Burckhardt, [1860] 1949), there is no reason to doubt the authenticity of his conversion (Drake, 2000; Fletcher, 1997). To the contrary, Christianity might have been far better served had Constantine's faith been pretended. For, in doing his best to serve Christianity, Constantine destroyed its most vital aspect: *its dependence on mass volunteerism.*

Although there is nothing factually revisionist in what follows, many contours are novel. Therefore, it will be useful to begin with an overview.

From a popular mass movement, supported by member donations and run by amateurs and poorly paid clergy, under Constantine Christianity was transformed into an elite organization, lavishly funded by the state, and bestowing wealth and power on the clergy. Thereupon, church offices became highly sought by well-connected men, whose appointments greatly reduced the average Christian leader's level of dedication. Subsequently, the task of completing the Christianization of the empire shifted from persuasion to coercion: laws against pagan practice, confiscation of pagan temples and property, and the use of the rapidly expanding monastic Christianity to provide shock troops to stamp out the last vestiges of nonconformity—including a variety of Christian heresies. As for taking the Good News to the "barbarians" beyond the borders of the empire, the new leadership sneered at the mere idea of attempting to do so; meanwhile, the means to do so—the missionizing spirit of the rank and file—had been allowed to decay. After the fall of Rome, there was renewed interest in spreading Christianity—especially to the powerful new "barbarian" kingdoms. This task was delegated to professional missionaries, to Christian monks who journeyed into non-Christian territories just as Buddhist monks had traveled to China and Japan, and with precisely the same failure to convert the masses. But, also as in the case of Buddhist monks in China and Japan, these efforts were quite successful among the ruling elites. Having baptized a king and his court, the Christian missionaries consigned the task of converting the public mainly to coercive efforts by the nobility. In the end, it is doubtful that the masses in northwestern Europe, and especially in Scandinavia, were *ever* truly converted. Now for the details.

The Christian Establishment

Constantine did not make Christianity the official religion of the Roman Empire, nor did he ban paganism. That came later. Constantine's "favor" was his decision to divert to the Christians the massive state funding on which the pagan temples had always depended. Overnight, Christianity became "the most-favoured recipient of the near-limitless resources of imperial favour" (Fletcher, 1997:19). A faith that had been meeting in humble structures was suddenly housed in magnificent public buildings—the new church of St. Peter built by Constantine in Rome was modeled on the basilican form used for imperial throne halls. A clergy recruited from the people and modestly sustained by member contributions suddenly gained immense power, status, and wealth as part of the imperial civil service. Consequently, in the words of Richard Fletcher (1997:38), the "privileges and exemptions granted the Christian clergy precipitated a stampede into the priesthood." Because Christian offices had become another form of imperial preferment, it was the sons of the aristocracy who usually won the race. Many contemporary accounts mention an extensive traffic in bishoprics, including payment of huge bribes. As early as the Council of Sardica (341), church leaders promulgated rules against ordaining men into the priesthood upon their appointment to bishop, requiring that bishops have previous service in lower clerical office. These rules were mainly ignored or were circumvented by a candidate's being rushed through ordination and a series of lower clerical ranks in a week or two prior to his becoming a bishop (Johnson, 1976). This did not always result in the elevation of an impious opportunist—St. Ambrose went from baptism, through ordination and the clerical ranks, and then was consecrated a bishop, all in eight days! But the overall result was a very worldly, political, and luxury-loving church hierarchy—as Eusebius (*ca. 260–339*) acknowledged in his unfinished *Life of Constantine*, wherein he noted the "hypocrisy of people who crept into the church" in pursuit of favor.

Constantine's lavish support of Christianity came at the expense of paganism. Unlike Christianity, the pagan temples were top-down rather than bottom-up organizations in that they were constructed and sustained by state funding and by gifts from a few very rich benefactors. Thus while Christianity had done very well without state or aristocratic support, paganism collapsed rapidly without it (Bagnall, 1993; MacMullen, 1984; Stark, 1996a). Nevertheless, throughout the fourth century many temples did survive, and Christianity coexisted with many other faiths. Had the church been weaker, and especially had it not gained such a potent role in secular politics, the result might have been a relatively stable pluralism, expanded periodically by the formation of new brands of Christianity (see Drake, 2000). Instead, with the exception of Judaism, all other religions, including all new or less powerful brands of Christianity, were soon suppressed.

At first, Christian attacks on "false" religions were merely condoned by the state; it was Christian activists who did the dirty work. In particular, the rapid growth of monasticism provided local church officials with ardent gangs to send against their opponents. Thus did the pagan poet Libanus complain to the emperor Theodosius in 390: "You did not order the temples to be closed, but the men in black [monks] attack the temples with stones, poles and iron crowbars, or even their bare hands and feet. Then the roofs are knocked in and the walls levelled to the ground, the statues are overturned and the altars demolished. The temple priests must suffer in silence or die" (in Johnson, 1976:97). Of course, pagans often responded with force and violence too. There were riots and street fighting in Alexandria, where a bishop was murdered in 356, while in Syria another bishop was lynched by a pagan mob following the destruction of a temple (MacMullen, 1984:91). However, as their numbers dwindled, pagans were increasingly the victims of Christian terrorism. Then, toward the end of the fourth century, even the hollow state policies of religious toleration came to an end. Many statutes were enacted against religious nonconformity, and the state officially assumed responsibility for their enforcement. Finally, in 407, it was proclaimed that if any pagan images remained, "they shall be torn from their foundations," all pagan altars "shall be destroyed in all places," and any remaining temples and shrines were to be confiscated "for public use" (in MacMullen, 1984:101). This edict was no more than a "cleanup" measure, as by then paganism had been driven out of public expression—at least within the cities of the empire.

However, pagans were not the only, or even often the primary, targets of official religious coercion. Rather, by the end of the fourth century and throughout the fifth, Christian heretics were the main target, often being the victims of atrocities. Augustine (*Epistle* 185.27–30, also 51.3 and 88.6) reported that many Donatist bishops and priests were blinded or had their hands and tongues cut off. Constantine himself had issued an edict that anyone possessing any of the writings of Arius, and who did not turn them in immediately, would be condemned to death. In 392 the death penalty was imposed in some eastern provinces on anyone who celebrated Easter on the wrong day of the year (MacMullen, 1984). Indeed, more often than they attacked pagans, gangs of Christian monks were dispatched to beat up Christian "heretics" and to threaten opposition factions at church councils. Thus "unscrupulous bishop[s]" often took bands of monks "to church councils to bully hostile delegates and try to influence the outcome"—and fatalities often resulted (Johnson, 1976:94).

Thus during the fifth century it was firmly and fiercely established by law and custom that everyone would worship the One True God in precisely the prescribed manner.

But not really *everyone*. The nonconformity of the Jews was generally tolerated, if highly circumscribed, as will be examined in depth in Chapter 3. And some others were ignored as beneath salvation.

Initially, Christians had considerable doubts about converting the rural peasantry—the word pagan is, in fact, simply a form of the Latin word for "rustic" or "country person" (*paganus*). Sharing the prevalent view of city-dwelling Romans (since early Christianity was an urban movement), the Christians regarded country people as subhuman brutes. Thus "the countryside simply did not exist as a zone for missionary enterprise. After all, there was nothing in the New Testament about spreading the Word to the beasts of the field" (Fletcher, 1997:16).

Soon, however, the proximity of country folk prompted efforts to lift them out of paganism, and the landed aristocrats were given the duty to do so, even if they needed to resort to force. As Maximus, bishop of Turin, put it in a sermon: "You should remove all pollution of idols from your properties and cast out the whole error of paganism from your fields . . . whoever knows that sacrilege takes place on his estate and does not forbid it, in a sense orders it" (reprinted in Hillgarth, 1986:55).

But barbarians—everyone living beyond the frontiers of the empire—were another matter. Educated Romans regarded them as incapable of even grasping, let alone adhering to, Christianity. St. Jerome dismissed Germans as cannibals. Even St. Augustine could not see any point in missions beyond the empire. Consequently, according to E. A. Thompson (1966:xvii), "[t]hroughout the whole period of the Roman empire not a single example is known of a man who was appointed bishop with the specific task of going beyond the frontier to a wholly pagan region in order to convert the barbarians living there."

Nevertheless, in the fourth century the "center of the world" began to shift northward in response to the increasing pressures imposed on the empire by these same barbarians. Indeed, Rome had been abandoned by the emperors long before it was sacked by the Vandals: "No emperor lived in Rome after the early fourth century A.D.; indeed after the reign of Constantine (306–337) there were only two imperial visits to the city in the course of the fourth century" (Beard, North, and Price, 1998:364). But even though the emperors massed their legions in the north to defend their frontiers, it was to no avail. And as Germans overwhelmed the empire, Rome was reduced to the status of a provincial city—distant from the Germanic power centers to the north and from the new imperial capital of Constantinople to the east.

The fall of Rome opened the eyes of churchmen to the need to convert the wider world or to once again become just another faith among many (Fletcher, 1997; Robinson, 1917). At first these efforts were directed entirely to those barbarians who took over and settled major areas within the empire—Burgundians, Ostrogoths, Visigoths, and then the Sueves and the Vandals. Obviously, these barbarian invaders did not arrive totally ignorant of Christianity. Prior to this time there had been, significant diffusion, or what Fletcher (1997:229) called "seepage," of Christianity across the frontiers. Moreover, the barbarian invaders were as impressed by the religion of Rome as they were by its buildings and other cultural achievements, and were rather easy to convert—although that often involved merely agreement by leaders to observe the Christian monopoly on public practice, and it is not at all clear when Christianization extended beyond the elites, or if it ever really did so.

Soon, however, power shifted from immigrant barbarian groups to the new barbarian kingdoms to the north. To make Christianity secure in these circles, more than seepage was needed. Thus monks were sent forth as professional missionaries.

Missionary Monks and the Barbarians

Asceticism is a universal religious current, having a marked "survival benefit" in the evolution of religious culture. As I have discussed at some length elsewhere (Stark, 1996a, 1999a; Stark and Finke, 2000; Stark and Iannaccone, 1993), ascetics always have an immense competitive advantage in terms of credibility, vis-à-vis other religious leaders. They appear to have very little to gain, and much to lose, through their commitment. Who could be more credible than someone advocating a faith who not only has no apparent material motives for doing so but is paying a high price in terms of personal sacrifices to do so? Thus ascetics are to be found in many polytheisms and even in response to divine essences—recall the credibility of Buddhist monks, especially of those who had obviously renounced a life of relative privilege to pursue enlightenment. But it is monotheism that seems capable of inspiring and sustaining the most intense, even extreme forms of asceticism. Ancient Judaism abounded in ascetic communities such as the Essenes, who observed many forms of abstinence, performed demanding ritual obligations, and often endured severe physical regimes.

From the start, the ascetic strain was strong in Christianity (Fletcher, 1997; Hannah, 1924; Hickey, 1987; Johnson, 1976; Knowles, 1969; Mayr-Harting, 1993; Smith, 1892). By the middle of the third century, monastic communities had been established in Egypt, whence they crossed the Mediterranean. By the fourth century, Christian monasticism was widespread throughout the empire, and tens of thousands of people were involved in an extensive and expanding network of monasteries, each housing dedicated and deployable servants of the faith. I have already noted how these servants were often sent to attack pagans and heretics in the fourth and fifth centuries. But as the need arose, they were also available to go forth to missionize and to baptize barbarian kings.

It is important to recognize that missions often require the use of professionals when the spread of a faith confronts social boundaries. Since conversion is a network phenomenon, faith ceases to spread when networks attenuate. This often occurs at the boundaries of very distinctive subgroups within a society—ethnic groups or castes, for example—and it is typical at the boundaries between societies. Sometimes these boundaries are overcome if conditions of trade or resettlement bring ardent amateur missionizers into a position to form network bonds to members of the group to be missionized—as the success of Jewish proselytism in the diaspora illustrates. But when such special conditions do not exist, then it is necessary to launch a mission via professionals. As has been mentioned, the success of professionals depends upon a two-step process. First, social bonds must be built between the missionaries and some members of the target society, and these attachments must result in conversions. Second, these initial converts must missionize others, spreading the faith through their networks. Thus the ultimate success of a mission depends in part on *with whom* the missionaries form their initial social bonds—whether to the general public, to a special subgroup or caste, or to a social elite. In the first case, because the missionaries build bonds to rank-and-file members of the target society (or group), when these people begin to spread the new faith through their own social networks, the result is the conversion of the masses. But, at least initially, mass conversion does not result when missionizing is restricted to a particular subgroup or caste. In the third case, when the missionaries focus on social elites in the target society, subsequent conversion of the masses is quite problematic. As for efforts to Christianize the barbarians, the initial focus was on the conversion of elites; as Ian Hannah (1924:178) acknowledged, the monks addressed "themselves in the first place to kings."

From the start, Christian monks had many advantages in their missions to the barbarians. Foremost was the fact that most of them were sincere ascetics. They had entered the church not in pursuit of power and glory but to serve God. Their obvious sincerity and their austere lifestyles led many to believe that, just as Buddhist monks were regarded as Holy Men by the non-Buddhist populace, Christian monks possessed magical and curative powers—even posthumously (Mayr-Harting, 1993).

Another advantage was that missionary monks began with "advanced bases" within the barbarian hinterlands. Some of these consisted of scattered Roman communities established during the imperial era that had already been substantially Christianized—some even had bishops. More important were the networks of monasteries that had been extended into pagan territories just as the string of Buddhist monasteries had crossed the mountains into China. As early as the fourth century, monastic communities had been established in Gaul, including a major complex at Tours. That same century St. Athanasius (*ca. 297–373*) crossed the Rhine to establish a monastic community at Trier, in a solidly Germanic pagan region. Athanasius was soon followed by other monastics, and by the eighth century major monasteries flourished in pagan surroundings at Fulda, Eichstätt, Utrecht, Echternach, Würzburg, Constance, Salzburg, Freising, and St. Gall. Meanwhile, British Christian missionaries were active on the Frisian coast (many European monasteries were founded by monks from Britain and Ireland). The monasteries were closely linked, and monks traveled back and forth frequently, just as Buddhist monks traveled the Asian trade routes. Also like the Buddhists, Christian monasticism was able to support itself locally from donations and to acquire lands, and even to recruit novices from among the local pagans. A major difference was that, unlike Buddhist monks, who were focused on their own enlightenment and recognized no divine mission, the Christian monks felt a profound responsibility to spread their faith. But, again like the Buddhists, their success tended to be restricted to barbarian elites.

In dealing with elites, the missionary monks had the advantage of being educated men. Unlike orthodox Christian monastics in the East, monasticism in the West stressed literacy, and monks tended to be recruited from the privileged classes (Hickey, 1987; Johnson, 1976; Knowles, 1969; Mayr-Harting, 1993). Consequently, they possessed what their barbarian hosts recognized to be superior culture, enabling them to provide all manner of sound advice and instruction, thereby gaining credibility for their religious convictions. Moreover, they represented a religion that was known to command the allegiance of the nobility in many other nearby kingdoms. But I believe that the greatest advantage possessed by the missionary monks was that they presented a far more plausible and valuable image of divinity. Theirs was no God or Goddess of here or there, or of this or that, but was the awesome, omnipotent Jehovah. Barbarian elites found this image of God very much to their liking—a King of Kings. Still, the conversion even of Europe's barbarian elites took many centuries.

The initial target of missionary monks was the expanding and powerful kingdom of the Franks, occupying most of Gaul. Late in the fifth century the great Frankish king Clovis (*ca. 466–511*) converted to Christianity, undergoing public baptism in his capital city of Rheims. The story of his conversion has come down to us in an account by St. Gregory of Tours (*538–594*) in his *History of the Franks* (2.20–22). Written nearly a century after the event, Gregory's report was probably based mainly on the *Life of St. Remigius*, who was the bishop who supervised Clovis' conversion, and on oral traditions (James, 1988). Moreover, as told by Gregory, several of the most significant aspects resemble the conversion of Constantine, and, in its general contours, the story greatly resembles many subsequent accounts of the conversion of medieval kings. Historians usually suggest that similarities such as these discredit all of the accounts as "fictionalized" according to a literary formula or topos. However, as Albert Baumgarten (1997:52) put it, topoi "derive their power because they describe a usual experience." Indeed, I see historical truth in the similarities across conversion accounts—they are similar because the behavior they report conforms to well-established principles and precedents. Before these are identified, it will be useful to recount the conversion of Clovis.

It was through his wife, Clotilde, that Clovis was linked to Christianity. The origin of her conversion was not reported, but there already was an island of Christians in Rheims, and we must assume that the monks had been busy instructing noblewomen. As the story begins, Clotilde is pushing Clovis to convert, but "the king's mind was nowise moved toward belief." But she keeps at it—"the queen without ceasing urged the king to confess the true God, and forsake his idols; but in no wise could she move him to this belief, until at length he made war upon a time against the Alamanni." During the battle everything goes wrong, and Clovis finds himself "being swept to utter ruin." As a last resort, Clovis prays to the Christian God for aid, promises to be baptized, and goes on to victory. Now he has proof that this Christian God is the real thing. Even so, once secure in his victory, Clovis procrastinates. But Clotilde will have none of it and arranges for the local bishop to instruct him. This is done in secrecy because Clovis is fearful that the Frankish nobility will turn against him if he forsakes the ancestral Gods—"the people that followeth me will not suffer it that I forsake their gods." But this is not the case. When Clovis announces his decision to be baptized, many members of the court proclaim that they will do so too. Immediately upon the public baptism of King Clovis, three thousand of his armed followers are also baptized. But about the Christianization of the several million ordinary Franks, not a word is said.

The Winning Prayer. King Clovis was losing the battle with the Alamanni when he prayed to the Christian God for victory, promising to be baptized.
© Bettmann/CORBIS.

Gregory's account includes six basic elements that occur again and again in medieval accounts of missions to pagan societies. Each is consistent with social science as well as good sense. First, professional missionaries establish a local base. Someone must bring the faith. Second, the initial converts are female members of the elite. The men are reached through their wives, mistresses, sisters, mothers, and daughters who proselytize and arrange for missionaries to instruct the men. There is a solid social scientific literature on the extreme overrepresentation of women in new religious movements (Stark, 2000). Third, the men tend to resist, often fearing negative responses from their peers and followers. Even kings are reluctant to risk offending their aristocratic allies and supporters. Fourth, their resistance is overcome when a perceived "miracle" convinces them that Christianity is true. This is entirely consistent with the tradition of "foxhole" conversions. Keep in mind, too, that any king whose emergency prayers for victory went unanswered is unlikely to have survived to leave a record of the failure. Since medieval kings engaged in chronic warfare, the spread of Christianity among them could easily have depended upon "miraculous" victories. Fifth, upon the baptism of the head of an elite household, the other members of the household usually convert too (or appear to do so), and, in the case of the conversion of the king, most of the court follows suit. Keep in mind that preferment depended upon the king's pleasure. Sixth, nothing is done to missionize the general public. Why? Perhaps because it was assumed that they would have no choice but to follow the example set by the elite. But it also seems to have been the case that once the Church was securely established by royal favor, the actual faith of the masses seemed rather unimportant. As Edward James (1988:127) recognized, "churchmen [in this era] do not seem to have thought in terms of [religious] instruction for the laymen. As far as they were concerned, so it seems, conversion meant acceptance of baptism and outward observance of Christian forms . . . rather than of any inner change in the soul." Thus Gregory (2.10) noted, without expressing much dismay, that a century after the conversion of Clovis "the people seem always to have followed idolatrous practices, for they did not recognize the true God."

The primary variation from these six elements in other accounts of medieval missions involves a prince's having been converted while living in a Christian society, often having been sent off for schooling, and then returning home to take the throne, whereupon he introduces Christianity. These instances often were very bloody, as the local aristocrats, lacking strong bonds to their new king, did resist—sometimes quite successfully. The "Christianization" of Norway is illustrative. Olaf Tryggvason, an English-educated Christian convert, seized the throne of Norway in 995, whereupon he attempted to convert the nobility by force, killing some who resisted and burning their estates. These and other repressive measures aroused sufficient opposition to defeat him in the Battle of Svolder (about the year 1000), during which he was killed. Fifteen years later, Olaf Haraldsson, who had been baptized in France, conquered Norway; he too used fire and sword in an effort to compel Christianization. And he too provoked widespread hatred, leading to rebellion, and was driven into exile. When he attempted to return, leading a new army raised in Kiev, he was defeated and killed at the Battle of Stikklestad in 1030. Despite this, he was soon canonized as St. Olaf and is credited with the Christianization of Norway, which seems to have consisted primarily of the reimposition of Olaf's official policies of intolerance (Jones, 1968; Sawyer, 1982).

In neither variant of the conversion of barbarian elites is the conversion of the masses given significant attention or effort—apart from the sporadic application of violent coercion. This neglect reflects the commitment of missionizing monks to what Fletcher (1997:236) has correctly characterized as the "trickle-down" theory of conversion. Having become dependent on state subsidies and governed by a privileged establishment, Christianity was by this time a top-down organization, and nothing could have seemed more obvious to the monastic missionaries than the wisdom of devoting all of their efforts to converting the elite. There were several additional reasons for this, safety being perhaps the most important. Successful conversion of a group of commoners would provide the missionary monks with no protection, either from the nobility, who may have feared that the group posed a religious challenge to their authority, or from other commoners offended by denunciation of their traditional Gods—often enough, monks evangelizing in barbarian areas were murdered by the locals. In contrast, successful inroads into the elite—even if just among the wives—offered substantial protection. An additional reason was perceived efficiency. The missions had limited personnel, and this "compelled them to be selective in their approach" (De Rue, 1998:17). Thus it seemed to make more sense to focus on the elite and wait for their example to eventually trickle down the ranks until the peasants were good Christians too—and if not, there remained fire and sword.

As a variation on this theme, the Frankish heirs of Clovis soon attempted to Christianize their neighbors by conquest. These efforts reached a zenith during the long rule of Charlemagne (*ca. 742–814*), who so extended the Frankish empire that he was crowned in Rome by the pope. Under the guidance of churchmen such as Alcuin of York (*735–804*), Charlemagne was determined to make his a truly *holy* empire. Therefore, as he incorporated new territories, he demanded the immediate Christianization of their inhabitants. His merciless campaign against Saxony (772–775) set new standards in religious brutality. Each victory was followed by forced mass baptisms, and thousands of captives who showed reluctance were beheaded.

Charlemagne's excesses eventually caused Alcuin to write a letter condemning forced conversions (Gaskoin, [1904] 1966). In particular, he argued that it was useless to baptize people who had no idea what Christianity meant, and that conversions were worthless unless they were the result of persuasion and therefore sincere. The truth of Alcuin's point lives on in the fact that the masses were not actually Christianized in many parts of Europe, but it was apparently an unacceptable truth to those whose zeal was matched by their power. Thus Charlemagne's successors continued to rely on forced Christianization, just as the Church continued to rely on the baptism of kings—an approach culminating in the so-called Northern Crusades of late medieval times, during which Christian rulers gradually conquered and subdued the remaining pagan peoples in the far north of Europe: Norse, Slavs, Balts, and Finns (Christiansen, 1980). Each conquest resulted either in the baptism of the defeated rulers or in their replacement with Christians.

As for the common people, they soon found that it was sufficient to add Jesus and various saints to the pantheon of Gods and spirits they used for their peace and protection. To some extent this was in keeping with church policy. In a letter dated 601 and preserved by the Venerable Bede (*Ecclesiastical History* 1.30), Pope Gregory the Great advised Abbot Mellitus, who was setting out to missionize in Britain:

> [I] have come to the conclusion that the temples of the idols among that people should on no account be destroyed. The idols are to be destroyed, but the temples themselves are to be aspersed with holy water, altars set up in them, and relics deposited there . . . In this way, we hope that the people, seeing that their temples are not destroyed, may abandon their error and, flocking more readily to their accustomed resorts, may come to know and adore the true God. And since they have a custom of sacrificing many oxen to demons, let some

other solemnity be substituted in its place such as a day of Dedication or the Festivals of the holy martyrs whose relics are enshrined there . . . If the people are allowed some worldly pleasures in this way, they will more readily come to desire the joys of the spirit. For it is certainly impossible to eradicate all errors from obstinate minds at one stroke.

One must wonder whether "obstinate minds" were ever changed by such an approach. As the great Danish historian Johannes Brøndsted (1965:312) noted, it was quite easy for Christianity to become the "public" faith in Scandinavia, "but far more difficult to overcome the complex culture beneath that religion." He quoted a twelfth-century Anglo-Danish monk: "As long as things go well and everything is fine, the *Sviar* and *Gautar* seem willing to acknowledge Christ and honor him, though as a pure formality; but when things go wrong," they turn against Christianity and revert to paganism (ibid.:312). Or, as was written in the Icelandic *Landnánabók*, Helgi the Lean "was very mixed in his faith; he believed in Christ, but invoked Thor in matters of seafaring and dire necessity" (in ibid.:306). Finally, Brøndsted suggested that to the extent it can be said to have taken place at all, the conversion of Scandinavia occurred "only . . . when Christianity took over old [pagan] superstitions and usages and allowed them to live under a new guise" (ibid.:307).

This illustrates the principle of *cultural continuity*, which I developed to help explain variations in the success of new religious movements: that they are more likely to succeed to the extent that they *retain familiar elements* of the religious culture of the group being missionized (Stark, 1987, 1996b; Stark and Finke, 2000). In effect, the more familiar a new religion, the less costly it is for people to adopt it—the less they must learn and the less they must discard. By thinly overlaying pagan festivals and sacred places with Christian interpretations, the missionaries made it easy to become a Christian—so easy that actual conversion seldom occurred. Instead, in customary pagan fashion, the people treated Christianity as an "add-on religion," and the popular Christianity that eventually emerged in northwestern Europe was a strange amalgam, including a great deal in the way of pagan celebrations and beliefs, some of them thinly Christianized, but many of them not Christianized at all (Davies, 1996; Jolly, 1996; Milis, 1998). Thus the influential French religious historian Jean Delumeau (1977b) listed many instances during the sixteenth and seventeenth centuries when church officials attempted to suppress obviously pagan festivals and celebrations, not only in northwestern Europe but in Italy and France as well. He noted that that among the people there was not only "a profound unfamiliarity with the basics of Christianity" but also "a persistent pagan mentality" and a persistence of "pre-Christian ceremonial" (ibid.:176). Indeed, the "rediscovery" of paganism by artists and writers during the Renaissance was nothing of the sort—the Gods and myths of paganism had never been forgotten. As Jean Seznec ([1953] 1972:3) put it in his classic work on the subject: "Above all, it is now recognized that pagan antiquity, far from experiencing a 'rebirth' in fifteenth-century Italy, had remained alive within the culture and art of the Middle Ages. Even the gods were not *restored* to life, for they had never disappeared from the memory or imagination of man." That elements of paganism survive is one of the remarkable omissions of contemporary perceptions of religion in Europe. For example, polls show that the majority of people in Iceland today (including intellectuals and church leaders) believe in "huldufolk" or hidden people, such as elves, trolls, gnomes, and fairies (Nickerson, 1999). People planning to build a new house often hire "elf-spotters" to ensure that their site does not encroach on huldufolk settlements, and planned highways are sometimes rerouted in order not to disturb various hills and large rocks wherein these pagan entities are thought to dwell (Nickerson, 1999; Swatos and Gissurarson, 1997). Moreover, the popular European right-wing movements that arose during the nineteenth and twentieth centuries involved "a rejection of Christianity and the affirmation of paganism" (Lixfeld, 1994; Poewe, 1999:388;). Even today, in both Germany and France, paganism "is the heart of fascism and the New Right" (ibid.:397). Keep in mind, however, that I reject contemporary Wiccan fantasies concerning an active pagan underground stretching back to pre-Christian times. Paganism did not linger as an organized or even a distinctive faith but survived only as part of the semi-Christian folk religion of northwestern Europe.

As for the Church in these parts of Europe, upon the conversion of the elite it became a fully subsidized state institution, and being entirely independent of popular support, the clergy were (and remain) quite unconcerned about evangelizing the masses. Thus neither the exclusive commitment to Christianity nor the high levels of personal piety exhibited by the early Christians ever developed among the majority of people in northwestern Europe. Marc Bloch ([1940] 1961:82–83) described the religion even of the "faithful" as "superficial," adding that "never was theology less identified with popular religion as it was felt and lived." Indeed, the Dutch historian Anton Wessels (1994:4) claimed that at least until the Reformation, popular religion in most of Europe "remained 'pagan animist' . . . and their [Christianity] was an outward veneer." In similar fashion, Delumeau (1977a:26) declared "mediaeval Christendom" to be a fiction. Indeed,he would allow at most that Europe was "superficially [C]hristianized" (1977b:161), concluding that the de-Christianization of Europe is but illusion (ibid.:227). The French sociologist of religion Gabriel Le Bras (in Delumeau, 1977b:227) agreed that "[d]echristianization is a fallacious term" and should be rejected as unhistorical.

Admittedly, Delumeau and some other Catholic historians have thought that significant Christianization was finally achieved as a result of the Reformation, especially by Catholic efforts to evangelize the masses as part of the Counter-Reformation. That is consistent with the fact that current levels of religious participation are higher in southern Europe. But the higher current levels of religiousness in southern Europe are also consistent with the explanation that it was only here that early Christianity spread as a mass movement; hence this was the only part of Europe *ever* to be Christianized.

In any event, there is little evidence that significant efforts to Christianize the masses occurred in Protestant areas during the Reformation. Certainly, local rulers mostly seemed able to shift back and forth between Protestantism and Catholicism without arousing any popular objections. Indeed, religion often seemed of very secondary importance during the "religious wars" associated with the Reformation, as monarchs made alliances across religious boundaries—for instance, when Catholic France made common cause with the Protestants of Holland against Catholic Spain.

Today, church attendance is extremely low in the Protestant areas of Europe. Although many have claimed that this represents the final stages of the secularization of these societies, such a conclusion is based on bad history—on the assumption that once upon a time religious participation was high in these societies. The truth seems to be that high levels of religious participation were never achieved because real, person-to-person Christian missions faltered in the fourth century and never reached these areas. This interpretation is supported by the fact that current levels of church attendance in European nations are strongly predicted by the date at which they are said to have been Christianized—the later, the lower their current rate of attendance. Date of "Christianization" also powerfully predicts whether or not an area turned Protestant (Stark, 1999c; Stark and Finke, 2000).

It is important to see that the doctrinal imperatives of monotheism were sufficient to prompt elites to attempt to impose religious conformity, even to the point of butchery. However, because reliance on professional missionaries to the elites did not convert and mobilize the rank and file, it can be said that the first era of real Christian missions ended sometime in the fourth century. Ironically, a new era of Christian missions did not begin until religious pluralism had developed within Christianity to the point that the various bodies had to compete with one another in order to prosper and, in doing so, once again became bottom-up, mass movements.

That part of the story awaits. To maintain historical sequence, I turn aside briefly to consider Muslim mission movements.

Muslim Missions

The essential aspects of Muslim missions are well recorded and fully consistent with the principles displayed by Jewish and Christian missions (Arnold, 1896; Cooley, 1965; Denny, 1993; Farah, 1994; Hodgson, 1974; Parrinder, 1983; Payne, 1959; Rahman, 1987; Waines, 1995).

It took early Christianity more than two centuries of growth via social networks to achieve significance, but Muhammad (570?–632) built Islam into a great movement within only a few years. This was possible because the flight of Muhammad and his tiny band of followers—probably numbering only sixty to seventy (Hodgson, 1974, 1:172; Payne, 1959:32)—from their homes in Mecca to the oasis community of Medina (Yathrib) soon enabled them to establish political control over a secure geographic base. This was facilitated by wealth acquired through a series of successful raids on caravans. Indicative of their tiny numbers, the first attack involved only eight Muslim raiders (Payne, 1959:33). But, using the booty and the promise of future profits, Muhammad was able to expand his forces. A major breakthrough came when he was able to increase his ranks very substantially by forming alliances with nearby Bedouin tribesmen. It should be noted that these alliances did not necessarily involve even nominal conversion—when the Bedouin agreed to follow Muhammad, they did not adopt his religion, as their defections following his death made obvious. Nevertheless, these alliances made Islam a military as well as a religious movement, enabling Muhammad to provide the spoils of war to his followers in addition to the promise of paradise. And spoils there were, as Muhammad's forces sacked and looted many communities on the Arabian Peninsula, each success bringing more tribes to his banner. The pattern of treaty and conquest was repeated again and again, long after Muhammad's death, as successive tribes, cities, and whole societies joined up in order to become military allies of the rapidly expanding new power, or they were annexed following their defeat.

Like Christianity, and unlike Judaism, Islam discarded its original ethnic identity, making the faith open to all who accepted its teachings and adhered to its moral code. As with Christianity this required some debate, but here too the decision for universalism was critical for growth, allowing people of all cultures and nations to become Muslims while retaining their diversity.

However, as mentioned, relatively little actual conversion was involved in this massive expansion. Instead, just as was the case during the post-Constantinian era of Christian expansion, conversion was limited mainly to the elites, and the vast Islamic "world" created by Muhammad and his immediate heirs consisted mainly of small Muslim ruling classes presiding over non-Muslim populations (Bulliet, 1979; Hodgson, 1974). Of course, being monotheists, the Muslim elites soon attempted to bring their subjects into the faith as well. These efforts consisted of various forms and degrees of coercion. Except for those whose religion was also "of the Book" (Jews and Christians), non-Muslims were usually classed as "idolaters" and forced to convert upon pain of death, although sometimes with the option of banishment—this rule was especially carefully enforced within Arabia. But even Jews and Christians were often exposed to intense pressures to convert.

Coercion of non-Muslims was facilitated by the fact that through most of its history, and especially in the early centuries, Islam was not simply the state religion, it also was the state. Consequently, laws and government policies could be employed to produce conversions. One popular and effective method was to tax people very differentially based on their religion. Usually this approach required non-Muslims to pay exorbitant rates, while devout Muslims were exempted from paying all or most of their taxes (Hodgson, 1974; Payne, 1959). Such schemes were often so effective that they were very short-lived because they resulted in government revenues' falling so rapidly as to be "ruinous to the state" (Arnold, 1896:104). There is considerable evidence, however, that these coerced conversions were often insincere (see Chapters 3 and 4).

Another form of coercion involved discrimination and harassment. It is true that Islamic states have often tolerated *some* other religions. But it must be recalled that within several years of Muhammad's death, his successor Unmar solved the "Jewish question" by expelling all Jews from the Arabian Peninsula. Moreover, even the most tolerant Muslim societies soon outlawed conversion to any religion other than the local brand of Islam. Even today it is a capital offense in many Islamic nations to proselytize Muslims or for Muslims to convert. But even within these limits Muslim toleration has often been grudging at best. Marshall G. S. Hodgson (1974, 1:268) wrote that from very early days Muslim authorities often exerted themselves to make non-Muslims "feel inferior and to know 'their place' . . . [imposing such laws as] that Christians and Jews should not ride horses, for instance, but at most mules, or even that they should wear certain marks of their religion on their costume when among Muslims." In addition, at various times, non-Muslims were prohibited from wearing clothing similar to that worn by Muslims, nor could they be armed, and if they were mounted, they must dismount whenever a Muslim passed by (Payne, 1959:105).

Comparative religion textbooks sometimes contrast a tolerant Islam with an intolerant Christianity, stressing that in 1492 Christians expelled the Jews from Spain where, it is often asserted, they had lived peacefully and prosperously for centuries under Muslim rule (Smith, 1991). These same textbooks ignore the fact that in 1148 Muslims also expelled the Jews from Spain under the same terms as the Christians did later, which surely demonstrates that these comparisons are at least uninformed and often probably disingenuous. As will be seen in Chapter 3, Muslim history includes its full share of bloody religious intolerance. For example, during his stay in Medina, Muhammad grew incensed at the unwillingness of the several local Jewish clans to accept his revelations and at their criticism of his understanding of the Bible. The conflict escalated until it resulted in the banishment of two of these clans. Two years later, Muhammad accused the remaining Jewish clan of consorting with their banished coreligionists, whereupon he enslaved all the women and children and murdered all the men (Hodgson, 1974; Parrinder, 1983; Payne, 1959). This was but the first of many such massacres. For example, following Muhammad's conquest of the rich Jewish colony of Khaybar, there was a general slaughter of the male inhabitants and indiscriminate rape. Following Muhammad, other Muslim conquerors sometimes acted as Charlemagne did when he encountered unbelievers—those unwilling to immediately profess the faith were killed. And this often included Jews as well as Christians. In the words of Marwan, an eighth-century caliph, "Whosoever among the people of Egypt does not enter into my religion and pray as I pray and follow my tenets, I will slay and crucify him" (in Arnold, 1896:8). Nor were attacks on Jews limited to the early days of Islam. As will be examined in detail in Chapter 3, in 1032–1033 there were recurring massacres in Fez, and about six thousand Jews died. In 1290 the Jews of Baghdad were massacred, and the butchery spread throughout the region. Indeed, given the frequent claims about the exemplary treatment of Jews by Muslims in Spain, it must be noted that four thousand Jews living in Granada were murdered in 1066, and in 1090 the Jewish inhabitants of Granada were wiped out again. A century later there were widespread massacres of Jews throughout the remainder of Islamic Spain. Chapter 3 will examine why these and similar massacres (including those by Christian Europeans) occurred when they did. Here it is sufficient to recognize that religious intolerance is inherent in *all* monotheisms.

In addition, heresy was as common and aroused as much violence and bloodshed within Islam as within Christianity. Hodgson (1974, 1:66–67) complained that comparative religionists have greatly exaggerated the prevalence of sects in early Islam, confusing the writings of what may well have been a single proponent with a social movement. He undoubtedly is correct, and in similar fashion the number of significant "heresies" in early Christianity has also been greatly inflated, especially those usually identified as gnostic (Williams, 1996). The confusion of heretical writings with heretical communities or movements does not apply, however, when armed conflicts break out. Hence just as "Donatists" and "Arians" were significant theological factions within early Christianity, and not merely dissenting texts (to say nothing of "Cathars," "Lutherans" or, indeed, "Papists"), so too does Islam have its bitter divisions, including "Sufi," "Shi'ah," "Sunni," "Isma'ili" and many others. Just as Christendom has often been ripped by religious conflicts, so has Islam, and if religious divisions within Islam have also often involved economic and nationalistic components, the same can be said of those found in Christendom (or anywhere) and does not eliminate the importance of religious motivations. Indeed, it is absurd to minimize the role of religion in the many collisions between Christian and Muslim armies.

Islam and Christianity also used similar tactics in their conversion efforts by incorporating elements of local belief and practice. Just as medieval Christians sought to entice the pagan peasants by reconsecrating their shrines and canonizing their local Gods and spirits, Islam did the same. In fact, all across the once-Christian areas of North Africa, where many originally pagan shrines had been Christianized, these were incorporated by Islam. Muhammad had set a precedent for this when he adopted pagan traditions such as an annual pilgrimage to Mecca and the observance of the holy month of Ramadan. As a result, the Islam to which the common people eventually assented was as amalgamated as the Christianity that prospered among northwestern European peasants. As Hodgson (1974, 1:305) put it, "A popular Islam thus arose, complete with its own history, ethics, and eschatology, drawing on the most striking notions found in all of the earlier traditions [Christianity, Judaism, and paganism] . . . and the mosque became the most lively, and certainly the most cosmopolitan, centre of all activities." In similar fashion the medieval Christian parish churches, especially in northwestern Europe, served an amazing variety of social and commercial functions, seldom having any religious significance (Stark, 1999c).

In the end, did the coercive and trickle-down approach to the conversion of the masses succeed in Islam while failing in Christianity? It has certainly been the conventional wisdom that the Muslim masses long ago became intensely pious. But I think this characterization is as faulty as the one, held with similar conviction for so long, about the intense piety of medieval "Christians." Although the Middle Ages were long known as the Age of Faith, as noted earlier historians now recognize that the average medieval European was, at most, lukewarm about religion (Bossy, 1985; Murray, 1972; Stark, 1999c; Thomas, 1971). There is every reason to think that the same was true of the Muslims. Compelling evidence is provided by Richard W. Bulliet's (1979) very creative analysis of the history of thousands of names of prominent people in Islam. Bulliet used biographical dictionaries (which abounded in medieval Islamic societies) to code the name of each entrant as Islamic or non-Islamic. By sorting names by year of birth, Bulliet could estimate the proportion of Muslims in the population at various dates and thus create curves of the progress of conversion in various societies. However, because only important people were included in these dictionaries, both the extent and the speed of conversions are very greatly overestimated. Nonetheless, these records trace a very slow rate of conversion—the curves for various places typically required many centuries to pass the 50 percent mark and typically leveled off at about 80 percent. Reality must have fallen far short of these curves. In addition, as noted, many of these conversions would have been quite literally nominal, having been of no greater significance than were most conversions to Christianity among the "barbarians." Thus Bulliet's research provides a very solid basis for the conclusion that Muslim efforts to convert the conquered masses were no more effective than were Christian missions to the barbarians.

Our contrary perceptions are based on European stereotypes of Muslims as fanatics, and on the very recent emergence of Muslim fundamentalism. I do not think that this is a *re*surgence of rank-and-file Muslim commitment. I think it is something quite new, a reaction against colonialism and too-rapid, top-down modernization (Martin, 1991). It was by recently becoming the focus of cultural and political resistance that Islam has gained militant rank-and-file support, just as in the nineteenth century the previously rather indifferent rank and file in Ireland and in French Canada became militant Catholics in reaction against English domination (Stark and Finke, 2000).

In contrast, Muslim immigrants and traders—especially in Africa and parts of Asia—seem to have been as effective at person-to-person proselytism as were the Jews of the diaspora. For example, Indonesia did not become a Muslim society through conquest, treaty, or the conversion of the elite. It was Arab traders who founded colonies along the coasts, and who brought Islam and shared it with their hosts. In similar fashion, Islam took firm root in the southern Philippines and Malaysia. T. W. Arnold (1896:369) provided this description of the conversion of Malay:

> It is to the proselytising efforts of Arab and Indian merchants that
> the native Muhammadan population . . . owes its existence. Settling

in the centres of commerce, they intermarried with the people of the land, and these heathen wives and the slaves of their households thus formed the nucleous of a Muslim community which its members made every effort in their power to increase . . . They did not come as conquerors, like the Spanish in the sixteenth century, or use the sword as an instrument of conversion; nor did they arrogate to themselves the privileges of a superior or dominant race so as to degrade or oppress the original inhabitants, but [came] simply in the guise of traders.

Indeed, the *failure* of Islam to penetrate portions of Indonesia testifies to the network, person-to-person character of the spread of the faith. The boundaries of Indonesian Islam are those separating the commercial coastal areas from the agricultural inland—the latter having remained Hindu through many centuries of Islamic presence. Some scholars attribute this to a special theological compatibility of Islam with commercial activities (Muhammad was, after all, a trader), while Hinduism is said to be more compatible with the hierarchical structure of agrarian societies (Geertz, 1956, 1960; Legge, 1965). This seems plausible until we look beyond this region and notice an abundance of agrarian Muslims elsewhere and notice too the many societies in which Hindus dominate the role of merchant. Rather more compelling is the explanation that Islam failed to spread beyond the commercial areas because Muslims did not become agriculturists in Indonesia; hence their social networks never extended into these regions. Only where rank-and-file Muslims formed network ties to the locals were high rates of conversion achieved. Why? Because only authentic missions get results. Which takes us back to Christianity and its second era of real missions.

The Rebirth of Christian Missions

The Reformation does not mark the rebirth of Christian missions. Sectarian rivalries, no matter how bitter, are about reaffiliation, not conversion. Like the Waldensians and other "heretical" groups before them, Protestants were trying to convince people not to accept a new God but to worship their traditional God according to somewhat different assumptions through new organizational arrangements. Of course, to the extent that Protestant sects brought the barely Christianized masses to God for the first time, their work may have amounted to missionizing. However, at least in the case of Protestantism, it seems unlikely that it did actually Christianize any substantial number of people—rather, only those already having significant Christian concerns ever really took part in the Reformation. As Andrew Greeley (1995:66) pointed out, that the peasants of northwestern Europe so often and readily switched back and forth across the Catholic/Protestant divide, according to the momentary affiliation of their rulers, suggests the superficiality of their Christianity. In any event, efforts by Protestant sectarians or by their Catholic opponents to arouse public enthusiasm took place in a Christian cultural environment and therefore are better identified as *evangelism* than as missionizing.

Evangelism is *an effort to intensify public commitment to the conventional religion(s) of a society.* Hence when Swami A. C. Bhaktivedanta, founder of the International Society for Krishna Consciousness (often referred to as the Hare Krishnas), came to the United States in 1965, he initiated a *mission*. He attempted to convince Americans to newly form an exclusive commitment to a Hindu God. In contrast, when American converts to this movement went to India to seek followers, they were *evangelizing*, attempting to arouse greater commitment among Hindus to their traditional God.

As defined, missions nearly always involve travel to a new society or at least the penetration of a distinctly different religious subgroup within a society.[8] Thus it was that the Age of Exploration confronted Christianity with an immensely expanded mission opportunity to spread the faith to millions of "heathen" in the New World, Asia, and Africa. However, during the first several centuries, these mission efforts were variations on the previously unsuccessful methods of conversion by conquest and colonization. And the results were no better (Drummond, 1971; Eddy, 1945; Griffiths, 1996; Herbert, 1971; Hutchison, 1987; Moran, 1993; Neill,

1986; Robinson, 1923; Ross, 1994; Stanley, 1992; Traboulay, 1994; Yates, 1994).

Initially, missions to the New World were almost exclusively a Spanish undertaking. The task was consigned mainly to priests and monks, and although they were often sensible and humane men, final authority always lay with their political masters, most of whom seem to have believed that coercion could solve anything (Griffiths, 1996; Traboulay, 1994). The brutal and deadly results of Spanish colonization are well known. What has been little known until recently is the amazing failure of Spanish efforts to coerce conversions. Centuries of illusions to the contrary, Latin America never became a "Catholic continent." For example, compared with Europe and North America, the number of priests serving Latin American nations has always been extremely small relative to the "Catholic" population (Stark, 1992). In 1995, for example, one diocesan Catholic priest was said to serve 29,753 Catholics in Guatemala, 20,552 in Bolivia, and 17,835 in Brazil (as compared to 1,833 in the United States, 1,956 in Canada, and 1,861 in Spain). There is nothing to suggest that priests were ever more abundant in Latin America—early Protestant travelers reported many large areas having no priests at all (Robinson, 1923). The lack of priests shows several things. First, the general level of Catholic commitment is so low that very few seek ordination— indeed, even today a substantial proportion of priests in Latin America are foreigners (Martin, 1990). Second, these small numbers of priests seem to have been adequate to meet the very modest demands for their services. Even baptism has been far from universal (and many who do bring their infants to the font do so primarily to ensure the child's "good luck"); church attendance has always been low; and there has been a widespread persistence of pre-Columbian and African religions (Griffiths, 1996; Murphy, 1996). As David Martin (1990:57–58) summarized:

> Curiously, in view of the stereotypical view of Latin America as securely and devoutly Catholic, the culture of the people has been quite resistant to Catholic teaching. This is very understandable in those areas where [indigenous] subject peoples have maintained an under-

ground resistance to their masters. But it is also evident among the Hispanic and Creole populations, for whom such practices as priestly celibacy are unintelligible and who regard actual attendance at church as suitable only for the very young, the old, and the women ... Perhaps less than 20 percent of Latin Americans are regularly involved in the [Catholic] church ... Catholic leaders themselves ... attribute the success of Protestantism to the inertness of conventional Catholicism.

In contrast, Catholic (and especially Jesuit) missionaries had some early success in Asia, particularly in Japan (Drummond, 1971; Moran, 1993; Ross, 1994). But, as top-down missions, these collapsed when the Christianized elites were destroyed by their enemies.

Meanwhile, other European nations began to stake out colonies, and they too were prompted to undertake some mission efforts in conjunction with colonial administrations. Hence French priests began working among the native peoples of Quebec as early as 1610. At about the same time the Dutch sponsored a few missionaries to various places in Southeast Asia. The first group sent by the Dutch made no headway and returned with most of them having failed even to learn a local language. Their replacements adopted a new approach in which tens and then hundreds of thousands were baptized—but without any instruction whatsoever as to what the rite meant (Robinson, 1923). Local chiefs were instructed to have the people drawn up and ready when the missionaries arrived. There were no individual ceremonies; instead, there was a general sprinkling of the crowd, and the baptismal liturgy was said only once, not that any of the "recipients" understood Dutch. Then, with their goal accomplished, the missionaries reported the total number of new Christians to their superiors and were paid a fee per baptism. Thus by the end of the seventeenth century there were alleged to be more than 300,000 Christians in Ceylon and 100,000 in Java. Not surprisingly, no evidence of these "conversions" has endured. Only in the nineteenth and early twentieth centuries did Dutch missionaries accomplish much in Asia (Legge, 1965).

In 1733 the Danes sent some Moravian missionaries to their Greenland colony, there to missionize the Eskimos. Unfortunately, the missionaries brought smallpox with them and caused a lethal epidemic. The Church of England accepted responsibility for the propagation of the gospel in New England, placing it in the hands of clergy most of whom had quite discreditable reasons for wishing to go abroad (Finke and Stark, 1992). These were not missions to authentic "heathen" but were meant to evangelize the unchurched colonists. That fewer than one American colonist in five was churched by 1776 is indicative of the ineffectiveness of these efforts (ibid.). However, despite being relatively unchurched, colonial America sustained a substantial effort to convert Native Americans. Some missions were quite successful in actually converting the rank and file but failed to be of lasting value in preserving the tribe from destruction by disease, expropriation, or defeat. Other missions resembled the Dutch missions in Ceylon or the Spanish in Latin America.

During this same era many Christians were attracted by the challenge of converting the immense populations of India, China, and Japan—and Africa soon beckoned them too. But actual attempts to missionize these continents were few and ineffectual. Aside from employing poor tactics, many mission efforts in the seventeenth and eighteenth centuries ended simply because the missionaries were unable to reach their destinations—as in the case of three English Quaker missionaries dispatched to China in 1661, who never arrived. Given the immense distances involved, and the uncertainties of sailing ships, the wonder is that missionaries attempted to reach these places at all.

But then, at the start of the nineteenth century, something new began (Bainbridge, 1882; Eddy, 1945; Hopkins, 1861, Robinson, 1923). In 1806, five American students at Williams College in Massachusetts met in a secluded grove for their weekly prayer meeting. An approaching thunderstorm caused them to seek refuge behind a haystack, whereupon Samuel Mills (*1783–1818*), who had been studying the geography of Asia, suggested that what they ought to do with their lives was take the gospel to all of the millions who had never had an opportunity to learn about Christ. Soon thereafter they formed a secret fraternity called the Society of Brethren in anticipation of becoming the first missionaries to Asia. Having graduated from Williams and entered Andover Theological Seminary, in 1810 Mills and his friends, now joined by several new members, attended the annual meeting of the Congregational Association of Massachusetts and offered themselves as foreign missionaries. The next day the American Board of Commissioners for Foreign Missions was founded, and the ABCFM continues to oversee all Congregational mission efforts, few as they have become, in a denomination now known as the United Church of Christ.

Although they were college-educated, these mission volunteers did not come from privileged backgrounds but were from the "lower classes in an infant college, at a place so secluded that no mail from any direction reaches it oftener than once a week, and [with] an ocean and a continent intervening" between them and their mission (Hopkins, 1861:16). Nevertheless, in 1812 these New Englanders became the first American foreign missionaries, as five young clergymen, three accompanied by their wives, set sail for Bombay, India.[9]

However, these young Americans were not the first Protestant foreign missionaries to achieve substantial results in India. That honor may belong to William Carey (*1761–1834*), a self-educated former shoe repairman who, as a young British Baptist pastor, convinced his coreligionists to found the Baptist Missionary Society. Unwilling to wait for the society to raise funding, in 1793 Carey went on his own to India, where he supported himself as manager of an indigo plantation and missionized in his spare time. Later, after several other missionaries had arrived from England, Carey moved to Calcutta, where he earned his living by teaching, translated the Bible into literally dozens of local languages, founded Serampore College in 1818, supervised newly arriving missionaries, preached, and led many relief efforts (Chatterjee, 1984; Smith, 1885; Walker, 1926).

Soon, many other groups in America and Great Britain organized missionary societies. The British and Foreign Bible Society began its work in 1804. In 1812 British Anglicans founded the Church Missionary Society for Africa and the East, and in 1815 it sent its

Going for God. In 1812 the first five American missionaries were ordained prior to their departure for India. © CORBIS.

first two missionaries abroad. The American Baptist Missionary Union was founded in 1814, the American Bible Society in 1816.

These professional missionaries were not the Protestant equivalent of monks. They were the vanguard of a real mission movement intending nothing less than to convert continents—every man, woman, and child. If these missionaries often went to places under colonial rule by European powers, usually they had no official standing, and surprisingly often the colonial administrators and Western traders objected to their coming. But they came and they stayed. And not only did they preach the gospel, they opened schools, colleges, and hospitals. To sustain these undertakings, they recruited and trained local teachers, doctors, and nurses—and they ordained growing numbers of local clergy. In the case of the British and Americans, the money for all of this came, not from government subsidies, but from the freewill offerings of rank-and-file Protestants (modest mission efforts mounted at this same time by Continental Protestants were financed by state-supported churches). The voluntary mode of funding was possible because, in the United States and to some extent in Great Britain, Christianity had once again become a bottom-up organization—or, more accurately, a collection of bottom-up organizations. Before I explain how that happened, it will be helpful for the reader to gain an overview of these new mission efforts.

During the first half of the nineteenth century, progress was slow, and the number of Protestant missionaries small. Then, the steamship changed everything. Relatively cheap and rapid travel made ventures to distant ports much more attractive, and the number of missionaries grew proportionately. By 1880, when William Folwell Bainbridge[10] went around the world to visit all Protestant missions, there were 2,657 British and 1,440 American Protestant missionaries serving abroad—plus a few hundred from northern European nations. Together, the British and American mission schools enrolled 365,632 students; the missions employed 26,030 local "helpers" and claimed nearly 400,000 "communicant" members (Bainbridge, 1882). It was possible for Bainbridge to visit all of the missions during his world tour because, initially, the missionaries located their stations on the coasts, or up navigable rivers. Then, the construction of railways, especially in China and India, allowed easy access to interior areas, and this led to the organization of several groups devoted to "inland missions."

Meanwhile, the ranks of missionaries grew rapidly. In 1900, the number of American missionaries serving abroad had risen to 5,278, compared with 5,656 from Britain and about 2,200 from Continental nations (Beach, 1903). The Continental missionaries served almost exclusively in their nation's colonies—nearly all of the Dutch missionaries were in the East Indies, the German missionaries were massed in German Southwest Africa and in German East Africa, and every one of the small band of Belgian Protestant missionaries was in the Congo. The British also tended to be in British colonies, but not nearly so exclusively. Collectively, these new mission efforts had provided schools and colleges enrolling more than a million students and about a thousand hospitals, which employed, in addition to missionary physicians, more than a thousand locally trained doctors (nearly three hundred of them women).

World War I dislocated the mission effort sufficiently that by 1923 it had become predominantly an American undertaking (Beach and Fahs, 1925)—there were 13,463 missionaries from the United States and 8,408 from Britain serving that year. The American dominance was not limited to areas outside the British Empire such as China, where the Americans by then outnumbered the British 4,492 to 1,351, but throughout the world—even in India there were 2,675 Americans compared to 2,455 from Britain.

World War II, and the postwar collapse of British and European colonialism, turned the world Protestant mission effort into a virtual American monopoly. By 1960 there were more than 30,000 full-time American missionaries abroad. In 1996 there were more than 40,000 American missionaries serving commitments of more than one year (Siewert and Valdez, 1997). In reality, the current American mission effort is far greater than even this total suggests. Earlier in the century, in far less affluent times and when travel was, relatively, far more expensive, most missionaries were sustained by denominational mission boards and societies that published full, reliable reports of their activities. But today there is a substantial (but unknown) number of self-supporting, self-appointed American missionaries serving abroad who do not show up in the published statistics. In addition, there are very many missionaries who are sponsored by a local congregation (both denominational and nondenominational), many of whom are not included in the statistics reported by any missionary agency (Barrett, 1998; Siewert, 1998). Moreover, there are many other large and well-tabulated omissions from this total (Siewert and Valdez, 1997). Not included are 28,535 persons *fully supported* by American funds who are serving as full-time missionaries in their own country—more than 10,000 of them in India alone. An additional 1,791 foreign nationals are employed by American agencies as missionaries in countries not their own. Moreover, the 1996 total does not include the 63,995 American Protestants officially serving shorter-term foreign missions of a year or less.

So how many American, or American-funded, foreign missionaries are out there? No one knows. But if we limit the total to full-time professionals (serving tours of more than a year), there are more than 70,000, plus perhaps another 15,000 or more not reported to mission boards. Then factor in another 100,000 volunteers doing tours of a year or less. This suggests that there currently are about 185,000 American Protestant missionaries abroad. And this total does not include tens of thousands of Mormons and Jehovah's Witnesses.

Of the millions of baptisms that these efforts have produced, few have involved kings. Instead, from the beginning, these have been missions to the people, and they really began to show results when the actual work of proselytism shifted from missionary-to-local networks to entirely local-to-local networks, as the first generation of converts began to draw in their relatives, friends, and neighbors. Nowhere has this been more dramatically demonstrated than in the "Protestantization" of Latin America (Gill, 1998; Martin, 1990; Stoll, 1990).

At the turn of the twentieth century, there was a heated debate among American and British mission officials about the propriety of sending missionaries to Latin America. Many believed that mission efforts ought to be limited entirely to non-Christian nations. Since Latin Americans were Christians, albeit Catholics, no missionaries should be sent. To signal their disapproval of missionizing Latin America, when an international conference on world missions was held in Edinburgh in 1909, its organizers excluded those involved in Latin America (Gill, 1998:82). In reaction, various American evangelical denominations and mission organizations held their own conference in Panama several years later and affirmed Latin America as a high-priority field on the grounds that the claim that these were Catholic nations was misleading. Based on their travels and observations, these mission leaders were sure that the masses in Latin America had yet to be Christianized in any meaningful sense. And so they went.

In 1900 there were already 610 American Protestant missionaries deployed in continental Latin America. By 1923 the total had risen to 1,627, and in 1996 there were nearly 12,000. To put this number in perspective, at present there are substantially more full-time American missionaries (nearly all of them from evangelical Protestant denominations) in many Latin American nations than there are Roman Catholic diocesan priests! In Honduras there are five missionaries per priest, and missionaries outnumber priests two to one in Panama and Guatemala. This does not include thousands of missionaries on shorter tours. It also ignores the fact that native-born evangelical Protestant clergy now far outnumber both missionaries and priests in many parts of Latin America. Consequently, in many Latin nations today, the great majority of people in church on any given Sunday are Protestants (given the very low attendance rates of Catholics), and in many nations from a tenth to a quarter of the population are now claimed as *active* evangelical Protestants (Siewert and Valdez, 1997; Stoll, 1990)—as even official Catholic statistics now concede. A generation ago, figures in the *Catholic Almanac* placed the percent Catholic in most Latin American nations in the very high nineties, allowing a percent or two for Protestants and Communists. The 1999 edition of the *Almanac* conceded that Chile is "only" 78.2 percent Catholic, that Brazil is only 86 percent, and that only 90.1 percent of the population of Argentina is Roman Catholic. Of course, these numbers are nearly as absurd as the old ones claiming 98 percent Catholic. Not only do they substantially understate the growth of evangelical Protestantism; what is more significant, they are computed on the assumption that aside from those who are explicitly not Catholics, *everyone else is*. Were this true, had most Latin Americans in times past actually been Catholics, the immense effects of Protestant missions would have been impossible. People are quite reluctant to shift from one religious commitment to another, but they are often quite ready to acquire a commitment in place of none, or to replace the rather weak commitments inspired by polytheism. As will be seen, this principle has been confirmed on other continents as Christian missions have gathered rapidly growing local conversion networks in Africa, in parts of Asia, and, indeed, in Europe.

Pluralism and Participation

An obvious question is, Why was an authentic mission impulse reborn in Christianity? And my answer is that the development of relatively free market conditions vis-à-vis religion results in the emergence of pluralism—of multiple religious organizations, which must compete for survival—and this always favors bottom-up organizations. I have written at length about the conditions governing religious pluralism, and how competition among religious "firms" maximizes the overall level of religious mobilization in societies, and will pursue these matters in Chapter 5 (Stark and Finke, 2000).

Here it is sufficient to note that in religion as in anything else, *effort is rewarded*. Other things being equal, the harder members of a religious group work to attract new members, the more their organization grows. Nothing makes a group work harder than knowing that they are challenged on all sides by other groups also prepared to work hard to grow—or to at least hold their own. In contrast, nothing destroys initiative more rapidly than the elimination of competition and thereby of the need to generate high levels of member support. Recall the contrast between the enthusiasm of rank-and-file Christians prior to the conversion of Constantine and the rapid loss of this enthusiasm once Christianity became the highly subsidized state church, governed by an affluent and powerful clergy who catered to the upper classes. Moreover, the clergy of any subsidized state religion are, as Adam Smith pointed out ([1776] 1981:789), inevitably content to repose "themselves upon their benefices [while neglecting] to keep up the fervour of faith and the devotion in the great body of the people; and having given themselves up to indolence . . . become altogether incapable of making any vigorous exertion in defence even of their own establishment." And that's precisely why the state churches of northwestern Europe never exerted themselves to Christianize and activate the masses—their privileges and affluence were guaranteed without their doing much of anything other than to remain within the good graces of the ruling elites. Indeed, it was only in conjunction with the international competition engendered by colonialism, and by Protestant-Catholic antagonisms, that the subsidized state churches of continental Europe bestirred themselves to any foreign mission efforts.

Without state subsidies, churches must depend on member support, and therefore the well-being of leaders rests upon their ability to satisfy and motivate the rank and file—ergo bottom-up organizations. When bottom-up groups are also committed monotheists, they are eager to proselytize, not only locally but ubiquitously, to bring their True Faith to everyone.

It was the emergence of religious pluralism and of religious competition in the United States, and to a somewhat lesser degree in Britain, that restored bottom-up Christian organizations. From the start, these contending Protestant sects eagerly pursued one another's members, and it was inevitable that eventually they would raise their goals to the conversion of the whole world. Here, too, they found much additional motivation in competition. No one put this so clearly and succinctly as William Folwell Bainbridge, a leading figure in American Baptist foreign missions, upon his return from the previously mentioned two-year trip (1879–1880) during which he visited all Protestant missions:

> The frequently-mooted plan of denominational division of labor among foreign mission stations needs reconsideration. Lately it has been proposed in Japan, that all the missions should be represented in a delegation that should map out the country, apportioning to each denomination its sphere of work. Anxieties are frequently felt both by missionaries and their home constituencies lest there be infringement upon pre-empted territory. But I have observed that, as a rule, those mission stations of whatever church or denomination, which are left entirely by themselves . . . do not show that activity and develop that strength, which are manifested in those mission fields where [there is competition]. It was evident in Yokohama that Presbyterians and Methodists were prompting each other to a larger measure of evangelizing enterprise than either would have commanded with all the responsibility in the hands of a single mission, even though reinforced to the full extent of the other denomination's men and means . . . In Burma the Baptists have never been so stirred up

in regard to their missions as since the advent of the Propagation Society and the Methodists . . . The American mission school work at Beirut has been stirred to still more efficiency by the British Syrian schools and Bible missions. It does seem there are greater advantages than having a mission all to one's dear denominational self. (1882:270–72)

Statistical confirmation of Bainbridge's point of view appeared in *Mission Frontiers* more than a century later. Wayne Allen (1999) compared subsidized and unsubsidized mission districts among the Dayaks of Indonesia—a society of preliterate animists who live by slash-and-burn agriculture. American missionaries have been active among the Dyak since shortly after World War II, and their missions were organized into districts in 1960. During the 1970s some missionaries began to challenge the policy that indigenous churches be self-supporting and to campaign for financial subsidies. Soon, subsidies were provided for several of the districts, where they were used to provide salaries for native clergy. Elsewhere, native clergy remained unpaid volunteers. Where there were no subsidies, the Dayak missions grew by an average of 5.75 new churches a decade (1960–1990). Where native clergy were able to devote full time to their duties because of American mission funding, growth amounted to 0.5 new churches per decade.[11] That's all it took to create a "state church" mentality among the Dayak.

In religion, as in all human endeavors, motivation is the key to success, and socialized religious "workers" are as unmotivated as those in socialized industries. It is no accident of history that the new era of Christian missions has been mainly an American affair. This becomes fully apparent when we contrast American religious bodies in terms of their participation in missions.

The Collapse of Liberal Missionizing

In the beginning, American missions were dominated by what have since come to be known as the liberal denominations, and which the press often mistakenly identifies as the "mainline" denominations (Finke and Stark, 1992). The very first Americans sent abroad went under the auspices of the Congregationalists. In 1880, as the missions grew rapidly, the United Presbyterian Church was the leader, with 34.3 percent of the 1,440 American missionaries. The Congregationalists were a close second, with 29.8 percent, followed by the United Methodists (15.0 percent) and the American Baptists (12.3 percent). Episcopalians made up 3.3 percent, and the Friends (all meetings) 1.4 percent. Hence 96.1 percent of all American missionaries were from the so-called liberal mainline. Very few missionaries were being sent by evangelical groups—the Southern Baptists had supplied only 19, or 1.3 percent.

But soon thereafter, grumbling began in leading divinity schools about the propriety of sending out missionaries at all. That is, churchmen who no longer believed in One True God, or perhaps in anything more Godly than an essence, began to express doubts as to whether there was any theological or moral basis for attempting to convert non-Christians. At first these qualms did not register in terms of absolute numbers of missionaries. Hence while the Congregationalists had supplied 429 missionaries in 1880 (Bainbridge, 1882), they supported 661 in 1916. But this was a small increase compared to the sudden influx of missionaries from evangelical groups. Thus in 1916 the Southern Baptist Convention had 307 missionaries abroad, and the overall percentage from the liberal mainline had dropped from 96.1 to 67.1 percent (U.S. Census, 1919).

In the aftermath of World War I, liberal condemnations of missionizing grew increasingly strident and public. Led by Daniel Johnson Fleming of New York's Union Seminary and Harvard's William Ernest Hocking, liberal Protestants charged that Christianity has no greater claim to religious truth than do other religions, and that the entire mission effort must accept the validity of non-Christian religions rather than try to replace them. In January 1930, a blue-ribbon commission (funded by John D. Rockefeller, Jr.) was convened to "re-think" Christian missions. When the final report appeared in 1932 (under the prestigious imprint of Harper and Brothers), it attracted national attention and was widely read. Written by Hocking, and signed by his wife and thirteen other commission members, *Re-thinking Missions* charged that "it is a humiliating mistake" for Christians to think their faith is superior, for there is nothing unique in Christianity, and anything in its teachings that "is true belongs, in its nature, to the human mind everywhere" (1932:49). Hocking went on to argue that if "the Orient is anywhere unresponsive," the fault lies with missionaries who attempt to teach complex doctrines that "are too little Christian, too much the artifacts of our western brains" (ibid.:49–50). Several pages later (ibid.:53), the commission warned against missionizing to the slogan "Our message is Jesus Christ," lest natives fail to realize that this is merely symbolic language "marking loyalty to a tradition." The report then proceeded to denounce all teachings that credit "intrusions from the supernatural" into "the realm of natural law"—that is, miracles.

As can easily be inferred from the report, the basis for Hocking's objection to missions, long shared by his fellow liberal theologians (Ahlstrom, 1972), was that he could no longer acknowledge God as an aware, conscious, concerned, active being. Rather, in his book *The Meaning of God in Human Experience: A Philosophic Study of Religion* (1912), Hocking devoted nearly six hundred pages to dispatching traditional conceptions of God, leaving a God having only vague, symbolic properties—anticipating Paul Tillich's (1951) notion of God as a psychological construct, the "ground of our being." Indeed, having reduced God to an essence of interior goodness, Hocking asserted that all religions are reflections of the same God, albeit in somewhat idiosyncratic ways.

Despite this, Hocking and his committee felt that, on the whole, missions were valuable and should continue. But what would such missionaries do? Perform Christian service! As Ralph Cooper Hutchison explained in the *Atlantic Monthly* (1927:621), who cares if even "from this day to the end of time not a single person surrenders his indifference or deserts his own faith to become a Christian . . . [for] service to needy men requires no pay in the form of conversion to Christianity." In fact, by this time, among eastern college students from whose ranks most missionaries had previously been drawn, "[p]hrases like 'evangelization of the world' . . . had become downright embarrassing," in the words of William Hutchison (1987:147), Harvard historian and son of Ralph Cooper Hutchison. Henceforth, the young idealists from the Ivy League should go forth on behalf of worldly good deeds—to spread knowledge of matters such as sanitation rather than salvation.

Whatever the theological virtues of these views, they are sociologically naive. As soon became obvious, people will seldom face the hardships of missionary service merely to do good deeds. Without the conviction that they were bringing priceless truths to those in need, the mission spirit quickly dissipated in liberal Protestant circles. Missionary recruitment "flagged" on college campuses; the "Student Volunteer Movement attracted declining numbers to its conventions, to the signing of pledge cards, and to actual missionary service" (Hutchison, 1987:147). Indeed, the younger Hutchison would have us believe that this was the end of the mission era, noting in his well-received history of American Protestant missions that their "heyday" occurred from 1880 to 1930. He made this absurd claim while fully aware that the mission movement was barely begun by 1930, and that there are far more missionaries in the field now than ever before. But *they* don't count! Why? Because, as Hutchison (ibid.:200) pointed out, most of these missionaries are nothing but "aggressive soul savers" and "extreme conservatives," while enlightened Christians long ago gave up such vulgar activities. Indeed, James Reed (1983:197) also claimed that the "Protestant missionary movement began to wane in the 1920s," justifying his statement on the basis that the influx of evangelicals is merely an "atavism."

Hutchison and Reed were correct about at least one thing: the liberals certainly did rapidly give up on missionizing, abandoning the field to evangelicals. Thus by 1935 barely half of all missionaries were from liberal denominations (Parker, 1938); this fell to 26.8 percent by 1948 (Grubb and Bingle, 1949), to 18.0 percent in 1966 (Coxill and Grubb, 1967), and to 4.2 percent in 1996 (Siewert and Valdez, 1997). And it isn't only proselytizing abroad that has become scarce in these same denominations. A national sample of Americans was asked in 1988, "Have you ever tried to encourage someone to believe in Christ or to accept Jesus as his or her savior?" Only about one in five members of liberal Protestant groups answered yes. But four of five did so among evangelicals

(Stark and Finke, 2000). I probably need not point out which denominations are growing and which have long been in decline (Finke and Stark, 1992).

New Vistas

Several years ago David Martin (1989:31) told one of his English colleagues that he was planning to write a book about Protestantism in Latin American. The response he received was "A very small book, surely." Yet when Martin's *Tongues of Fire: The Explosion of Protestantism in Latin America* appeared in 1990 it was in fact the *second* book on the topic that year, preceded by David Stoll's *Is Latin America Turning Protestant? The Politics of Evangelical Growth*.

Until these books were published, the successful entry of aggressive Protestant missions into most of Latin America had gone largely unnoticed in scholarly circles. Indeed, according to most social scientists, such a thing was impossible. Some could accept that the Catholic Marxism known as Liberation Theology had a small future (at least in the short term) in Latin America, but a successful outbreak of evangelical Protestantism was dismissed as absurd—hence the haughty reactions Martin experienced when he began his study. Ironically, neither Martin's nor Stoll's book was all that timely. A very good study could have been written thirty years earlier, for evangelical Protestants had already achieved an impressive "liftoff" by 1960. Moreover, much was being written about the rapid growth of Protestantism in Latin America as early as the 1950s. However, because these reports appeared only in sectarian publications, the millions of American evangelicals who regularly contributed funds to support missions in Latin American were the only ones who knew. It took the scholarly world another thirty or forty years to catch on.

Today, these same evangelical publications are filled with news about "the astonishing growth" in sub-Saharan Africa, where local-to-local networks are currently bringing in millions of converts, and where about half of the population is now Christian (Johnstone, 1993:34). Indeed, there are more than five thousand different *indigenous* Protestant sects, some of them very large, now operating in sub-Saharan Africa (Barrett, 1968; Gifford, 1998). One would hope that lessons learned from Latin America would prompt social scientists to pay attention before another thirty years have passed.

One group that has been paying attention is the Roman Catholic Church. In Latin America, local Catholic mission and evangelizing efforts have increased in direct response to the success of local Protestant missions (Gill, 1998). Indeed, just as competition resulted in an extremely aggressive and effective American Catholicism (Finke and Stark, 1992), so too the Catholic Church in Latin America has recently been energized by Protestant pressures. For example, in many nations the rates of seminary enrollments and of ordinations have been rising—probably for the first time in history (Gill, 1999)—and there has been a quite dramatic outburst of Catholic evangelizing (Clarke, 1999).

It also needs to be acknowledged that from the start, Catholic missions in Africa have been real missions in the sense that they have been aimed at the masses and based on persuasion, and with real success—approximately half of African Christians are Catholics. One reason for this may be that these Catholic missions began much later than missions to Latin America or even to Asia and thus were influenced by rather different attitudes about coercion. Moreover, unlike the circumstances they faced in Latin America, the Catholic mission orders in Africa were not controlled by brutal political regimes or by an entrenched colonial upper class. Free to follow their own course, the orders sought to win souls, not to force conformity—as they might have done in Latin America, too, had they been free to do so. Of immense importance is the fact that Africa was from the start a highly competitive mission field—even in the Belgian Congo there were Protestant as well as Catholic missions—and often there was Muslim competition as well. As Bainbridge recognized, monopoly missions always underachieve.

The same is true of monopoly state churches, which helps explain one of the most telling and least noticed mission developments since World War II: Europe has become a very active mission target. As American soldiers returned from service in Europe, espe-

103

cially service in the postwar European garrison forces, many of them enrolled in evangelical colleges and seminaries, where they made it common knowledge that church attendance is extremely low and appreciation of basic Christian culture is largely lacking in much of Europe. Indicative of this growing concern, in his very influential textbook on Christian missions published in 1971, J. Herbert Kane (1971:535) quoted Hans Lilje, bishop of the German Evangelical Church and a president of the World Council of Churches, as admitting that "[t]he era when Europe was a Christian continent lies behind us." For evangelical Americans, this presented an irresistible challenge, and forthwith "Europe came to be regarded as a mission field."

So, in the late 1950s and early 1960s, one after another of the major evangelical mission boards began to shift resources to European missions. By 1975 there were 2,363 American Protestant, full-time, long-term missionaries in Europe. By 1985 this total had grown to 3,898. Then the Berlin Wall came down and Communist prohibitions of mission activity collapsed; American mission boards reacted. In 1996 there were nearly 5,000 missionaries in Western Europe and another 2,400 in the East. This total does not include many thousands of independents and short-term volunteers. Nor does it include thousands of Jehovah's Witnesses. Although mission periodicals express considerable concern about restrictions being imposed on missionaries in the former Soviet Union, they are aglow with enthusiasm about Christianizing Europe.

The important point is that Christian missionaries today are not devoted primarily to "Christian service." As need dictates, of course, they bring medical services, schools, basic public health, and sanitation techniques. But that's not why they go. They go because their conception of God justifies and motivates their mission efforts. Unlike liberal Protestants whose vague ideas about God no longer let them "presume" to tell someone else they have the wrong religion, evangelical Protestants remain confident that it is God's plan that "all the nations and tongues" shall be Chosen People.

Finally, something must be said about efforts to depict Christian missionaries as servants of colonial capitalism. This is a very old refrain. In his play *The Man of Destiny* (1897), George Bernard

Shaw had Napoleon say that when an Englishman "wants a new market for his adulterated Manchester goods, he sends a missionary to teach the natives the Gospel." Of course, not only was Shaw a dedicated atheist and socialist, he also worked hard at "offending" the conventional public, much as did Mark Twain (1901), who made similar charges about ties to imperialism in several nasty essays about missionaries. Anyone who believes the notion of missionaries as the agents of Western imperialism has probably never met missionaries or read an informed account of missions (e.g., Neill, 1986), and certainly has not read any sampling of the letters, diaries, or autobiographies of missionaries. Four themes dominate these materials. Love of God. Loneliness for family and friends. The satisfactions of forming attachments to those to whom they have been sent, and the resentment the missionary feels toward all Westerners or local rulers who exploit or impose on the people. It was not at all unusual for missionaries to become deeply involved in bitter conflicts with commercial and colonial leaders in support of the local populations (Hiney, 2000). Even so ardent an opponent of the mission movement as William Hutchison (1987:92) could grudgingly admit that the missionaries were quite opposed to "the evil" of "exploitation or colonization," although he was quick to characterize any efforts to Christianize as imperialism per se. Hutchison made it clear that his objections to missions had to do only with efforts to spread the gospel; he approved of missions modeled on the Peace Corps. What he failed to grasp, even though efforts by his father and many others to create such missions were complete failures, is what Mother Teresa made clear when a reporter referred to her sisters as social workers: "We are not social workers. We do this for Jesus!"

Hindu Missions

Western devotees of Eastern religion often quote Ramakrishna Paramahansa's (1836–1886) eloquent claims that all religions are true and all Gods are one and the same, in order to display the superior tolerance and wisdom of Hinduism. In the best-selling textbook ever written for comparative religion courses, Huston Smith (1991:74–75) devoted most of two pages to an excerpt from Ramakrishna, which included the following passages:

> *God has made different religions to suit different aspirations, times, and countries. All doctrines are only so many paths . . . one can reach God if one follows any of the paths with whole-hearted devotion . . . the one Everlasting-Intelligent-Bliss is invoked by some as God, by some as Allah, by some as Jehovah, and by others as Brahman.*

> *People partition off their lands by means of boundaries, but no one can partition off the all-embracing sky overhead. The indivisible sky surrounds all and includes all. So people in ignorance say, "My religion is the only one, my religion is the best." But when a heart is illuminated by true knowledge, it knows that above all these wars of sects and sectarians presides the one, indivisible, eternal, all-knowing bliss.*

As a preface to this excerpt, Smith (ibid.:73) expressed his own sentiments: "To claim that salvation is the monopoly of any one religion is like claiming that God can be found in this room but not in the next, in this attire but not another."

Authors who don't quote Ramakrishna often quote his disciple Swami Vivekananda *(1863–1902)*, especially his lecture at the World Parliament of Religions in Chicago in 1893, in which he proposed that Hinduism is not only the most ancient of the world religions but the "mother" of all of the others and, for that reason, the most tolerant (Hanson, 1894; Seager, 1993).

These views, especially the one that all religions are the same religion, have struck a very sympathetic chord among Westerners seeking alternatives to the Judeo-Christian religious tradition, especially when, as Simon Weightman (1984:193) explained, they are "coupled with the notion of the spiritual East and the materialistic West, as if there were no spirituality in the West and no materialism in the East." Of particular interest is the additional claim that, because Hindus realize that all religions and Gods are one, Hinduism is *not a missionizing* religion. Ironically, this claim is made most often by people who are in the act of missionizing on behalf of

Hinduism, as in: "You should embrace my faith because it is so much wiser and more tolerant than that narrow and disgusting creed of yours."

Contrary to the textbooks, Ramakrishna and Vivekananda actually represented a very unusual, liberal brand of Hinduism. As the Danish religious historian Johannes Aagaard put it:

> The nature of Hinduism is normally described in connection with the liberal reformers . . . Therefore, the whole nationalist and revivalist line is tuned down and the expansion and mission of Hinduism is not seen. The result is a complete caricature of Hinduism and its nature and mission . . . for which the scholars are to be made responsible . . . It is not a minor mistake. (In Mathew, 1987:7–8)

It would be appropriate to identify Ramakrishna, Vivekananda, and their followers as the Indian counterparts of William Hocking and his colleagues, whose attacks on Christian exclusivity were written partly in response to the "ecumenical" example set by Ramakrishna and Vivekananda. But just as American missions did not eschew conversionism when Hocking said they should, the missionizing spirit of Hinduism did not disappear in response to assertions of its nonexistence. Rather, entirely in keeping with its essential monotheism, Hinduism claims to possess exclusive religious truth. As Maharishi Mahesh Yogi, founder of Transcendental Meditation, put it, "I felt a strong desire to spread the true religion" (in Mathew, 1987:6). The very idea that Yahweh, Jehovah, and Allah are alternative names for Brahman is anathema even to most Hindu intellectuals, let alone to the rank and file (Mathew, 1987). Were it otherwise, how would one explain the chronic and brutal violence against non-Hindus that has gone on so long in India, especially since the British left, and the need to partition the subcontinent into Hindu and Muslim nations? Should anyone propose that this was entirely in response to Muslim violence (which it wasn't), one might ask that person for an account of the recent attacks on Sikhs and the desecration of their most sacred temple, and of the rash of anti-Christian violence in Hindu India—church burnings and missionary murders. No! Conventional Hindus regard theirs as the *true* faith to the same extent as do Muslims, Christians, and Jews and are just as inclined to missionizing. And the reason is that Hinduism at least approximates monotheism.

There is a general impression among Westerners that Hinduism is polytheistic, and hence relationships with any given God are short-term and utilitarian, as is typical in polytheistic religious economies. But this is a quite erroneous (Fowler, 1997; Knipe, 1993; Parrinder, 1983; Smart, 1984; Weightman, 1984). First of all, the Hindu Gods really number only two: *Vishnu* and *Shiva*. Each of the many other apparent Gods is regarded as an additional aspect, avatar, or incarnation of one of these two. Thus while there exist many different Hindu sects devoted to different incarnations, it is understood that each really is either Vishnu or Shiva. The popular Krishna, for example, is an avatar of Vishnu. Some scholars claim that, in fact, Hindus *do not worship both* Vishnu and Shiva (Fowler, 1997; Weightman, 1984). Following a principle known as *ishtadeva*, "the chosen deity," the individual Hindu worships one or the other "exclusively as the supreme God": "[O]ne could spend a lifetime in India and never find a 'polytheist' in Western terms, because even an unlettered peasant who has just made offerings at several shrines will affirm that ... God is one" (Weightman, 1984:212). Indeed, many Hindus do not really believe that there are two Gods, but only Brahman, the creator of the universe, who can be worshiped in the form of either Vishnu or Shiva (Bowker, 1997; Smart, 1984). Thus Hinduism at least approximates monotheism.

It is worth recalling that once it got its monotheistic bearings, Hinduism extinguished a thriving Buddhist establishment in India. It also sustained missionizing efforts in Southeast Asia, often taking the form of conversion by conquest and colonizing (Kane, 1953; Majumder, 1963). Moreover, just as the Jews have repulsed many centuries of Christian and Muslim efforts to convert them, Hinduism withstood centuries of conversion efforts by Muslim conquerors. As Willard Oxtoby (1996a:544–45) noted, "the Muslims in India were minority rulers of a subcontinent that remained dominantly Hindu."

But the definitive proof that Hinduism is a missionizing faith is to be found in the presence of literally hundreds of Hindu mission organizations and centers in Europe and North America—many of which frankly include the word "mission" in their names. Just as the steamship made it feasible for Christian missionaries to go to India, Hindu missionaries were soon booking themselves aboard the return voyages. By the end of the nineteenth century, Hindu missionaries enjoyed a considerable vogue among intellectuals in Europe and America. Ironically, their way had been prepared by Christian missionaries to India who had translated many sacred Hindu scriptures, including the Bhagavad Gita, in order to better understand the "opposition." The circulation of these scriptures in Europe and the United States had considerable impact, especially among secularists who regarded themselves as "too sophisticated" to accept Christianity or Judaism (Oppenheim, 1988; Washington, 1995). Thus the New England "Transcendentalists" who gathered around Ralph Waldo Emerson (*1803–1882*), poet and failed Unitarian minister, were deeply and obviously influenced by Hindu teachings. The first Hindu guru to visit America gave his first lecture in the home of Emerson's widow in Concord, Massachusetts, on September 2, 1883. From Concord, Protap Chunder Mozoomdar went on to make a number of appearances in other parts of New England (Melton, 1988). On his way to America, Mozoomdar had stopped in England, where he also found a ready audience—Hinduism having attracted some devotees among those who had served as colonial civil servants in India. Nevertheless, the early days of Hinduism in England were dominated by very unauthentic adaptations such as the Theosophy concocted by Helena Petrovna Blavatsky (*1831–1891*).

Ten years after Mozoomdar's American tour, several Hindu missionaries appeared at the World Parliament of Religions in Chicago, and among them was, as mentioned, Swami Vivekananda, who became the star of the gathering (Hanson, 1894; Seager, 1993). After the Chicago affair ended, Vivekananda toured America for two years and founded the first Hindu mission movement in America—the Vedanta Society. Thus began a substantial influx of Hindu missionaries to the West, lasting until travel became virtually impossible because of World War I.

Of course, to missionize in the West, Hindus faced many barriers. In addition to colonialism and ethnic prejudice, two devastating wars interfered greatly (as was true for Christian mission efforts too). There have also been a variety of legal restrictions. In many European nations, even Protestant missionizing was illegal until quite recently, let alone proselytism on behalf of "heathenism" (Stark and Finke, 2000). Hindu missionaries faced no such barriers in the United States, if only they could get a visa. From the early 1920s until 1965, it was almost impossible for Hindu missionaries (or anyone else from India) to become residents of the United States, and the swamis and gurus were limited to short stays on visitor visas. This afforded an opportunity for local initiative—the immensely popular books on Hindu teachings by Swami Ramacharacka (some of which are still in print) were in fact written by an American named William Walker Atkinson, and Oom the Omnipotent, founder of the Tantrick Order of America, was an American using the name Pierre Bernard, who had been born as Peter Coons (Melton, 1989). Americans posing as Indians were not a very effective substitute for the real thing. Thus it was a matter of great significance when the immigration laws were modified in 1965 so that once again authentic gurus could missionize America. Indeed, before the year was out, Swami Bhaktivedanta had taken up residence in New York City and had begun to instruct several potential converts to his International Society of Krishna Consciousness (ISKCON), and Satguru Sant Keshavadas had founded the Temple of Cosmic Religion[12] in Washington, D.C. Also in 1965, the first center of the Society for Transcendental Meditation was founded in Los Angeles, and Maharishi Mahesh Yogi, leader and founder of the movement, began the first of his long stays in America the next year. Before the 1960s ended, many other Hindu teachers flocked to America; more have come since, including Bhagwan Shree Rajneesh, whose community in Antelope, Oregon, attracted several thousand devotees, many of them upper-middle-class professional women (Goldman, 1999).

It can be argued that Hinduism in America is still in the stage of missionary-to-local networks, and that real growth lies ahead when the local-to-local conversion process gains momentum.

However, that ignores the hard going faced by missions to societies having a deeply entrenched monotheism, as is clearly revealed by the very small numbers of converts thus far to these various Hindu missions and the "religious" backgrounds of those who do join. As to numbers, there have probably never been more than four thousand members of ISKCON (Hare Krishna) in the United States, and most of the other missions have never attracted more than a thousand. Americans who do join are overwhelmingly from irreligious backgrounds. Young Americans from "secular" Jewish homes are many times more likely to be recruited by Hindu missionaries than are Americans of any other background. The other highly susceptible group consists of those who give their parents' religion as "none" (Judah, 1974; Stark and Bainbridge, 1985). Given the high level of active religiousness in America, one would expect Hindu missionaries to have done far better in Europe, and they have. Proportionate to population, there are far more Hindu mission centers operating in most Western European nations than in the United States (Stark, 1985, 1993). Indeed, they already are quite active in Eastern Europe (Carden, 1998; Krindatch, 1995; Ross, 1995; Zagorska, 1998).

Conclusion

The common element in all of these authentic instances of missions is monotheism. The logic involved is elegant and compelling. If there is only one God, then anyone who worships other Gods is profoundly wrong. Surely one owes it to them, as well as to God, to bring them the truth. So far, so good. But it also seems to follow that one has an obligation to protect people from error and from false prophets. "Here be monsters."

Notes

1. Also spelled Ikhnaton.
2. The principle of diffusion should not be confused with the theory known as diffusionism, that civilization developed in only one center and spread from there.

3. In previous work I have defined conversion as a long-distance shift in religious allegiance—a shift *across* religious traditions, as when one "converts" from Christianity to Islam. In doing so, I took an exclusive commitment, at least to the new faith, for granted. Here I make that assumption explicit. In keeping with Nock, one does not convert from one God to another within a polytheistic system. That would constitute what I have previously defined as reaffiliation. As stated, this new definition fully covers conversions across monotheisms as well as conversion to a monotheism from irreligion or polytheism.

4. For centuries it was anti-Semites who denied that Jews once missionized, preferring to cast them as too exclusive and selfish to do so. Edward Gibbon (*The Decline and Fall . . .* 1.15) is representative, writing of the "Jewish religion" that it was of "narrow and unsocial spirit, which, instead of inviting, had deterred the gentiles from embracing the law of Moses . . . The sullen obstinacy with which they maintained their peculiar rites and unsocial manners . . . that unsocial people was actuated by the selfish vanity . . . that they alone were the heirs of the covenant, and that they were apprehensive of diminishing the value of their inheritance, by sharing it too easily with the strangers of the earth." Ironically, today it is Jews who deny that ancient Judaism missionized, seemingly in order to claim that only Christianity was capable of such an inherently arrogant activity. Indeed, Martin Goodman (1994) claims that to the very small extent that Jews ever proselytized, they learned it from Christians and did so out of self-preservation. I think it not irrelevant that the denial of Jewish missions seems to enlist greatest support from less religious and "secular" Jews, while more religious Jews such as Louis Feldman (1993) are entirely comfortable writing chapters with titles such as "The Success of Proselytism by Jews in the Hellenistic and Early Roman Periods."

5. The Pentateuch had been translated into the Greek—the Septuagint.

6. This passage inspired me to undertake projections of early Christian growth and to infer that Jews probably converted to Christianity in far greater numbers and over a substantially longer period than has been assumed (Stark, 1996a).

7. The recognition that conversion is a network phenomenon, spreading through structures of direct and intimate interpersonal attachments, is no longer limited to sociologists. The historian Robin Lane Fox (1987:316) noted, albeit concerning Christian conversion, that "[a]bove all we should give weight to the presence and influence of friends. It is a force which so often escapes the record, but it gives shape to everyone's personal life. One friend might bring another to the faith . . . When a person turned to God, he found others, new 'brethren,' who were sharing the same path." Peter Brown, also a historian, expressed similar views: "Ties of family, marriages, and loyalties to heads of households had been the most effective means of recruiting members of the church, and had maintained the continued adherence of the average Christian to the new cult" (1988:90).

8. Sometimes this involves missions from a smaller to a larger subgroup (or subculture), as in the case of Mormon missionaries in the United States, or Christian missionaries in ancient Rome.

9. Samuel Mills was not among them, having been asked to remain home to recruit others to mission work. In 1819, at age thirty-five, he died at sea while returning from his first trip abroad—a brief visit to West Africa.

10. Great-grandfather of my colleague and frequent coauthor, William Sims Bainbridge.

11. District 2, which received subsidies for part of the period, is omitted.

12. Originally named the Dasashram International Center.

"Enemies of Christ." Knights preparing to leave for the First Crusade attack a
Jewish neighborhood. © Christel Gerstenberg/CORBIS.

. 3 .

God's *Wrath*: Religious Conflict

Soldiers of Hell, become soldiers of the living God!
—Pope Urban II

Religious differences have fueled some of the most brutal intergroup conflicts in human history. Often, even minor variations in doctrine unleash the dogs of war and "justify" mass butchery. Yet, at other times and in other places, what would seem to be immense differences in religious doctrine and ritual coexist, and potential conflicts are muted by norms of civility. Why?

Generations of social scientists have defined this question in terms of prejudice and have sought explanations of religious conflict within the human psyche. The result is a vast literature on such constructs as authoritarianism, stereotyping, scapegoating, projection, and the like (Taylor and Pettigrew, 1992). But, as should have been clear from the start, the psychological approach to questions involving cross-cultural and historical variations necessarily is a cul-de-sac. The causes of phenomena such as religious conflict are not to be found primarily within the human head, *unless* we make the patently false assumption that basic psychological processes differ greatly by time and place.

Ironically, while literally hundreds of social scientists have invested their careers in studies of religious prejudice, elements of a model to explain variations in religious conflict and civility have been available to economists for more than two centuries—clearly expressed by Adam Smith (*1723–1790*) in *The Wealth of Nations*. Unfortunately, generations of economists following Smith mostly ignored his forays into "peripheral" topics (Radnitzsky and Bernholz, 1987). In fact, these sections of *The Wealth . . .* are omitted from most of the available editions, and only recently has much attention been given to Smith's writings on religion (Anderson, 1988; Finke and Stark, 1988, 1992; Iannaccone, 1991; Stark, 1992; Stark and Finke, 2000; Stark and Iannaccone, 1994; Stark and McCann, 1993). But if economists long neglected Smith's insightful legacy on these topics, presumably his work on religious conflict was available to noneconomists who did concern themselves with the matter. Yet early in my career when I published several well-received books on religious prejudice, I knew nothing of Smith's work and encountered no trace of it in that literature (Glock and Stark, 1966; Stark et al., 1971). I did not discover the critical passages on religious conflict in Smith's masterwork until I was well along on the theory presented below, long after I had begun to collaborate with an economist and to publish articles quoting Smith on the inefficiency of established churches (Stark and Iannaccone, 1993, 1994, 1996).

In this chapter I attempt to isolate essential concepts and link them with theoretical principles sufficient for a theory of religious conflict—clarifying that some of the propositions were anticipated more than two centuries ago by Adam Smith. Once the theory of conflict is in place, I devote the rest of this chapter to applying it to some significant historical cases.

A Theory of Monotheism and Conflict

The image of God that is most potent in terms of social effects is, for that very reason, the most dangerous. It is precisely God as a conscious, responsive, good supreme being of infinite scope—the One True God as conceived by the great monotheisms—who prompts awareness of idolatry, false Gods, and heretical religions. *Particularism*, the belief that a given religion is the *only true religion*, is *inherent in monotheism*.

In *Christian Beliefs and Anti-Semitism* (Glock and Stark, 1966), I developed the notion of particularism at some length, using it to explain not only Christian anti-Semitism but classical anti-Semitism as well. If salvation comes only through faith in Christ, then

Jews are outcasts, bound for hell for practicing a false religion. By the same logic, if Yahweh is the One True God, then the ancient Greeks and Romans were idolaters—and even polytheists will take offense when others dismiss their Gods as fantasies or falsehoods. Thus the two sides of particularism: the contempt for other faiths and the reaction by those held in contempt.

But if monotheists believe there is only One True *God*, they have been unable to sustain One True *Religion*. Rather, from the start all of the major monotheisms have been prone to splinter into many True Religions that sometimes acknowledge one another's right to coexist and sometimes don't. Hence *internal* and *external conflict* is *inherent* in particularistic religion.

Not only did the Pharisees denounce Sadducees while the Essenes condemned them both, the Talmud noted the existence of twenty-four disputatious Jewish theological factions in this era (Cohen, 1987; Georgi, 1995). So, too, did the early Christians devote a lot of energy to denouncing one another—among very early Christian documents are *catalogs of heresy*! In about the year 180 (when I estimate the entire Christian population to have numbered no more than 100,000), Irenaeus produced his famous five-volume attack on heresy wherein he lists nearly two dozen groups of Christians who had gone astray. A few years later Hippolytus issued an expanded catalog listing nearly fifty heretical groups (Williams, 1996). Given the limited communications of that time as well as a canon still in flux and a shortage of written scriptures, it probably isn't too surprising that in a substantial number of places the tiny local Christian groups drifted into doctrinal differences. What is striking, however, is that this doctrinal drifting resulted in such intense antagonism. Not content to call one another names, Christian factions sometimes engaged in mayhem and mass murder on behalf of truth. In similar fashion, Islam has always been plagued by bitter and often violent sectarianism. Conflicts among major factions such as the Sunni, the Shi'ites, and the Sufis are well known, but Islam abounds in minor, and often very militant, sects as well.

Even so, there was far more diversity of doctrines and practices among the various pagan groups than has ever existed within Judaism, Christianity, or Islam. But in the absence of claims to exclusive truth, these pagan differences produced no sparks. The priests of various pagan temples undoubtedly regarded one another as competitors for patronage, and I am sure that sometimes priests of one temple were a bit contemptuous of those serving in another, but this was far more like the feelings a modern auto dealer has for another dealer down the street. As a perceptive pagan told St. Augustine (*Epistle* 16), the temples existed in a state of "concordant discord." Moreover, whenever there exist many nonexclusive Gods, each with a religious organization, most people will patronize a variety of divinities since many offer specialized services. In addition, most people will seek help from many Gods, simply to hedge their bets. Laurence Iannaccone (1995) has aptly described this as assembling a "religious portfolio." But even polytheistic tolerance has limits. Just as had the "Atenites" before them, Jews and Christians outraged pagan opinion by denying all of their Gods, and consequently they were sometimes severely persecuted for their "atheism." Indeed, Plato advocated solitary confinement and, in extreme cases, execution for anyone who denied the existence of the Gods (*Laws* 10).

But it is among those committed to the particularistic principle— that there is only one authoritative belief system—that truly dangerous religious antagonisms arise. Moreover, where particularism rules, bitter antagonisms are inevitable because *theological disagreement is inevitable*. Let me stress that doctrinal differences of the kind cataloged by Irenaeus and by Hippolytus usually are not masks for other, more basic causes such as class. These disputes are the normal consequences of theological study, for heresy is inherent in the act of seeking to fully understand and to reconcile the deeper meanings of scriptures and revelations within any context wherein there can be only one correct answer.

For this reason, even within the confines of monotheism, pluralism is the "natural" or "normal" religious state of affairs—in the absence of repression, there will be multiple religious organizations (Stark, 1983; Stark and Bainbridge, [1987] 1996; Stark and Finke, 2000; Stark and Iannaccone, 1994). In addition to doctrinal diversity, pluralism arises from the apparent fact that in any normal population people seem to differ according to the intensity of their religious desires and tastes. That is, some people are content with a religion that, although it promises less, also requires less. Others want more from their religion and are willing to do more to get it. Max Weber expressed this point by noting that "people differ greatly in their religious capacities . . . in every religion," and those who make the greatest efforts he identified as "religious virtuosi" ([1922] 1993:162). Building on this observation, I have proposed that the religious diversity in all societies is rooted in social *niches*, groups of people sharing particular preferences concerning religious intensity. I argue that these niches are quite stable over time and quite similar in their fundamental outlook across societies and history (Stark and Bainbridge, [1987] 1996; Stark and Finke, 2000).

Put another way, in all societies people can be ranked according to the intensity of their religious concerns and tastes, and hence in the level of demands they are willing to fulfill in order to satisfy their needs. Most people want some intensity in their religion and will accept some costs, but not too much of either. Some people will have little religious interest and will prefer to be involved as little as possible. But in any society, as Weber noted, some people will aspire to a high-intensity faith. Given the diversity of religious *demand*, other things being equal there will be a corresponding diversity in religious *supply*: hence pluralism, the existence of multiple religious organizations. Thus in any society where diversity is not suppressed by force, the religious spectrum will include a full range of religious organizations, from some that demand little and are in a very low state of tension with their surroundings to some that offer very high-intensity faith. Enrollment in these groups will tend to resemble a normal curve, with the moderate faiths commanding the largest followings (Stark and Finke, 2000).

As will be seen in Chapter 5, pluralism can be quite stable and even civil, so long as there are many religious organizations, none of them very powerful. However, if there exist only a few very powerful religious groups, intense conflicts must ensue as each attempts to suppress the other(s). Yet because of the inherent forces impelling pluralism, no single religious organization can impose a monopoly, *unless* it is able to enlist the *coercive power of the state* on its behalf.

Adam Smith recognized that no religious organization possesses the means to impose a monopoly—that "monopoly" religious organizations exist only when it suits the interest of a political elite to sustain them. Sometimes this is because the political and religious elites are one, as has often been the case in Islamic societies. More typically, this occurs during a contest for political power when a contending "political party has either found it, or imagined it, for its interest to league itself with some one or other of the contending religious sects. But this could be done only by adopting, or at least by favoring, the tenets of that particular sect. The sect which had the good fortune to be leagued with the conquering party, necessarily shared in the victory of its ally" (Smith, [1776] 1981:792).

The result is that the victorious sect successfully appeals to the victorious ruling elite "to silence and subdue all its [religious] adversaries" (ibid.). This was, of course, how Christianity rose to become the only licit religion in the latter days of the Roman Empire.

Because religious monopolies depend upon state coercion, to the degree that a religious monopoly exists, religious conflict will involve *a political challenge to the state*. That is, to the extent that the political elite support the monopoly faith, to challenge it is to challenge them, so *heresy* inevitably becomes *treason*. For example, during the reign of Frederick II (*1194–1250*), any person who was excommunicated by a German bishop was automatically deprived of her or his civil rights six weeks later (Holborn, 1982:23). Conversely, direct challenges to the political elite will be defined as *heresy*. It was not the Church that declared the Knights Templars heretics. It was King Philip IV of France (*1285–1314*) who, fearing the rapidly growing political and economic power of the order, initiated the heresy charges and rushed Grand Master Jacques de Molay and Geoffroi de Charney, preceptor of Normandy, to the stake in defiance of Pope Clement V (Read, 1999). Subsequently, the pope accepted this judgment and signed a bull suppressing the order, but only after a satisfactory division of the Templars' property between Church and State had been agreed. Thus do political elites and established churches reinforce one another. This union has been the cause of some of the most virulent "religious" conflicts, for, as Adam Smith ([1776] 1981:791) noted, "times of violent religious controversy have generally been times of equally violent political faction."

The many massacres of dissenting Christian movements were achieved by secular armies on behalf of the Church (although sometimes rulers allowed the Church to employ mercenaries against dissenters), and Luther's Reformation survived only because it was successfully defended by secular forces. Indeed, Luther's experience demonstrates that not only must religious rebels seek secular protectors, political rebels must make common cause with religious dissenters in order to offset their religious illegitimacy. Thus Lutheranism provided northern European princes with a sufficient shield against excommunication, while they, in return, protected Luther from the stake. As Adam Smith ([1776] 1981:806–7) explained:

> The success of the new doctrines was almost every where so great, that the princes who at the time happened to be on bad terms with the court of Rome, were by means of them easily enabled, in their own dominions, to overturn the church, which, having lost the respect and veneration of the inferior ranks of people, could scarce make any resistance. The court of Rome had disobliged some of the smaller princes in the northern parts of Germany, whom it probably considered as too insignificant to be worth managing. They universally, therefore, established the reformation in their own dominions.

Given the involvement of both Church and State in all efforts to impose and sustain a religious monopoly, the focus of repression will be much more on power than on theology. Indeed, where a relatively secure monopoly exists, a substantial amount of *religious nonconformity* will be *tolerated* to the extent that dissenters are perceived as posing no threat to the power of the religious elite.

Atenists posed a profound threat to the other Egyptian temples, as Pharaoh Akhenaten cut off their funding. Similarly, by their condemnation of the Greco-Roman Gods, Jews and then Christians made it clear that they wished for their elimination, and the Christians eventually made good on their threats. Conversely, Christian laxity in rooting out rural paganism or in evangelizing the rank-and-file "barbarians" can be understood as the "lazy" behavior of a secure monopoly. The Christian clergy of northern Europe served the state church. The elite did conform. The peasants paid their tithes. Outward signs of nonconformity were minimized. What did it matter what people actually thought or even what they did in private? Moreover, that Jews posed no institutional threat to Christianity was an important element in the policies allowing Jews to persist in their nonconformity, as circumscribed and inconsistent as these policies were.

But Donatists—that was another matter altogether. Such dangerous heretics must be crushed! Why? Because they were led by an elite who controlled much of North Africa, and who posed a direct and serious institutional threat to Roman domination of the Church. This is also why the English Protestants were so militant in their hunt for Catholics—the latter had controlled the state and meant to do so again.

In contrast, popes and bishops have often tolerated quite extensive "heresy" so long as it was clearly contained within the institutional framework of the Church. The founders of many religious orders were only held to be in "error" for variant theological views that would have been declared heresy on the part of laity. In this manner, religious orders have often served as an acceptable form of sect movement. Many who might otherwise have broken away and formed a dissenting religious movement instead founded a new religious order, thereby accepting and acknowledging their submission to institutional authority. This illustrates that power and authority can be more important to the definition of heresy than variations in theology.

Finally, we arrive at the two theoretical principles on which the rest of the chapter is based. The first notes that religious *conflict will be maximized* where, other things being equal, *a few powerful and particularistic religious organizations coexist.*

Adam Smith saw this very clearly. Religious differences, he wrote, "can be dangerous and troublesome only where there is, either but one sect tolerated in the society, or where the whole of a large society is divided into two or three great sects" ([1776] 1981:792–93). As Smith realized, the latter tends to be a very unstable situation, as one group usually attempts to wipe out the others or drives them underground. Moreover, such conflicts will tend not to be restricted to the main contenders but will generate a *climate of general religious intolerance* extending to minor religious groups that would ordinarily tend to be tolerated. Hence the second major principle: during periods of substantial religious conflict, *toleration will be withheld or withdrawn* from *nonthreatening* but *nonconforming* religious groups.

I cannot claim to have been ignorant of European history when I initially formulated these principles. It was my intention that they should shed substantial explanatory light on major religious conflicts, especially the religious wars. But it was not until I actually began to apply them to the historical record that I realized how efficiently and fully they unite countless bloody events over many centuries into an integrated dynamic process.

As I continued to sift these historical materials, it became apparent that the most revealing thread to pursue is that of anti-Semitism, because while other "sides" and "factions" came and went (Arians, Waldensians, Cathars, Hussites), the Jews were always present and invariably became deeply, if unwillingly, involved. Indeed, through an attempt to explain why episodes of lethal violence against Jews were restricted to only certain times and places, it will be possible to expand the focus beyond the boundaries of Christendom and to show that the same principles apply within Islamic history—and, further, that periodic intensifications of the conflicts between these two major faiths brought bad times not only upon Jews but on all forms of religious nonconformity.

To sum up: When several powerful particularistic faiths threaten one another, conflict will be maximized, as will levels of intolerance. Whatever degree of toleration had been formally or informally extended to nonthreatening religious nonconformists will tend to be overridden by the intensification of particularism generated by the larger conflict. Hence in the following sections I will test these three primary hypotheses:

First, I propose to demonstrate that the historical record of violent attacks on Jews by Christians reveals that most were "collateral" actions during times of maximum conflict involving major contenders for institutional religious power.

Second, I will attempt to establish that the renewal of conflicts over Christian heresy in the eleventh century also began as a "collateral" action to more distant conflicts with Islam. These initial disputes over heresy then generated the era of religious wars, culminating in Luther's Reformation.

Third, I will show that many episodes of Muslim violence against Jews occurred in unison with those in Christendom, as each major religious power responded to the other.

By pursuing these hypotheses, I will have the opportunity to examine revealing aspects of religious conflicts in general, including the interplay between religious and political elites.

Anti-Semitic Violence as "Collateral" Conflict

Let me be clear: my intentions do not include writing even a brief history of anti-Semitism. I will ignore nearly all of the common aspects of prejudice and discrimination against Jews, limiting my analysis to the *outbursts* of *fatal violence*. I imposed the criterion that an episode involve murders because I wanted, as far as possible, a complete (thus unbiased) set of events, and those involving deaths are far more likely to have been included in the contemporary sources than are less severe outbursts. Moreover, I wished to eliminate commonplace, chronic anti-Semitism and identify periods of unusually intense expressions of religious hatred. The analysis begins in the year 500 and ends in 1648, when the Treaty of Westphalia concluded the era of Europe's major religious wars.

Given Christians' intolerance of religious nonconformity, the appropriate question is not why they persecuted Jews, but why they tolerated them at all. For, unlike the Donatists, Montanists, Pelagians, Waldensians, Cathars, or, indeed, the pagans, Jews were the only sizable, openly nonconformist religious group who endured other than by force of arms. As Robert Chazen (1986:29) noted, despite negative stereotypes and many forms of discrimination, the "essential fact remained . . . that Jews were to be permitted to exist within Christian society and to fulfill their religious obligations as Jews." Christians made an exception for Jews because of the theological doctrine that the Second Coming would be ushered in by the conversion of the Jews. That was usually interpreted to mean that Jewish nonconformity was part of the divine plan, and that their eventual conversion was in God's hands. Thus, as Augustine put it, "the continued preservation of the Jews will be a proof to believing Christians."

This formula must not be dismissed as "mere words," given the very frequent and vigorous intervention by popes and local bishops to protect Jews. Because several attempts to condemn the Church for not doing more to save the Jews during the Holocaust have so misrepresented the position of the medieval Church, it seems worthwhile to quote the most respected of all Holocaust historians, Steven T. Katz (1994:318–19), on this matter. Calling "Thou Shalt Not Annihilate the Jews" the "Eleventh Christian Commandment," Katz wrote:

> Though Christendom possessed the power, over the course of nearly fifteen hundred years, to destroy that segment of the Jewish people it dominated, it chose not to do so . . . because the physical extirpation of Jewry was never, at any time, the official policy of any church or of any Christian state. Rather . . . Christian dogmatics entailed protecting Jews and Judaism from extinction . . . with the quasi exception of Pope Leo VII (936–939), no pope permitted the use of force in attempts to convert Jews, whereas Pope John XVIII (1004–1009) openly defended Jews against hostile Christian forces. In doing so his protective actions were consistent with by-then ancient papal precedents. As Pope Gregory the Great had written centuries before to the bishops of Arles and Marseille, "I praise your missionary intentions, but you have erred in using force to baptize Jews."

Of course, although the rules varied by time and place, nowhere in Europe did Jews enjoy the same freedoms and rights as Christians, just as they were not treated as equal to Muslims in Islamic societies. In general Jews were forbidden to proselytize, to have

Christian slaves or servants (in Islam they were forbidden Muslim slaves), or to celebrate Passover earlier in the year than Easter, and they were excluded from public office, from military service, and from many professions. Intermarriage was prohibited (and often so was sexual intercourse), and Christians were typically prohibited from taking part in any Jewish celebrations or festivals. Indeed, physical separation soon became the norm as in most cities Jews were segregated into their own quarter (eventually to be known as the ghetto)—although this arrangement was often voluntary and had as much to do with protecting Jews as with limiting their influence on Christians. And, adopting the Muslim practice, European Jews were often required to identify themselves by wearing a badge or a distinctive hat (Baer, 1961; Baron, all vols.; Chazen, 1986, 1996; Flannery, 1985; Gidal, 1988; Graetz, 1895, 1894a, 1894b; Keith, 1997; Long, 1953; Oberman, 1984; Poliakov, 1965, 1973, 1975).

For all that these were onerous impositions, they were endurable. My interest here is with the unendurable, with *outbursts* of *collective* and *fatal* anti-Semitic violence. I ignore incidents involving Jews who were arrested, tried, and executed for crimes, even if they might have been innocent. For example, I have excluded Jews executed by the various Spanish inquisitions who were tried and condemned for "false" conversions to Christianity, since these were judicial proceedings, not collective outbursts. I have also excluded murders of a specific individual, such as the assassination of a Jewish public official, regardless of the motivation. Instead, I have attempted to identify all instances in the historical record for the period in question when *groups* of Christians, whether organized forces or mobs, spontaneously attacked a group *because* they were Jews, and brought about Jewish fatalities. I will also examine similar attacks by Muslims on Jews.

To assemble a record of lethal Christian attacks on Jews, I began with the very valuable list compiled by Paul E. Grosser and Edwin G. Halpern (1983). Because their list included many varieties of anti-Semitic activities, it was often difficult to know whether an event only involved attacks on property and/or physical assaults or involved murders as well. Consequently, I assembled all of their sources and reassessed each episode (Baer, 1961; Baron, 1952, 1957, 1965, 1967, 1969; Dubnov, 1920; Flannery, 1985; Graetz, 1895, 1894a, 1894b; Marcus, 1969; Poliakov, 1965, 1973; Raisin, 1949; Roth, 1965, 1963, 1959, 1930; Runciman, 1951; Runes, 1968; Wurmbrand and Roth, 1966). I also consulted other sources, many of them subsequent to Grosser and Halpern's study (Barnavi, 1992; Chazan, 1986, 1989, 1996, 2000; Cohn, 1961; Eidelberg, 1977; Gidal, 1988; Keith, 1997; Long, 1953; Oberman, 1984; Poliakov, 1975; Tuchman, 1979). My list differs somewhat from Grosser and Halpern's. It was necessary to revise some of their estimates of fatalities, and it was sometimes possible to be more accurate about the location or date of an event. I eliminated several episodes that were included twice with different dates, and I added some episodes they missed. I have also eliminated some episodes in which violence was directed at people not because they were Jews but because they were on the losing side of battles or wars. For example, Grosser and Halpern reported that eight thousand Jews were slain in Toledo in 1368. However, these deaths were battle casualties or were caused by privation during the siege and conquest of the city at the climax of a civil war. In the long power struggle between Henry II and Don Pedro, the Jews of Christian Spain supported (and many fought for) Don Pedro, who was killed in battle about three months before the city fell, and thousands of residents, Christians and Muslims as well as Jews, shared the fate of their king (Baer, 1961, 1:367).

Grosser and Halpern also offered a very short and poorly documented list of Muslim attacks on Jews. I rechecked their sources and consulted other works devoted in whole or in part to Jews under Islam (Alroy, 1975; Bat Ye'or, 1985; Deshen and Zenner, 1996; Fischel, 1969; Goitein, 1964; Lewis, 1984; Patai, 1986; Spuler, 1968; Stillman, 1979; Siddiqi, 1969), and I drew upon a substantial number devoted to Jewish-Christian-Muslim relations in Spain (Ashtor, 1973; Assis, 1997; Bendiner, 1983; Fletcher, 1992; Lourie, 1990; Montalvo, 1993; Paris, 1995).

I am confident that the historical record of lethal episodes of collective Christian violence against Jews in western Europe is reasonably complete. Unfortunately, it was impossible to identify a satisfactory set of episodes for Byzantium or, subsequently, for eastern Europe. It is known that some Byzantine emperors were extremely hostile toward Jews, but very few actual episodes were recorded. Many attacks on Jews are known to have occurred in eastern Europe during the past several centuries, but records are sparse and unreliable for the era with which I am concerned. Consequently, episodes listed in the upper sections of Figure 3.1 are limited to western Europe and to one instance of actions taken by western Europeans in the East.

The lower portion of the figure offers a very incomplete record of episodes involving Muslim attacks on Jews. One reason that this list is so incomplete is that until very recently it was not a topic of much interest to Western historians. Another reason is, as will be seen, that for a considerable time historians displayed a very marked anti-Christian bias in contrasting the situations of Jews under Islam and Christianity.[1] A comparison of the death tolls from the atrocities listed for Muslims and for Christians makes it obvious that I have been able to list only major massacres committed by Muslims, and I have probably missed some of these as well.

I have grouped individual episodes on the basis of general precipitating events, such as the Crusades, and have tried to order these by period, although there is overlap. Within each grouping, I have ordered episodes by year and alphabetically.

As I assembled episodes, it soon became clear that historians long recognized the collateral connection of anti-Semitic violence and major religious conflicts, but they recognized this in a piecemeal way and without fully comprehending why. That is, historians of the Crusades know that they were accompanied by a wave of Jewish massacres, and recognize that this was because the antagonism toward Islam somehow expanded to include Jews. Indeed, Chazan (1986:29) understood that the medieval policy of "tolerating Jews was perhaps feasible" in "untroubled times," but that toleration "was apt to disintegrate" during "periods of agitation and stress." In similar fashion, historians of the Christian reconquest of Spain know that it prompted violent attacks on Jews, and some even know that these occurred on *both* sides. And histori-

Figure 3.1
Fatal, Collective Anti-Semitic Outbursts

ATTACKS BY WESTERN EUROPEAN CHRISTIANS

Tranquil Times: 500–1000

554   Clermont: "many" Jews killed and 500 submitted to forced baptism.

The Crusades
1095–1099: First Crusade

1096   Cologne: attack thwarted, 2 Jews killed. Several weeks later, a second attack results in the death of perhaps 1,000 Jews.
Mainz: 1,000 Jews killed.
Metz: 22 Jews killed.
Regensburg: some Jews killed, number unknown.
Speyer (Spier): 12 Jews killed plus 1 suicide.
Worms: 500 Jews killed.
Eller, Geldern, Kerpen, Neuss, Wevelinghofen: perhaps 3,000 Jews killed.

1099   Jerusalem: massacre of Muslims, during which a synagogue in which Jews were gathered was burned.

1146–1149: Second Crusade

1146   Cologne: many Jews killed, number not known.
Mainz: many Jews killed, number not known.
Speyer: 3 Jews killed.
Strasburg, Worms, and other communities in the Rhine valley: some Jews killed.

1147   Carenton: Jews massacred, number unknown.
Würzburg: more than 20 Jews killed.

1188–1192: Third Crusade

1188   London: looting of Jewish quarter with 30 deaths.
York: looting of Jewish quarter with some deaths.

Figure 3.1
Fatal, Collective Anti-Semitic Outbursts (cont'd)

ATTACKS BY WESTERN EUROPEAN CHRISTIANS

1188–1192: Third Crusade (cont'd)

1189	Lynn: Jews massacred (number unknown) and Jewish quarter looted and burned.
	York: murders and mass suicide, 150 to 500 Jewish deaths.
	Colchester, Lincoln, Ospringe, and Thetford: some Jews killed in each town.
1191	Bray (in France): questionable accounts claim that either 80 or 99 Jews were burned.

1236: Failed Attempt to Organize a Crusade

1236	Angouleme, Anjou, Bordeaux, and Poitou: over 3,000 Jews killed.

1320: The "Shepherd's Crusade"

1320	Southern France: a mob of peasants, many of them shepherds, march from Agen to Toulouse, killing all Jews along the way: number killed is unknown, but 120 communities destroyed.

Disorder in Germany

1270	Coblenz, Erfurt, Magdeburg, Weissenberg, and other cities in Germany: Jews murdered "by the thousands."
1283	Mainz: 10 Jews killed.
	Bacharach: 26 Jews killed.
1285	Munich: at least 180 Jews killed.
1286	Oberwesel: 40 Jews killed.
1298	Beginning in the Rhineland, the "Jew killers" move from city to city, looting, burning, and killing thousands of Jews. Cities specifically mentioned: Augsburg, Heilbroun, Nuremberg, Regensburg, Röttingen, and Würzburg.

Figure 3.1
Fatal, Collective Anti-Semitic Outbursts (cont'd)

ATTACKS BY WESTERN EUROPEAN CHRISTIANS

The Reconquest of Spain

1066	French knights kill Jews whenever they encounter them, until ordered to cease by Pope Alexander II.
1109	Toledo: "murder and pillage of the Jews."
1328	Navarre: 5,000 Jews perish in riots throughout the province.
1366	Briviesca: 200 Jews killed.
1391	Aguilar de Compo and Villadiego: Jewish communities slaughtered.
	Barcelona: 400 Jews killed.
	Castille: many Jews slaughtered and others sold to Muslims as slaves.
	Cordova: many Jews killed, number unknown.
	Cuenca: many killed, number unknown.
	Madrid: Jews "slaughtered," number unknown.
	Majorca: 300 killed.
	Seville: 4,000 killed.
	Toledo: a rabbi, his students, and several prominent Jews murdered.
	Valencia: 230 Jews killed.
1392	Albarracin: several Jews killed.
	Barcelona: 500 Jews killed.
	Gerona: 40 Jews killed.
	Lerida: 78 Jews killed.

The Black Death: 1347–1350

1348	Barcelona: 20 Jews killed.
	Cervera: 18 Jews killed.
	Catalonia and Aragon: many deaths.
	Southern France: Jewish congregation burned to death.
	Basel, Berne, Constance, Freiburg, St. Gall, Zurich: Jewish communities burned, many deaths, numbers unknown.

Figure 3.1
Fatal, Collective Anti-Semitic Outbursts (cont'd)

ATTACKS BY WESTERN EUROPEAN CHRISTIANS

The Black Death: 1347–1350

1349	Erfurt: 3,000 Jews killed.
	Mainz: 6,000 Jews die when "ghetto" burned.
	Speyer: some Jews killed, some convert, many commit suicide.
	Strassburg: 2,000 Jews killed.
	Augsburg, Cologne, Munich, Nuremberg, Würzburg: all or many Jews killed, number unknown.
	Dresden, Frankfurt, Nordhausen, Oppenheim, Stuttgart, Ulm, Vienna, Worms: Jewish communities commit suicide.
	Brussels: 500 Jews killed.

Revolt in Paris

1380	Paris: mob rioting against high taxes turns on Jews, at least 10 murdered.
1381	Paris: uprising of "Maillotins" includes violence against Jews, at least 15 murdered.

Heresy Reborn

1209	Beziers: 200 Jews killed (and perhaps 20,000 Albigensians).
1384	Nordlingen: Jewish community burned, number of deaths unknown.
1421	Rhineland: Jewish communities slaughtered as troops march to fight Hussites.
	Vienna: 100 Jews killed during campaign against the Hussites; many others commit suicide.
1431	Lindau, Ravensberg, Ueberlingen: anti-Hussite preaching also targets Jews, and the Jewish community in each town is destroyed.
1614	Frankfurt: about 2,000 Jews killed

Figure 3.1
Fatal, Collective Anti-Semitic Outbursts (cont'd)

ATTACKS BY MUSLIMS

The Crusades

1291	Acre (Palestine): after a long siege, Muslim forces under al-Ashrif Khalil take the city, and there is a general massacre of Christians and Jews.

The Reconquest of Spain

1032–1033	Fez (Morocco): 6,000 Jews killed.
1066	Grenada: 4,000 Jews killed.
1090	Grenada: several thousand Jews massacred.
1447–1460	Morocco and Islamic Spain: widespread massacres.
1148	Islamic Spain: all Christians and Jews required to convert, leave, or die. Many convert. Many pretend to convert. Some leave. Some die.
1465	Fez: Massacre of Jews in Fez and throughout Morocco.

Mongol Conquest of Persia

1290–1291	Baghdad: upon death of Grand Khan, Muslim mobs kill Jews and Christians throughout the country.

ans are aware of the eruption of anti-Semitism during the various internal European religious wars. But historians have tended to examine each of these periods of anti-Semitism in isolation and have often proposed ad hoc (and too often ad hominem) explanations or none at all. Perhaps this merely reflects the useful division of labor between the focus on the particular by historians and the search for the general among sociologists. Let me readily acknowledge that, of course, events *are* always shaped by the personal idiosyncrasies of particular individuals and by particular local circumstances, and some events may be due almost entirely to these factors—including some instances of anti-Semitic violence. However, as very similar cases begin to pile up and to occur in various times and places, it becomes likely that a more general explanation is needed. As we view this collection of cases as a whole, it will be obvious that most of them seem to have a common basis.

Tranquil Times: 500–1000

In accord with Grosser and Halpern (1983) I began my catalog of anti-Semitic violence in the year 500, at the start of the era during which Jewish-Christian relations were quite "tranquil," as Robert Chazan put it (1986:29). I could uncover only *one* episode of collective Christian anti-Jewish violence resulting in fatalities between the years 500 and 1000. This outburst occurred in 554 in Clermont, a city in southern Gaul (now France). Fully in accord with the theory, it was collateral to a more major religious conflict.

While Christian missionaries were hard at work to convert the Franks in northern Gaul (Clovis converted in about 497), the Visigoths who controlled Spain and southern Gaul already were Christians—but not of the Roman Catholic variety. Instead, they adhered to the Christian heresy known as "Arianism." Arians embraced a highly qualified notion of the divinity of Jesus. They did not believe that he was the "begotten" Son of God, but merely that he had been created by God and that he achieved divinity only through perfect obedience to God. Thus, as Arians were fond of telling Trinitarians, if Jesus is divine, "there was a time when he was not." Trinitarians would have none of this—Jesus was conceived as the Son of God, and Arianism was condemned as a heresy at the Council of Nicaea in 325.

Meanwhile, however, Ulfilas, a Gothic convert to Arianism, returned to his people with a Gothic translation of the Bible and had immense success as a missionary, especially among the elites. Thus when the Visigoths conquered Spain and lower Gaul in 416, they constituted a powerful nation of heretics. However, their rule did not include many of the cities within this area, which remained under the control of Trinitarian bishops, loyal to Rome. This set the stage for religious conflict. As such things go, the conflict was generally rather mild. The Visigoths did often confiscate Trinitarian churches for their own use, and some of the more zealous among them sometimes forcibly rebaptized Trinitarian Catholic children. And from time to time fighting did break out, and some Trinitarian cities were destroyed. But most of the time relations were merely tense (Johnson, 1976; Wolfram, 1997).

At the turn of the sixth century, the Christianization of the Frankish king and court to the north of them encouraged the Trinitarian bishops in their armed opposition to the Arian Visigoths and in their efforts to convert them to Catholic orthodoxy. Among these bishops was Avitus of Averna, who controlled the city of Clermont. It was within the context of the larger religious power struggle with the Arians that Avitus turned his concerns about religious conformity toward the local Jews, demanding that they choose between Christian baptism and expulsion. When only one Jew appeared for baptism, a Christian mob attacked the Jewish quarter. "Many" Jews were killed, five hundred accepted baptism, and the rest fled to Marseilles (Graetz, 1894b).

That incident aside, Jewish-Christian relations were so tranquil that Israeli historian Nachum T. Gidal (1988:30) described the tenth and eleventh centuries in Europe as the "Halcyon Days" of Christian-Jewish relations. In similar terms, Léon Poliakov, one of the most respected contemporary historians of anti-Semitism, wrote of the "favorable status of Jews" during this era: "Kings, nobles, and bishops granted Jews a broad autonomy: thus they administered their own communities and lived according to their own laws. Talmudic scholarship flowered again on the banks of the Rhine and the Seine at the very period when it was falling into decay in Babylonia . . . they continued to mix freely with the Christian populations and to live on excellent terms with them" (1965:35). Then he added, "[U]ntil the eleventh century, no chronicles mention outbursts of popular hatred of the Jews" (ibid.:36).

The Crusades

In 1009, at the direction of Fatimid Caliph al-Hākim,[2] Muslims destroyed the Church of the Holy Sepulchre in Jerusalem—the splendid basilica that Constantine had erected over what was believed to be the site of the tomb where Christ lay before the Resurrection (Biddle, 1999).

As word of the desecration of the holiest of all Christian shrines reached Europe, it prompted several outbursts against Jews—in Rouen, Orleans, Limoges, Mainz, "and doubtless other Rhenish villages" (Poliakov, 1965:36). The timing makes it apparent that anger against "all enemies of Christ" precipitated these episodes. Unfortunately, information on these events is so scanty that we do not know whether there were fatalities. But given the detailed and mutually supporting accounts provided in both Christian and Jewish chronicles of events later in the century (see Chazan, 1986, chap. 2), it seems reasonable to assume that the lack of coverage reflects that little or no blood was shed. In any event, the crisis soon passed. Al-Hākim was killed by political opponents, and religious tolerance was restored in Jerusalem, thus permitting resumption of the substantial flow of Christian pilgrims. Indeed, the value of the pilgrim traffic was probably a major factor in the very liberal policies that had prevailed in Muslim-controlled Jerusalem through the centuries. Despite the great distances involved and the limited means of transportation, pilgrimages to Jerusalem were surprisingly common. In the first of his distinguished three volumes on the Crusades, Sir Steven Runciman reported that "an unending stream of travellers poured eastward, sometimes travelling in parties numbering thousands, men and women of every age and every class, ready . . . to spend a year or more on the [journey]" (1951, 1:49). A major reason for going to the Holy Land was the belief that a pilgrimage would absolve the pilgrim of even the most terrible sins. Thus many came all the way from Scandinavia—some even from Iceland. As Runciman explained, the Norse "were violent men, frequently guilty of murder and frequently in need of an act of penance" (1951, 1:47).

But then, later in the eleventh century, everything changed. The Seljuk Turks, recent converts to Islam, became the new rulers of Asia Minor, pushing to within a hundred miles of Constantinople. Perhaps because they were new to Islam, or perhaps because they were still seminomadic tribesmen untainted by city dwelling, the Turks were unflinching particularists. There was only One True

God and his name was Allah, not Yahweh or Jehovah. Tolerance was at an end. Not that the Turks officially prohibited Christian pilgrimages, but they made it clear that Christians were fair game. Hence every Anatolian village along the route to Jerusalem began to exact a toll on Christian travelers. Far worse, many pilgrims were seized and sold into slavery, while others were tortured, seemingly as much for entertainment as for edification. Those who survived these perils "returned to the West weary and impoverished, with a dreadful tale to tell" (Runciman, 1951, 1:79).

Thus anger and anxiety about the Holy Land grew. It is important to understand just how vivid was the image of the Holy Land to sincere medieval Christians. It was where Christ and the disciples had lived and, to an almost palpable degree, still did. In the words of Robert Payne (1984:18–19), in Palestine Christians "expected to find holiness in a concrete form, something that could be seen, touched, kissed, worshipped, and even carried away. Holiness was in the pathways trodden by Christ, in the mountains and valleys seen by Christ, in the streets of Jerusalem where Christ had wandered." In Jerusalem, a Christian had even been able climb the hill on which the cross had borne the Son of God. But no longer. Living "enemies of Christ, the spawn of Satan," now barred Christians from walking in Christ's footsteps.

It was in this climate of opinion that Alexius Comnenus, emperor of Byzantium, wrote from his embattled capital to the count of Flanders requesting that he and his fellow Christians in the West come to the rescue. In his letter, the emperor detailed gruesome tortures of Christians and vile desecrations of churches, altars, and baptismal fonts. Should Constantinople fall to the Turks, not only would thousands more Christians be murdered, tortured, and raped, but "the most holy relics of the Saviour," gathered over the centuries, would be lost: "Therefore in the name of God . . . we implore you to bring this city all the faithful soldiers of Christ . . . in your coming you will find your reward in heaven, and if you do not come, God will condemn you" (in Payne, 1984:28–29).

When Pope Urban II (*ca. 1042–1099*) read this letter, he was determined that it be answered in deeds. He arranged for a great gathering of clergy and laity in the French city of Clermont on

November 27, 1095. Standing on a podium in the middle of a field, and surrounded by an immense crowd that included poor peasants as well as nobility and clergy, the pope gave one of the most effective speeches of all time. Blessed with an expressive and unusually powerful voice, he could be heard and understood at a great distance. Subsequently, copies of the speech (written and spoken in French) were circulated all across Europe. Five major versions of the speech exist, each incomplete, and there are several translations of each into English (Peters, 1998). I have selected excerpts from several versions in order to reveal the means by which the pope aroused thousands in attendance to commit themselves to sew a cross onto their clothing as an emblem that they would serve. Since the Turks had conquered Persia before invading Byzantium, Pope Urban referred to them as "Persians." He began:

> Distressing news has come to us . . . that the people of the Persian kingdom, an accursed race, a race utterly alienated from God . . . has invaded Christian lands and devastated them with sword, pillage, and fire. Some of these Christians have been made captive and taken to Persia, and some have been tortured to death. Many of God's churches have been violated and others have been made to serve their own religious rites. They have ruined the altars with filth and defilement. They have circumcized [sic] Christians and smeared the blood on the altars or poured it into baptismal fonts. It amused them to kill Christians by opening up their bellies and drawing out the end of their intestines, which they then tied to a stake. Then they flogged their victims and made them walk around and around the stake until their intestines had spilled out and they fell dead on the ground . . . What shall I say about the abominable rape of women? On this subject it may be worse to speak than to remain silent . . .
>
> Who shall avenge these wrongs . . . if not you? You are the race upon whom God has bestowed glory in arms . . . Rise up, then, and remember the virile deeds of your ancestors, the glory and renown of Charlemagne . . . and all your other kings who destroyed the kingdoms of pagans and planted the holy church in their lands. You should be especially aroused by the knowledge that the Church of the Holy Sepulchre is now in the hands of unclean nations and that

holy places are shamelessly misused and sacrilegiously defiled with
their filth. Oh, most valiant knights, descendants of unconquerable
ancestors, remember the courage of your forefathers and do not dis-
honor them.

At this point Pope Urban raised a second issue, one to which he
had already devoted years of effort—the chronic warfare of medieval times. The pope had been attempting to achieve a "Truce of
God" among the feudal nobility, many of whom seemed inclined
to make war, even on their friends, just for the sake of a good fight.
After all, it was what they had trained to do every day since early
childhood. Here was their chance!

> Christian warriors, who continually and vainly seek pretexts for war,
> rejoice, for you have today found a true pretext. You, who so often
> have been the terror of your fellow men, go and fight against the
> barbarians, go and fight for the deliverance of the holy places . . . If
> you are conquered, you will have the glory of dying in the very same
> place as Jesus Christ, and God will never forget that he found you in
> the holy battalions.

Then he hit them with it:

> If you must have blood, bathe in the blood of the infidels . . . Soldiers
> of Hell, become soldiers of the living God!

Now, shouts of *"Dieu li volt!"* (God wills it!) began to spread
through the crowd. Thereupon the pope raised his crucifix and
roared:

> It is Christ himself who comes from the tomb and presents you with
> this cross . . . Wear it upon your shoulders and your breasts. Let it
> shine upon your arms and upon your standards. It will be to you the
> surety of victory or the palm of martyrdom. It will increasingly re-
> mind you that Christ died for you, and that it is your duty to die for
> him! (In Payne, 1984:33–35)

At once, the crowd began to cut up cloaks and other pieces of cloth
to make crosses and to sew them on their shoulders and chests.
Everyone agreed that next spring they would march to Jerusalem.
And they did.

However, it wasn't only knights and lords who marched. In fact, well before the regular forces set out for the Holy Land, thousands upon thousands of peasants (including many women and children) headed east behind Peter the Hermit. This strange figure emerged from obscurity and displayed an immense talent for stirring up enthusiasm among the very poor to reclaim the Holy Land from the heathen. Unfortunately, Peter's ability to attract a following was not matched by any sense of logistics or tactics. Nor was he able to maintain any discipline in his ranks. Consequently, his march east was sustained by his adherents' looting the towns and countryside along the way. When Peter's "crusade of the poor" came to a tragic end, slaughtered by the Turks at Civetot, they were unmourned. Nevertheless, whatever their other shortcomings, Peter's followers kept their focus exclusively on Islam as the enemy. So did the other crusader armies of knights and lords, with several terrible exceptions.

At the start of 1096, as Godfrey of Bouillon, duke of Lower Lorraine, began to assemble his forces at Verdun, the rumor went around that before he marched east, he would avenge the death of Christ by killing the Jews of the Rhineland. Alarmed, the chief rabbi of Mainz wrote to Henry IV, the Holy Roman Emperor and Godfrey's overlord, asking him to prevent the massacre. Henry wrote to all of his vassals, including Godfrey, commanding them to guarantee the safety of all Jews in their domains. Meanwhile, the Jews of Mainz and Cologne paid Godfrey five hundred pieces of silver to insure their safety. In return, Godfrey guaranteed their security. But then he marched away, leaving behind a minor Rhineland count, Emich of Leisingen, to follow with additional forces.

Emich had believed the rumor about an attack on the Jews and thought it made sense to start with the "original enemies" of Christ. So, on May 3, 1096, he led an attack on the Jews of Speyer (Spier). However, the bishop intervened and took the local Jews under his protection, so Emich's forces could lay their hands on only twelve, whom they murdered; and one Jewish woman committed suicide when she realized she was to be raped. Two weeks later Emich and his followers arrived in Worms. There he launched an attack on the Jewish quarter, killing all of the Jews who could be found. Here, too, the bishop opened his palace to the Jews. But this time Emich would have none of it. His forces broke down the gates and slaughtered the Jews. A total of about five hundred died.

As Emich's cohort moved down the Rhine, the same pattern was repeated the next week in Mainz. The archbishop attempted to protect the Jews but was forced to flee for his life, and another thousand Jews died. Then on to Cologne: there, Emich's marauders had been thwarted a few weeks previously when the bishop had protected the Jews, and they were forced to settle for burning down the synagogue and killing two Jews. This time the local Jews had gone into hiding in several nearby villages. But they were betrayed, and hundreds were slain. Next, in Metz, Emich's forces managed to kill twenty-two more Jews.

Word of Emich's actions spread, soon reaching another band of crusaders led by a barely remembered person named Volkmar. Entering Prague, Volkmar's forces immediately launched a massacre of Jews, unrestrained by the attempts made by the bishop to stop them. Just behind Volkmar came Gottschalk (a disciple of Peter the Hermit) with a somewhat larger force. Upon reaching Ratisbon (Regensberg), they massacred the local Jews. Meanwhile, part of Emich's forces had broken away from the main column at Mainz to purge the Moselle valley of Jews. Moving very rapidly through towns known to have Jews, but *without a resident bishop*, they were far more successful, killing several thousand.

In volume 4 of his monumental fifteen-volume *A Social and Religious History of the Jews*, Salo Baron (1957:105) cites the sixteenth-century historian Gedaliah ibn Yahya as estimating that during these episodes in 1096, five thousand Jews were murdered. This is entirely consistent with Figure 3.1.

It must be mentioned that Volkmar and his followers were wiped out in Hungary when they attempted to continue their murders of Jews. Soon thereafter the Hungarians annihilated Gottschalk and his followers too. And when Emich's column finally arrived at the Hungarian border, they were denied passage, and, attempting to force their way through, they too were routed by Hungarian knights and most of them killed.

"Stubborn Jews." From earliest days, many sincere Christians have been perplexed by the refusal of the Jews to accept Christ. This illumination from an early medieval manuscript portrays the Jews covering their ears so as not to "hear the Word of God." © Gianni Dagli Orti/CORBIS.

Runciman (1951, 1:141) reported that these defeats struck "most good Christians" as "punishment meted out from on high to the murderers of Jews." That is consistent with the efforts of local bishops to preserve the Jews, and with the fact that most of the armies gathered for the First Crusade did not molest Jews.

Aside from the actions by Emich, Volkmar, and Gottschalk, only one other episode of lethal attacks on Jews occurred. In 1099, Godfrey of Bouillon (he of the five hundred pieces of silver, and whose reinforcements had been led by Emich) took Jerusalem and unleashed his troops to massacre not only Muslims but Jews as well. The account written by the great Christian historian William, archbishop of Tyre, estimates the Muslim dead as numbering at least twenty thousand and tells of "headless bodies" everywhere and of "the victors themselves, dripping with blood from head to foot, an ominous sight" (in Baron, 1957, 4:109). As for Jewish casualties, all we know is that a substantial number gathered in the synagogue, which the crusaders then set on fire, killing everyone inside.

Unfortunately, while the attacks on German Jews were the work of a few, they set a pattern by directing attention to the issue of continuing to permit Jews to reject Jesus in a context where religious conformity was of growing concern. Consequently, by the time of the Second Crusade, Abbé Pierre of the great French monastery at Cluny pointed out, "What is the good of going to the end of the world at great loss of men and money, to fight Saracens, when we permit among us other infidels who are a thousand times more guilty toward Christ than are the Mohammedans?" (in Poliakov, 1965:48). Nevertheless, it was only in Germany that these views led to violent actions, and it was only in the same part of the Rhine valley where Emich and his killers had set a bloody precedent that massacres took place during the Second Crusade—in such cities as Cologne, Mainz, Würzburg, Worms, Speyer, and Strassburg (see map). The death toll would have been far greater had it not been for the very vigorous intervention of St. Bernard of Clairvaux, who rode to Mainz and ordered an end to the killings. We have accounts of this event from two chronicles, one by a Christian, the other by a Jew. It seems useful to compare them.

From the chronicle of Otto of Freising:

Meanwhile the Monk Radulph . . . entered those parts of Gaul that touch upon the Rhine and inflamed many inhabitants of Cologne, Mainz, Worms, Speyer, Strasbourg, and other neighboring cities, towns, and villages to accept the cross [go on the Crusade]. However,

German Cities in Which Jewish Massacres and Mass Suicides Occurred,
1096–1614. Numbers in parentheses indicate multiple episodes.

he heedlessly included in his preaching that the Jews whose homes
were scattered throughout the cities and towns should be slain as
foes of the Christian religion. The seed of this doctrine took such
firm root . . . that a large number of Jews were killed in this stormy
uprising, while many took refuge under the wings of the prince of
the Romans [the bishop] . . . But the aforesaid abbot of Clairvaux
. . . dispatched messengers and letters to the people [of the Rhine-
land] . . . to point out clearly by the authority of the sacred page that
the Jews were not to be killed for the enormity of their crimes . . .
call[ing] attention also to the . . . fifty-seventh Psalm: "God shall not

144

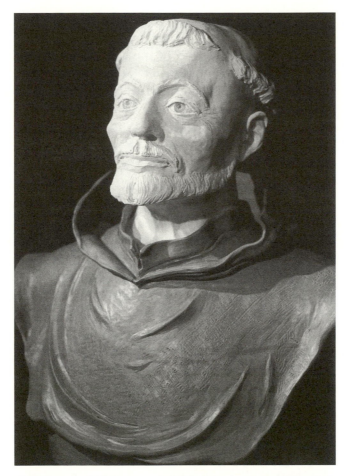

St. Bernard of Clairvaux. As with many important historical figures, there is no contemporary likeness of this enormously influential abbot. However, this bust is not a "hypothetical" depiction. Instead, it is a work of forensic science—a reconstruction made in 1999 from the saint's skull.
© AFP/CORBIS.

let me see my desire upon mine enemies. Slay them not." . . . Coming to Mayence (Mainz) . . . he summoned [Radulph] and warned him [and] . . . prevailed upon him to the point where he promised to obey and return to his monastery. The people were very angry and wanted to start an insurrection, but they were restrained by regard for Bernard's saintliness. (Chazan, 1980:106–7)

145

From the chronicle of Ephraim of Bonn:

> [Radulph] went about preaching—he was a preacher in the name of
> Jesus—that they must go to Jerusalem to battle the Muslims. Wher-
> ever he went, he spoke evilly of the Jews in the area . . . He said:
> "Avenge the Crucified upon his enemies who live among you. After-
> wards you shall journey to battle against the Muslims." We heard
> this and our hearts melted . . . We called out to the Lord saying . . .
> "Not yet fifty years have passed since our blood was spilled . . . "
> Then the Lord heard our sigh . . . He sent after the evil priest a decent
> priest, a great man . . . His name was Abbot Bernard, from the city
> of Clairvaux . . . Then [the abbot] said to them: "It is fitting that you
> go forth against Muslims. However, anyone who attacks a Jew and
> tries to kill him is as though he attacks Jesus himself. My pupil Ra-
> dulph who advised destroying them did not advise properly. For in
> the Book of Psalms is written concerning the Jews: 'Kill them not,
> lest my people forget.'" Everyone esteemed this priest as one of their
> saints. Moreover we have found no indication that he took a bribe
> for speaking up on behalf of Jews . . . Were it not for the mercies of
> our Creator Who sent the aforesaid abbot . . . there would not have
> been a remnant or survivor among the Jews. (Chazan, 1980:107–8)

Two things stand out in each account. First, St. Bernard did not
suggest that the Jewish religion was an acceptable or "alternative"
religion. He preached tolerance, not ecumenicity. (Chapter 5 explores conditions under which particularistic faiths can be tolerant.) Second, the high level of agreement between the Christian and
the Jewish accounts is quite typical of the medieval sources and
lends credibility to Figure 3.1.

Then came the Third Crusade, and the scene of attacks on Jews
shifted across the channel to London and York, in response to the
coronation of Richard the Lion-Hearted (*1157–1199*), who was
preparing to lead his forces to the Holy Land. As Runciman (1951,
3:7) noted about these episodes, "Crusading fervour always provided an excuse for killing God's enemies." Although King Richard
punished the perpetrators (hanging several of them), his protection
sufficed only until he left the country. So the next year, as groups
of crusaders assembled to follow Richard, the sentiment spread

that "it was not right to allow Jewish infidels to enjoy their ill-gotten riches undisturbed at home, while soldiers of the Cross were facing untold dangers to combat Moslem infidels overseas: the redemption of the Holy Sepulchre, and the avenging of the Crucifixion, should begin in England itself" (Roth, 1941:20). Jewish sections in many towns were looted, and many Jews who did not leave in time were murdered.

A final episode connected to the Third Crusade is claimed to have occurred in France two years later. Just days before setting sail to also join the Crusade, the king of France is said to have become enraged at reports concerning a Christian hanged for murdering a Jew in the small town of Bray, and to have led a small force thither, where he burned all the Jews above the age of thirteen. Baron (1957, 4:129) noted that despite this story's having been reported by both Hebrew and Latin chroniclers, the king of France was already engaged in battles in the Holy Land when this episode is alleged to have occurred. Baron concluded that something must have happened at Bray, but that it was "magnified out of all proportion by the contemporary chroniclers."

In 1236 Pope Gregory IX attempted to raise a new Crusade; in response, some crusaders gathered in Aquitania. Not enough showed up, however, and no Crusade took place. With their hopes dashed, the knights, attempting to salvage something of their dreams of glory before they dispersed, compelled all the Jews in several towns in that area to be baptized. About three thousand who resisted were murdered. Finally, crusader enthusiasm swept through farm laborers in southern France in 1320. Having neither money nor arms, participants in this "Shepherd's Crusade" decided to rob the Jews. Roaming eastward from Agen, they ended up killing a substantial number of Jews but never actually left for the Holy Land.

Thus ended Jewish killings directly associated with Crusades to the Holy Land. Unfortunately, as already noted, these attacks on the Jews became self-perpetuating. In some places, the idea of killing the Jews, looting their community, and invalidating all debts to Jewish lenders became a part of the popular culture, especially along the Rhine River, where the massacres prompted by the First and Second Crusades had been concentrated. As has been seen, most of the time the religious and political authorities were able to prevent this culture from expressing itself in action. But not always, and seldom in the fragmented political and ecclesiastical jurisdictions along the Rhine.

Disorder in Germany

In 1250, Frederick II, the Holy Roman Emperor, died unexpectedly following his many years of intense conflicts with the Church and while engaged in a civil war in Germany. After his death his "empire" broke apart, ushering in "a long period of political chaos and contested succession" (Duffy, 1997:116) or what Holborn described as a century of "anemic and at times defunct central government" (1982:24). Adding to the confusion, this was also a period of extreme crisis and disorder in the Church—between 1252 and 1296 there were thirteen popes. Within this power vacuum, the militant anti-Semitic tradition of the Rhineland reasserted itself as local rabble-rousers, who proudly claimed to be descendants of "*Judenbreter*" (Jew-roasters), stepped forward (Graetz, 1894b, 3:611). So, in 1270, once again thousands perished, in the same places as before. In 1283, the militant anti-Semites in Mainz got out of hand at Easter and killed 10 Jews before the archbishop could reach the scene and disperse them. That same day in Bacharach, 26 Jews were murdered as revenge for the Crucifixion. Two years later in Munich the rumor that the Jews had purchased a Christian baby to sacrifice at Passover prompted a mob to burn about 180 Jews to death by setting fire to the synagogue. In 1286, in Oberwesel, 40 Jews died in a similar event.

But the worst still lay ahead. In 1298, in the town of Röttingen, a man named Rindfleish organized a lethal attack on the local Jews, killing all of them. Rindfleish is identified as a minor noble in some accounts, as a butcher in others (his name means "beef flesh" in German), and a proud butcher of Jews was he. Rather than disband once they had killed all the Jews in Röttingen, Rindfleish and his followers adopted the name *Judenschächter* (Jew killers) and set off on a six-month orgy of killing Jews and looting and burning their communities—all across the same old area along the Rhine and then east into Bavaria. The death rate was huge—the *Memorbuch* (memory book) of the Jews in Nuremberg lists more than 5,000 victims killed between April and October, 1298, in forty-one different communities, and there must have been thousands more (Poliakov, 1973:316). Nor, sad to say, was this the last time Christians in this part of Germany became Jew killers.

Of course, these massacres cannot be claimed as directly collateral to the Crusades. In my view, it seems valid to assume that they would not have occurred had there been no Crusades to the Holy Land and no intensification of intolerance for religious nonconformity generated thereby. Alternatively, one can propose other explanations or simply settle for the assumption, hated by those of us who seek generalizations but apparently true: some things just seem to happen.

Meanwhile, the long campaign against the Muslims in Spain had also begun to precipitate attacks on Jews.

The Reconquest of Spain

Muslim invaders seized Spain from the Visigoths early in the eighth century, and, having ventured north into Frankish territory, they were defeated at the Battle of Tours in 732. Many later historians elevated Tours into one of the "world's most decisive battles." Edward Gibbon ([1788] 1994, 3:336) believed that had the Franks not triumphed at Tours, "the Koran would now be taught in the schools of Oxford," while Frederick von Schlegel believed that Tours "delivered the Christian nations of the West from the deadly grasp of all-destroying Islam" (in Creasy [1852] 1987:158). Even a generation ago, every schoolchild in America (and probably in Europe) learned that Charles Martel had saved Western civilization by winning at Tours. Indeed, no "history of Europe" written during my childhood would have failed to devote many pages to Tours, but Norman Davies (1996) did not mention either the Battle of Tours or even Charles Martel in his immense *History of Europe*; and, even in a long paragraph summarizing Martel's military career, Timothy Reuter (1999:14) barely mentioned Tours. This is because it is now understood that Tours was actually of minor strategic importance and remains of interest only to historians of military technology for being the first major engagement of armored knights. As was understood by the Franks at the time, the Saracen push north was far more of a raid than an invasion (Becker, 1913). Moreover, it was the worst sort of anachronism when Gibbon and other historians imputed a profound religious dimension to a conflict not so defined by those who actually took part. Whatever the Saracens may have thought, the Franks did not see themselves as the defenders of Christianity: the Frankish nobility were barely Christianized at this time, and the rank and file had not given up open paganism (see Chapter 2). In fact, most of the other battles involving Martel and his Frankish host were with pagan European opponents, and issues of conversion by conquest had not yet arisen. Nor did religion play a leading role in Frankish confrontations with Muslim invaders in Italy, which occurred in this same era. "Holy Wars" take serious, particularistic religious convictions, and these had not yet taken root among the Franks.

Following their defeat at Tours, the Muslims soon withdrew behind the Pyrenees. Subsequently, Frankish forces periodically began slowly to push into Spain, and for several centuries the advantage swung back and forth as the Franks made minor inroads only to retreat. But even these conflicts lacked religious interpretation, and for that reason *they did not generate any collateral religious intolerance.*

But then, in the eleventh century, as the Christianization of the Frankish nobility had progressed *and* as concern grew about Muslim abuses in the Holy Land, things changed. Religious sentiments to drive the infidel from Spain became ascendant at the immense monastic center at Cluny (in France), and from there monks went forth to campaign for a Holy War in Spain—the concept of Holy War was probably adopted from Islam. Urged by the abbot of Cluny, in 1063 Pope Alexander II announced "an indulgence [forgiveness for sins] for all who fought for the Cross in Spain" (Runciman, 1951, 1:90).

In 1066 a few French knights responded, the largest group being led by Guy-Geoffrey, count of Aquitaine. Upon their arrival in northern Spain, the French knights directed their efforts against *all* infidel and were inclined to slay both Muslims and Jews. When he learned of this, Pope Alexander II ordered them to let the Jews alone, and they obeyed. However, this expedition accomplished very little in terms of reconquest. Hence ten years later Pope Gregory VII promised that in addition to heavenly rewards, Christian knights who served in Spain would be entitled to all of the wealth and "lands that they conquered from the infidel" (Runciman, 1951, 1:91). Nevertheless, only a few minor nobles responded, and little or nothing was achieved.

Let me pause here to emphasize how the inability of two popes to generate a "Spanish Crusade" is a devastating counterproof of materialist claims concerning the basis for the Crusades. Throughout the twentieth century, many social scientists, non-Marxists and well as Marxists, maintained that the knights crusaded not for God but for land and loot. For example, having summarized many economic problems said to be facing Europe in the eleventh century, including the increasing population pressures and land shortages that supposedly beset the knightly class, the prominent Hans Eberhard Mayer[3] (1972:22–25) stressed the "lust for booty" and the "hunger for loot" that motivated the crusaders: "Obviously the crusade acted as a kind of safety valve for a knightly class which was constantly growing in numbers." He went on to emphasize the need to recognize "the social and economic situation of a class which looked upon the crusade as a way of solving its material problems." Mayer's materialist interpretation is wrong in all respects.

If the knightly class had really been squeezed financially at this time, about the last thing they would have done was march off on Crusades to the Middle East. As Peter Edbury explained, "Crusading was expensive, and the costs were borne by the crusaders themselves, their families, their lords and, increasingly from the end of the twelfth century, by taxes levied on the Church in the West" (1999:95). Even the network of crusader castles and the garrisons by which Christians held the Holy Land for two centuries were sustained not by local extractions but by funds sent from Europe. Indeed, the great wealth of the knightly crusading orders—the Hospitallers and the Templars—was not loot but came from donations and legacies in Europe (Edbury, 1999; Read, 1999). All told, "large quantities of Western silver flowed into the crusader states" (Edbury, 1999:95). The Crusades were possible only because this was not a period of economic decline but one of *growth*, "which put more resources and money into the hands of the ruling elites of Western Europe" (Gilligham, 1999:59).

Moreover, as hundreds of surviving letters and eyewitness accounts uniformly testify, the crusaders *believed* they were going because God willed it, and that their success was nothing less than miraculous. As Jonathan Riley-Smith (1987:38) put it: "The crusaders were not fools. They . . . knew how much at a disadvantage they were. They lacked provisions and had constantly to forage. They lost their horses and had to fight much of the time on foot. They had no firm leadership and at times their army disintegrated into anarchy. Yet still they won through. There could be no satisfactory explanation of this other than that they had experienced God's interventionary might."

Of course, materialists will argue that it doesn't really matter what the crusaders believed, since they would have been victims of false consciousness. It may be ungracious of me to suggest it, but perhaps it is claims of false consciousness that are the best example thereof.

In any case, even if we ignore these compelling objections to the materialist claims, there remains a devastating counterproof. Unlike the Holy Land, Moorish Spain was extremely wealthy, possessed an abundance of fertile lands, and was close at hand. But hardly anyone responded to the call to crusade against the Moors. Yet, only twenty years later, tens of thousands of Europeans set off for the dry wastes of faraway Palestine—and did so again and again. Why? Because Spain was not the Holy Land! Christ had not walked the streets of Toledo, nor was he crucified in Seville.

Meanwhile, as the Crusades to the Holy Land ran their course, the struggle for Spain was at a standstill. Then, more than two centuries after Pope Alexander's efforts to promote a Crusade to Spain, Christian forces launched successful offensives and began to seize new territories having substantial Jewish populations.

When a period of political disorder occurred (Montalvo, 1993), there was a major outburst of anti-Semitic violence. But it lasted for only two years (1391–1392). Thereafter, owing to vigorous actions taken by the nobility (Baer, 1961, 2:95–169), with support from the bishops and the pope, murderous outbursts by Christians against Jews ceased in Spain, never to resume—even though the expulsion of all unconverted Jews from Spain and the executions of people convicted of being insincere converts who still secretly practiced Judaism were yet to come.

The "Black Death"

In 1347 the bubonic plague[4] broke out in Sicily and then in several Italian port cities. Within a year it had spread across Europe, reaching England in 1349. By the time it was over in 1350, about a third of the population had died. Pope Clement VI (*1291–1352*) added up reports indicating that 23,840,000 had perished (Tuchman, 1978), and modern historians estimate the total at 30 million (Cartwright, 1972; Ziegler, 1971).

It is difficult to comprehend such a disaster. Everyone lost relatives and friends. Everyone must have wondered whether he or she would be next. Worst of all, no one knew why it was happening. Of course, various "explanations" prospered. One of the earliest and most widely accepted of these explanations was that God was punishing humanity for their sins. Perhaps the "cure" was to be found through penance. Thus in 1348 there rapidly arose a mass movement of flagellation. Tens of thousands of Christians organized themselves in companies and began to travel from town to town, beating themselves and one another as atonement for sins. At first the Church supported the flagellants, and, in hopes of warding off the plague, Pope Clement IV ordered public flagellations in Avignon (where he was in exile from Rome). Although the flagellants did not stem the plague, often they did have rather pronounced moral effects on communities through which they passed, as locals became stricken with guilt: adulterers made public confessions; thieves returned stolen goods (Ziegler, 1971).

Soon, however, the flagellants' concern with sins began to include the sins of the clergy and of the Church hierarchy. Unordained leaders of the movement began to hear confessions, grant absolution, and impose penances, while others seized churches and even stoned priests who resisted them. As Barbara Tuchman (1978:115) explained, "Growing in arrogance, they became overt in antagonism to the Church . . . and [soon] aimed at taking over the Church." In 1349 the pope responded by condemning the flagellants as a heretical sect, whereupon many of their leaders were seized and executed. Meanwhile, the plague continued.

In the midst of this incredible epidemic, and fed by the violent conflict within the Church, suspicion turned to groups who might have motives to inflict such a vengeance (Ziegler, 1971). Thus in Christian areas of Spain the story spread that the Muslims were behind it all, poisoning wells with the plague. In southern France the English were accused. Even pilgrims came under suspicion. But, inevitably, attention turned to the Jews. The story began to circulate that the Black Death was being spread by the Jews, who were seeking revenge against Christians by secretly poisoning the wells. The story had the ring of truth because it was obvious to all that the Jews had a lot to be angry about. It appears that the idea originated in Spain (adapted from the charge against the Muslims), and the story spread from there. And not surprisingly, that's where the first attacks on Jews took place. What is surprising is that the attacks in Spain were so few, as were the deaths they caused. This was due to effective intervention by local bishops, supported by Pope Clement IV, who issued a bull directing the clergy to protect the Jews, denouncing the claims about poisoned wells, and directing that those who spread that rumor, as well as those who harmed Jews, be excommunicated.

But papal authority failed in some Germanic areas. There the massacres began in the area around Lake Geneva. In the small town of Chillon the charge of well poisoning was leveled against several Jews. They were arrested, and under torture they confessed, implicating all Jews in the area, whereupon all the Jews were rounded up and burned. From there, once again a wave of massacres swept down the Rhine through the familiar list of cities: Speyer, Mainz, Worms, Cologne. And, in at least seven German towns, the Jews committed mass suicide.

It strikes me as significant that, aside from events in Spain, Jewish massacres during the Black Death were limited to the area along the Rhine River. In part this reflected the terrible grip of tradition— where else in Europe did families identify themselves as Jew-roasters? But it also reflected the prevailing weakness of both Church and State authority in this region. In her brilliant reconstruction of the Jewish community of Cologne, Shulamit S. Magnus (1997:18) described the Rhine basin as "the most politically fractured area" of Germany, portions of which were sometimes part of France. The area consisted of a patchwork of tiny political units (at times totaling more than seventy) ruled by independent princes or, in many instances, by "prince-bishops," the latter being bishops and abbots appointed by the German emperor and whose "double loyalty" to both pope and emperor made them "weak allies" of either (Holborn, 1982:21). The weakness of authority in this region is clearly demonstrated, not only in the frequency with which secular and religious authorities were unable to prevent mobs from killing Jews (Mainz and Cologne both had prince-bishops), but also in the concentration of Christian heretical movements in these same Rhineland communities—as will be seen.

A very useful essay could be devoted to why the nobility and the Catholic hierarchy did so consistently attempt to suppress violence against Jews. In my judgment, there were two primary reasons. First, elites are usually more tolerant of diversity, having expanded horizons and a greater range of experience. Second, and more important, ruling elites fear disorder—particularly spontaneous popular outbursts. Once the "people" take affairs into their own hands, there may be no stopping them. If mobs are allowed to loot, burn, rape, and murder their way through the Jewish quarter, where might they strike next? It is instructive that many recent historians believe that a major reason for the creation of the Inquisition was that it "substituted the rule of law for mob violence" (Hamilton, 1981:57). For, as Richard Southern (1970:19) noted,

Flaming Bigotry. This woodcut made in 1496 of a man carrying logs to throw on the fire consuming a group of Jews reflects the virulent anti-Semitism that developed along the Rhine River where many families claimed the title of "Jew-roasters." © Bettmann/CORBIS.

"on the whole the holders of ecclesiastical authority were less prone to violence, *even* against unbelievers, than the people whom they ruled" (also see Kieckhefer, 1989:112).

Revolt in Paris

Brief mention must be made of violence against the Jews of Paris that took place in 1380 and 1381. This appears not to have stemmed from a larger religious conflict but from a revolt by the poor against high taxes. During the initial riots in 1380, members of the nobility intervened to blame poverty and high taxes on the Jews, whereupon the mob attacked the Jewish quarter, causing at least ten deaths. The next year, the poor rose again; armed with heavy mallets (hence becoming known as the "Maillotins"), this time they turned against the Jews without any coaching, and perhaps fifteen were killed (Tuchman, 1978).

Heresy Rediscovered

In his fine study *Medieval Heresy*, Malcolm Lambert (1992:25) suggested that after the Visigoths were converted away from Arianism late in the sixth century, heresy essentially disappeared from Christendom for many centuries. He explained that the circumstances by which "the heresies of early centuries had once spread" no longer applied, and heresy "of the old pattern virtually ceased to exist." But then, in the eleventh century, heresy "reappeared in the West after a long gap."

Lambert is surely correct that something very important happened at this time. But while he and other historians have blamed such things as chronic warfare and the lack of "a cultivated laity" for the absence of heresy, I think that what really happened, and needs to be explained, is the sudden *rediscovery* of heresy. I will argue that this was a direct result of the rapid increase in religious intolerance, prompted by men preaching the Crusades. Let me summarize the analysis to follow.

Just as the nonconformity of the Jews was ignored for more than five hundred years, so was that of Christian heretics, and for the same reason: they posed no institutional threat. And just as the nonconformity of the Jews suddenly became an issue, at that same moment so too did Christian nonconformity. Furthermore, when the demands for conformity and orthodoxy *were applied to the Church itself*, as was bound to happen, mass heretical movements were born in protest against the official heresies. That is, the new heresies reflected a sudden, mobilized intolerance of the remarkable nonconformity of the official Church to its own standards. In that sense, the heretics were the victims of their own intolerance.

Slim though it is, the historical record reveals that during the eighth and ninth centuries there were some quite pronounced instances of heresy that aroused very little concern (Lambert, 1992;

Moore, 1976, 1985; Russell, 1965, 1971). For example, in the eighth century a certain Aldebert attracted large crowds as he traveled in northern France proclaiming himself a saint and distributing his hair and nail clippings to his followers. He was so popular that, after the bishop of Soissons prohibited him from preaching in churches, he set up crosses in the countryside and preached beneath them to large crowds. As Jeffrey Burton Russell (1965:103) reported, eventually his followers built him churches, "which Aldebert himself consecrated, so that his support among the population must have been wide and enthusiastic." Eventually, several Church synods demanded that Aldebert cease preaching, and threatened to excommunicate him, but he continued and nothing was done. Three centuries later he might have been burned. Or consider the case of Claudius, who, during his tenure as bishop of Turin from 814 to 820, denounced the use of all images in worship, ordering them removed from all his churches. He particularly opposed veneration of the cross, denounced the cult of saints, dismissed the value of pilgrimages, and questioned the pope's authority. Claudius' contemporary, Agobard, bishop of Lyon, held similar views about images, writing, "Whosoever adores a picture or a statue, whether carved or cast, does not worship God, nor does he worship angels or saints; he is an idolater" (in Russell, 1965:14). Two centuries later, both bishops would probably have been defrocked, or worse, but in the ninth century their "puritan" heresies were tolerated. During that same century a woman named Theuda attracted many followers by claiming to have received special revelations from God, including the date of the Second Coming. As with Aldebert, the Church allowed her to proceed for a considerable time before ordering her to stop.

What these events demonstrate is that the heretical impulse wasn't dead, but that this was an era in which the religious and secular authorities (and hence the chroniclers) didn't perceive heresy as a significant matter. In fact, Lambert (1992.:25) noted that during this era, "outbreaks of doctrinal dissidence that did occur were treated mildly by the authorities, presumably because they presented no significant challenge to the church." Hence, exactly as predicted, nonconforming groups were tolerated to the extent that they were perceived to pose no institutional threat. Neither the Jews nor wandering Christian mystics could conceivably challenge the religious establishment; hence the centuries without attacks on heresy were the same centuries that historians of anti-Semitism have identified as "tranquil." Then suddenly, in the eleventh century, there was substantial violence against both heretics and Jews. This is fully in accord with the proposition that religious toleration will be withheld or withdrawn even from nonthreatening nonconforming groups during periods when powerful religious groups collide.

Two "Churches"

When the eleventh century began, there had long been two major religious elements, or "churches," in Christendom—their existence being the inevitable result of niches in the religious "market," as discussed earlier in the chapter. The first of these, which I will name the *Church of Power,* was by far the largest and consisted of most of the official Roman Catholic hierarchy, from parish clergy through popes, and the masses of nominal Catholics. Since the days of Constantine, the majority of clergy (especially at the higher levels) consisted of worldly, ambitious, and often quite flagrantly immoral men (Cheetham, 1983; Duffy, 1997; Murray, 1972). As for the masses, they were at best "slightly" Christianized (Stark, 1999c). Most would have professed their belief in Jesus, but as part of a supernatural pantheon including all manner of spirits and godlings. Since very few medieval priests could even list the sins forbidden by the Ten Commandments, let alone actually recite the commandments (Thomas, 1971), obviously most laymen had little awareness of sin. Few ever attended mass, and when they did, it was often conducted by a priest who was known to lead a dissolute life. As for bishops, cardinals, and popes, many were openly devoted to opulent living and vice (Cheetham, 1983; Duffy, 1997).

But, of course, there were also devout Christians in medieval times, and they constituted a second, if far smaller, element, which I will call the *Church of Piety.* At the head of this church were the monks (and sometimes nuns played leading roles as well). An immense structure of monasteries crisscrossed medieval Europe as monasticism continued to attract the most ardent Christians from each generation. Most monks did not lead a sequestered life but were a very influential social force—in the eleventh century they were still busy missionizing the pagan political elites of northern Europe. Monks also served as chaplains and even as pastors to various groups of laity, for the fact is that while the people as a whole were quite lacking in piety, there were significant numbers of devout laypersons, many of whom had been led to serious commitment through instruction from a monk. Indeed, periodically monks embarked on preaching tours—an early form of revival campaign that added to the "membership" of the Church of Piety.

Preaching the Crusades and Heresy

Through the centuries there had always been tension between the two "churches," but the chronic criticisms by the Church of Piety had been kept under control by the official clerical hierarchy's allowing a proliferation of new orders that functioned as encapsulated sect movements, by occasional reforms, and simply by superior political power. Then, into this delicate balance of forces, suddenly along came several popes who wanted to inspire an enormous outburst of *popular* piety—the Crusades. In fact, all of the popes of the second half of the eleventh century were monks who wished to reassert the Church of Piety, and who themselves often stressed the moral shortcomings within the Church. So when Pope Urban II wanted knights to fight for the Holy Land, he did not try to hire mercenaries. Instead, he stood in the field at Clermont and challenged "[s]oldiers of Hell, [to] become soldiers of the Living God."

Preaching the Crusade was not a onetime thing. Rather, hundreds and then thousands of preachers took up the pope's message (Maier, 1994). Appearing in every hamlet, village, and town, they preached the duty to serve or help finance the liberation of the Holy Land. And, as had the pope, they did more: they stressed the *evil of nonbelief*—"Bathe in the blood of the infidels," the pope had thundered to the thousands in Clermont. "Kill the unbelievers" and "Avenge Christ," echoed those who preached the Crusade all across Europe.

Moreover, these preachers (and those who preached all of the Crusades that were to follow) were not clergy of the Church of Power—overwhelmingly, they were the monks of the Church of Piety (Lambert, 1992; Maier, 1994; Moore, 1976, 1985). And the longer they thundered about the infidel, the more they began to include as infidel *all* who were insufficiently faithful to Christ— including unworthy priests and bishops! Just as some had noted that it made no sense to march all the way to the Holy Land to rid the world of infidels while leaving behind whole communities of Jews, so too the revivalists preaching the Crusades also began to denounce infidels within the bosom of the Church. This was not the preaching of some dissenting sect; it was that of men who were so deeply committed to Catholic orthodoxy that they could see nothing controversial in their calls for reform. Indeed, the most influential of these early "reformers" had been specifically commissioned by Pope Urban II to preach the Crusade. Robert of Arbissel, Vitalis of Mortain, and Bernard of Tiron had each turned away from successful clerical careers to live as ascetics in the Forest of Craon. At the invitation of the pope, each emerged from seclusion to preach the First Crusade but soon turned most of his attention to denouncing the sins of the clergy in the most graphic fashion. These three, soon joined by many others, traveled from village to village for years, preaching against the sins of the clergy more than in support of the Crusades, never being reluctant to name dissolute local clergy. Despite the anger they aroused among the regular clergy, not only did these three monks survive, but each became a successful founder of a monastic order (Moore, 1976, 1985). Nevertheless, each must have ended his days knowing that he had failed to root out even most of the worst clerical offenders. By then, however, hundreds more were preaching reform.

Slowly, and out of frustration, the reformers begin to venture toward the old Donatist position that sacraments are of no value if received from unworthy priests. The orthodox view is that no matter how sinful your local priest, all sacraments received from him are valid, so long as his ordination was valid. To those committed to following in Christ's footsteps, such legalisms failed to satisfy—many asked, how can one be absolved of sins by an insincere, venal libertine doomed to hell? Thus Church "reform and heresy were twins" (Lambert, 1992:390).

The increasingly vigorous efforts to bring reform had two potent consequences. First, they voided the previous general toleration of Christian nonconformity. Attacks by clergy of the Church of Piety on "sinful" clergy prompted counterattacks on clerical "heretics," since the latter now posed a very serious institutional threat to the official hierarchy. Indeed, many critics had begun to preach that there should be no hierarchy at all, and that only those willing to lead lives of absolute chastity and abject poverty should be allowed to administer the sacraments. No wonder they were condemned. But, as a result, the Church of Piety gave rise to organized and truly threatening dissent: Waldensians, Cathars (called Albigensians in southern France), Lollards, Hussites, Lutherans, and Calvinists— to name only some major movements in what eventually came to be known as Protestantism.

Of course, the Church of Power responded to each of these challenges with fire and sword, to the fullest extent possible. But in the end an unlikely coalition of pious religionists and opportunistic politicians secured the survival of Protestantism. The Catholic response was the Counter-Reformation, during which many of the "sins" condemned by the heretics were corrected as the Church purged unobservant clergy and began serious efforts to Christianize its remaining laity.

Collateral Conflicts

Not only was the rediscovery of heresy collateral to the larger religious conflict with Islam, but some lethal attacks on Jews occurred as side effects of these religious wars. In 1209 French forces overwhelmed the fortress city of Beziers, the center of the massive Albigensian heresy in France. During the subsequent massacre approximately 20,000 died, among them 200 Jews. There is no evidence, however, that the troops were concerned with killing Jews, since they had been instructed to kill all inhabitants. Two centuries later, the Jewish community at Nordlingen was burned by a Christian mob; Heinrich Graetz (1894b:162) blamed this on the "passionate strife" that had divided "the whole of Christendom into two huge, bitterly hostile camps."

The war against the Hussites produced new massacres of Jews in the same old places—communities along the Rhine. As Graetz (1894a:222) put it, "The crusades against the Hussites, like those against the Mahometans and the Waldenses, commenced with massacres of Jews." As they marched up the Rhine valley to attack the Hussites in Bohemia, an army of German and Dutch mercenaries was prompted by locals to deal with Jewish heretics too. "We are marching afar to avenge our insulted God, and shall those who slew him be spared?" said one mercenary leader (Graetz, 1894b:225). So they laid waste the Jewish communities on their route. That same year, other soldiers making war on the Hussites attacked the Jewish community in Vienna, killing about a hundred and causing others to commit suicide. As the conflict continued, many Dominicans "thundered against heretics and Jews alike" (ibid.:226), with the result that in 1431, in the same area where massacres prompted by the Black Death had begun, the Jewish communities in three towns were murdered.

Of course, the Dominicans had good reason to be concerned with heretics in the Rhineland. For, as already mentioned, in addition to being the area where Jewish massacres were concentrated, this was also the area where, in the very same era, heresy flourished in Germany. It was in Mainz that Theuda gathered followers and proclaimed the date of the Second Coming. It was only in the Rhineland, in Cologne and Mainz particularly, that the Cathars gathered German congregations during the twelfth century, and it was also primarily in the Rhineland that the German Waldensians found support during the thirteenth century—especially in Mainz, Strassburg, Speyer, Worms, and Würzburg (Kieckhefer, 1989). During the thirteenth and fourteenth centuries it was in these same Rhenish towns that the heresy of the Free Spirit flourished—in about 1320 there may have been two thousand members of the Beguines, a female Free Spirit group, living in Cologne (Bynum, 1982; Cohn, 1961; Johnson, 1976; Kieckhefer, 1989; McDonnell,

"Heretic!" On July 6, 1415, Jan Hus was burned at the stake for his advocacy of Church reform. He soon became the martyred hero of a movement demanding both religious and political reforms that resulted in the Hussite Wars. © Archivo Iconografico, S.A./CORBIS.

1954). Again in the fifteenth century, it was here that the Hussites found receptive Germans, and such cities as Nuremberg, Mainz, Worms, Speyer, and Ratisbon were sites of conflict (Kieckhefer, 1989). And, of course, it was in Speyer that the term "Protestant" was first applied to the followers of Martin Luther (*1483–1546*), and in Worms that Luther told the Diet, "Here I stand, God help me. Amen." Then, in the next century, it was only in the Rhineland that Calvinism gained a foothold against Lutheran dominance (Holborn, 1982). Whatever else all this heretical activity may indicate, it clearly reveals the same lack of political and ecclesiastical control that failed when faced with anti-Semitic mobs. Indeed, in work presently underway, I have found that witch-hunts, sustained by mob violence, were concentrated here too.

It also seems significant that as Luther's defiance led to a new and truly major religious conflict, it too kindled the fires of collateral intolerance. Early in his career, Luther was a vigorous defender of Jews. But as the conflict with Catholics heated up, he became increasingly hostile toward all nonconformists: "But now I am not astonished at the Turks' or the Jews' blindness, obduracy, wickedness. For I see that same in the holiest fathers of the Church, pope, cardinals, bishops" (in Oberman, 1992:296). Soon he began repeatedly to accuse the Jews of various sorts of blasphemy, such as calling Mary a whore and Christ a bastard, and charged that "if they could kill us all, they would gladly do so" (in ibid.:293). Although Luther was unflinching in his opposition to any mob actions against Jews, that his charges did not prompt Lutheran massacres of Jews was fortunate. Furthermore, in 1614 about two thousand Jews were massacred by members of a dissident Protestant sect in Frankfurt, known as the Reformers, who sought to demonstrate that their virtue was superior to that of the Lutherans, who only talked about the Jews but did nothing about them.

It must be noted that just as massacres of the Jews were concentrated in the towns and cities of the Rhineland, that's also where there were substantial Jewish populations. Indeed, Nachum T. Gidal (1988:30) identified "the cities of Speyer, Worms, and Mainz" as "spiritual centers for the Jews of central Europe" in the tenth and eleventh centuries. That these same cities were especially notorious as the sites of Jewish massacres, starting in 1096, could suggest a sort of *opportunity thesis*: that the local availability of Jewish victims was a major cause of Christian violence. However, aside from the obvious fact that massacres of Jews could not occur where there were no Jews, the evidence is contrary to such an explanation. Gidal's fine map shows 102 significant Jewish communities in Germany in this era. While many of these were in towns and cities along the Rhine, most were not. Why did Christian mobs not form and attack the Jewish communities in most other German towns? Why weren't there periodic slaughters of Jews in the hundreds of Jewish communities elsewhere in Europe? Probably because local elites were sufficiently powerful to prevent a tradition of Jew killing from ever getting started. For, once begun, traditions of religious and ethnic violence are extraordinarily lasting: Munich, where the Jews were massacred in 1285 and again in 1349,

is less than twenty miles from Dachau, site of one of the most notorious Nazi death camps.

This seems the appropriate point to discuss why lethal attacks
on Jews ended early in the fifteenth century, except for the episode
in Frankfort in 1614. Two major factors can be cited. First, there
was a massive migration of the Jews from western to eastern Europe. By the middle of the fifteenth century there were very few
Jews left in those areas of western Europe where the attacks had
been concentrated. Indeed, in 1424 Cologne expelled all Jews, and
the other principal cities along the Rhine soon followed suit; Jews
were not permitted to return until the middle of the nineteenth
century! The second reason is that heretic hunting absorbed most
of the attention and animosity toward religious nonconformists
that had been directed against Jews. Indeed, as I will demonstrate
at length in future work, as heresies grew into serious political and
military challengers of the Church, the result was the appearance
of a new group of collateral victims: the seemingly endless supply
of local witches.

Heresy and "Class Struggles"

Many historians who are of sociological inclination, Marxists and
non-Marxists alike, have claimed that these great heretical movements were not primarily about doctrines and morals, if, indeed,
religious factors were of any real significance at all. Instead, they
argue, the religious aspect of these movements masked their real
basis, which was, of course, class struggle. Friedrich Engels (in
Marx and Engels, 1964:97–123) identified some of these movements, including the Albigensians, as urban heresies in that they
represented the class interests of the town bourgeoisie against the
feudal elites of Church and State. But most of the other heretical
movements were, according to Engels, based on the proletariat,
who demanded restoration of the equality and communalism of
early Christianity (Engels and many other Marxists have claimed
that the early Christians briefly achieved true communism). Engels
granted that these class struggles were embedded in religious and

mystical rhetoric, but dismissed this as false consciousness. Following Engels, many other Marxist historians have "exposed" the materialism behind the claims of religious dissent. Thus in 1936 the Italian historian Antonino de Stefano claimed that, "[a]t bottom, the economic argument must have constituted, more than any dogmatic or religious discussions, the principle motive of the preaching of heresy" (in Russell, 1965:231). Even many historians not committed to orthodox Marxist reductionism have detected materialism behind medieval dissent. For example, the non-Marxist historian Norman Cohn (1961:xiii) reduced medieval heresies to "the desire of the poor to improve the material conditions of their lives," which "became transfused with phantasies of a new Paradise." And, to be honest, some years ago I expressed similar views (Stark and Bainbridge, 1985, chap. 22).

It is hardly necessary to deny that class conflicts existed in medieval times, or to suppose that people participating in heresy never paid any heed to their material interests, to reaffirm that religion was at the heart of these conflicts. Had their primary concerns been worldly, surely most heretics would have recanted when this was the only way out. It was, after all, only their religious notions they had to give up, not their material longings. But large numbers of them chose death instead. Moreover, these movements drew participants from *all* levels of the class system. For example, contrary to Engels the Albigensians enlisted most of the nobility as well as the clergy of southern France along with the "masses" (Costen, 1997; Lambert, 1992; Mundy, 1985). Third, claims that the majority of participants in any given heresy were poor are quite lacking in force, even in the instances for which it might be true. Almost *everyone* in medieval Europe was poor. Gauged against this standard, it appears that the "proletariat" was *under*represented in most of these movements (Lambert, 1992). Finally, the emphasis these groups often placed on the virtues of poverty was not, as Russell (1965:234) pointed out, reflective of "a trades-union program or a grange" but found expression in calls for "holy poverty" in opposition to the worldly corruption of the Church. Indeed, I cannot improve on Russell's conclusion:

167

It is of course possible to press materialist interpretations farther and maintain that though the program of the dissenters was explicitly religious it was implicitly social. The "real" motivations are social, the materialists say, but in their naïveté the dissenters could do no more than express their discontent in religious terms. These historians make an a priori philosophical assumption about what is "real," an assumption that may or may not be justified. And in this question of medieval dissent, the burden of proof lies with the materialists who, in almost gnostic fashion, seek the esoteric explanation in preference to the simple one.

Muslim Attacks on Jews

For generations, scholars identified the situation of Jews in Muslim Spain as a "Golden Age" (Cohen, 1996; Goiten, 1964). No one disagreed with Stanley Lane-Poole when in 1897 he claimed that "[t]he history of Spain offers us a melancholy contrast. For nearly eight centuries under her Mohammedan rulers, Spain set all Europe a shining example of a civilised and enlightened state . . . Whatever makes a kingdom great and prosperous, whatsoever tends to refinement and civilisation was found in Moslem Spain" (in Fletcher, 1992:172). Lane-Poole went on to contrast this shining example with the cruel and fanatical Spain that expelled the Jews following the final defeat of the Moors by Ferdinand and Isabella in 1492.

Nor did anyone challenge the celebrated Jewish historian Heinrich Hirsh Graetz (1894b, 3:214) when he asserted, "Judaism ever strove towards the light, whilst monastic Christianity remained in darkness. Thus in the tenth century there was only one country that offered suitable soil for the development of Judaism, where it could blossom and flourish—it was Mahometan Spain." In the middle of the twentieth century, Rudolf Kayser (1949:50) still exulted, "It is like a historical miracle that in the very same era of history" in which "orgies of persecution" against Jews occurred in Christian Europe, the Jews in Moorish Spain "enjoyed a golden age, the like of which they had not known since the days of the Bible." As recently as 1991, Anthony Burgess wrote that after the fall of Granada "the magnificent Emirate of Córdoba, where beauty, tolerance, learning and order prevailed, was only a memory" (in Fletcher, 1992:171).

In a distinguished volume commemorating the five hundredth anniversary of the expulsion of the Jews from Christian Spain, Vivian B. Mann (1992:xi) noted that the "Golden Age of Spanish Jewry . . . was personified above all by Maimonides." But despite the intellectual achievements of Moses Maimonides (*1135–1204*), his biography makes a travesty of claims concerning a "Golden Age" of Judaism in Moorish Spain. As Gil Carl Alroy (1975:185) pointed out, "Maimonides fled to Egypt—not from Christian persecution, but from Muslim terror in Spain—and was later forced to hide his Judaism from the Muslims of Arabia and other places so as not to endanger his safety." Indeed, in 1148 the Maimonides family pretended to convert to Islam when the Jews of Córdoba were told to become Muslims or leave, on pain of death. After eleven years, fearing that their double life had become too dangerous, the family moved to Fez in Morocco—still pretending to be Muslims. Their story clearly demonstrates that, as Richard Fletcher (1992:173) put it, "Moorish Spain was not a tolerant and enlightened society even in its most cultivated epoch." Indeed, it should be noted that when the Maimonides family and other Jews were required to convert or leave Moorish Spain, many Jews migrated to the Christian areas of northern Spain—something that is seldom mentioned.

Aside from anti-Christian motives, a major reason that so many have celebrated what Mark Cohen (1996) has frankly identified as the "myth" of the Golden Age is that from the initial Muslim conquests in Spain in 711 until the second half of the eleventh century, there were no massacres of Spanish Jews by Muslims, and Jews often held high government posts, especially as tax collectors. These peaceful days are contrasted with the brutalities inflicted on the Jews in Christendom. However, this comparison works only if one ignores the calendar. For the peaceful era in Spain occurred at precisely the same time as the one known as the "tranquil" period in Christian-Jewish relations. That is, on *both* sides of the Pyrenees the Jews were reasonably secure during these centuries. Even more compelling is the fact that the alleged Golden Age of Jews in Moorish Spain ended in a massacre in 1066, the very same year that Jews were first massacred in Christian Spain!

That four thousand members of the Jewish community of Granada were butchered by Muslims in 1066, the same year in which Pope Alexander had to intervene to stop French knights from killing Muslims and Jews in northern Spain, was not a coincidence. Nor was it coincidental that a successful new Christian offensive, which resulted in the fall of Toledo, was soon followed in 1090 by the second massacre of the Jews of Moorish Granada. What these events demonstrate is that Muslim-Christian collisions escalated religious intolerance on both sides. In similar fashion, fatal Muslim attacks on Jews in the Middle East coincided with the Muslim conquest of the crusader fortress city of Acre in 1291.

New circumstances for religious conflict were created by the Mongol conquest of Persia in 1260. The Mongols were pagans and, as such, not much concerned about religious conformity. However, Grand Khan Argun chose to exclude Muslims from official positions, relying instead on local Christians and Jews to help him govern, placing a Jew named Saad-Addaula in charge. As Graetz (1894b, 3:648) described the situation: "The Mahometans, who were shut out of every office, beheld, with deep vexation, that Jews and Christians, whom they were accustomed to despise as infidel dogs, were in possession of the government. They were, moreover, urged by their priests and learned men to a most violent hatred of the Jewish statesman [Saad-Addaula], to whom they imputed their humiliation." Soon the incredible rumor spread that Saad-Addaula planned to proclaim the khan as a religious lawgiver and head of a new religion, and to send an expedition to Mecca to establish it as the center of a new paganism to which all Muslims would be forced to convert. In 1290 Argun died suddenly, and Saad-Addaula's enemies (including many powerful Mongols) seized the opportunity to have him executed. Meanwhile, the Muslim population "fell upon the Jews in every city of the empire" (Graetz, 1894b, 3:649). Not far away, Muslims forces also butchered the Jews and Christians in Acre.

Conclusion

Overall, it seems to me that the historical record is very consistent with the three hypotheses outlined earlier in this chapter. Both Christian and Muslim attacks on Jews, as well as the rediscovery of heresy within Christendom, can be linked to a common, underlying social process. Even such highly particularistic faiths as Christianity and Islam were able to accommodate religious nonconformity as long as it posed no significant institutional threat. But when confronted with significant threats from one another, Muslims' and Christians' tolerance evaporated, and Jews and heretics paid the price.

It would be wrong to conclude that during this era only the Muslims and Christians were militant monotheists ready to go to extreme lengths in behalf of their True Faith. As a weak and scattered minority, Jews were seldom in a position to attack unbelievers. But they fully demonstrated their unrelenting particularism by their unrelenting resistance. It was the power of particularism that made it possible for the Jews to resist assimilation despite their being a dispersed minority for more than two millennia. Of course, many Jews in the diaspora did convert, including some whose descendants became Christian kings or even popes.[5] What is remarkable is that identifiably Jewish communities endured at all. It must also be recognized that in virtually all of the bloody episodes reported in Figure 3.1, any Jew who would convert was spared. It is no surprise that many took that option. What requires explanation is that thousands upon thousands remained steadfast, choosing death over conversion. Indeed, again and again whole Jewish enclaves opted for mass suicide rather than be baptized or embrace Islam.

Thus, to return to the discussion that opened Chapter 2, monotheism has two social sides: the power to inspire conflict among groups and the power to sustain intense solidarity within groups. It is to this issue—the capacity of religion to generate unwavering loyalty—that the next chapter is devoted.

Notes

1. In the new *Macmillan Encyclopedia of World Religions* (1998), Alan Davis largely dismissed Muslim anti-Semitism as an "infiltration of Christian and Western influences" (38). But there is no record that the Prophet invoked charges of Jews' being "Christ-killers" when he attacked Jewish communities. Rather, he accused them of affronts to *his* divine mission.

2. Al-Hākim was undoubtedly insane and also persecuted Jews and all Muslims who openly doubted his claims to semidivinity.

3. Mayer is the classic intellectual moderate who agrees with everyone's theories, accepting the religious causes of Crusades on one page and the materialist causes on the next.

4. It was not called the "Black Death" until several centuries later (Ziegler, 1971).

5. Queen Isabella's husband King Ferdinand II (1452–1516) was Jewish through his mother, and "most Spanish noblemen [at this time] had Jewish blood" (Thomas, 1979:493). The very powerful Roman family the Pierleonis were of Jewish origins, and several of them became popes (Cheetham, 1983:84).

Keeping the Faith. Father and son participate in Simchat Torah (Festival of the Bibles) in the synogogue on Djerba Island, off the coast of Tunisia. The Jewish settlement on Djerba predates both Christian and Muslim rule.
© Hulton-Deutsch Collection/CORBIS.

· 4 ·

God's *Kingdom*: Religious Persistence

And ye shall be unto me a kingdom of priests and a holy nation.
—Exod. 19:6

Groves that once sheltered Druid rites are empty, the Parthenon is merely a tourist attraction, and only archaeologists frequent the sacred caverns of Mithra. The supernatural beings who once prevailed in these places have long since fled to the graveyard of the Gods, but there are no headstones there for Yahweh, Jehovah, or Allah—each lives on in the hearts of millions. Why do some religions survive for millennia, while others come and go? Or, to both narrow and intensify the question: How do minority religions *persist*? That is, how does a minority religious group *resist* the pressures and temptations to *assimilate*?

Many minority groups are *sects*, which I define as nonconforming religious bodies surrounded by a majority who adhere to the *same religious tradition*. The Amish are a sect in Christian societies, just as the Sufis are a sect within Islam, and the Karaites a Jewish sect. Sects are nourished by their agreement on the fundamentals of religious culture with those around them, although this doesn't always spare them from persecution even to the point of mass murder.

The theory developed in this chapter applies fully to sects, but the emphasis is on explaining the survival of groups whose nonconformity lies *outside* the conventional religious tradition, thus placing them in *fundamental opposition* to their religious environment, as the Jews have stood firmly as religious outsiders around the world. Indeed, because the diaspora is the quintessential example of religious persistence, I will give it my full attention in the historical portion of the chapter, confident that the lessons learned generalize to all monotheistic faiths under similar circumstances.

A Theory of Religious Persistence

Key elements of a theory of religious persistence are already in place, having been postulated in previous chapters. The most basic premise concerns the conception of God. People do not risk it all for "add-on" Gods of limited scope and dubious character. Rather, the extreme capacity for persistence with which this chapter is concerned requires belief in a *God of infinite scope* such as Yahweh, Jehovah, or Allah: *Belief in One True God maximizes the capacity to mobilize human actions on behalf of religion.*

As we have seen, missionizing is a primary aspect of religious mobilization. But sometimes missionizing is unavailing or even impossible, and the primary focus of a group's mobilization is to endure—to keep the faith. Their ability to do so depends upon the ability of their God to command the *extended exchange relations* necessary to sustain unwavering loyalty. Hence religious persistence is proportional to the *scope* of the Gods and the expected *duration* of exchange relations with the Gods.

Max I. Dimont ([1962] 1994) argued that the Jews have persisted throughout three millennia of wandering and tribulations because they broke with tradition and conceived of Yahweh as a "portable God." Unlike pagan Gods who ruled a specific location, Yahweh accompanied the Jews wherever they went, sustaining their faith and defining their community. Hence Judaism became a religion that could be practiced faithfully *anywhere*. Soon, however, it was unnecessary to believe merely that Yahweh traveled with them, because the Jews came to regard Him as of infinite scope, being equally and entirely present *everywhere*.

As noted, the power to produce otherworldly rewards is associated with Gods of infinite scope, and this, in turn, justifies not only an exclusive exchange relationship with the One True God but an *extended* exchange relationship. That is, the hope of obtaining rewards of immense value and everlasting benefit requires the individual (and the group) to accept a lifelong obligation to make periodic payments (usually in the form of sacrifices, rites, and conformity). Thus the key to religious persistence lies in extended exchange relationships with Gods—with the need to maintain a lifelong favorable balance in one's religious account.

The most valuable otherworldly reward is eternal life. Christianity and Islam offer very explicit and attractive promises of a paradise that ensues at the moment of death. The traditional Jewish view has been less immediate, providing for the resurrection of the faithful following the advent of the Messiah (Gillman, 1997). No doubt this is why Judaism has always been so prone to messianic movements—people become impatient for fulfillment of the otherworldly reward (Sharot, 1982). Even so, the promise of a messiah has always been sufficient to sustain unwavering commitment. In his classic study *The Pursuit of the Millennium*, Norman Cohn (1961:61) explained the durability of the Jewish diaspora:

> [T]he solution to this sociological puzzle is to be found in Jewish religion which not only—like Christianity and Mohammedanism— taught its adherents to regard themselves as the Chosen People of a single omnipotent God, but also taught them to regard the most overwhelming communal misfortunes—defeat, humiliation, dispersal—as so many tokens of divine favour, so many guarantees of future communal bliss. What made the Jews remain Jews was, it seems, their absolute conviction that the Diaspora was but a preliminary expiation of communal sin, a preparation for the coming of the Messiah and a return to a transfigured Holy Land.

Notice, however, Cohn is discussing not the beliefs of Jewish individuals but the shared beliefs of a Jewish *community*. People do not remain loyal to a particular religion primarily because of the appeal of specific doctrines. Rather, they find these doctrines appealing because they share them with an intimate network of believers. Religious persistence is a group phenomenon, because religion itself, and especially monotheism, is a group affair.

Otherworldly rewards are impervious to disproof, but by the same token they cannot be demonstrated to exist. Therefore, exchanges involving long-term expenditure of tangible costs here and now, in hope of otherworldly rewards to come, involve substantial *risk*. Hence the universal problem of religion is one of *confidence*. No exchanges with a God will occur until or unless people are sufficiently confident that it is wise to expend the costs required. In polytheistic societies, risk is dealt with by diversification—a portfolio pattern wherein people seek religious benefits from a variety of Gods simultaneously (Iannaccone, 1995). But even when one must choose a single divine supplier, or choose not to exchange with any God, people will still behave like all investors: they will seek assurance. Not surprisingly, they are able to obtain it in a number of ways, both secular and sacred.

Quite simply, an individual's *confidence* in religious explanations concerning otherworldly rewards is strengthened to the extent that *others* express their confidence in them. As Darren Sherkat (1997:68) put it, "Religious goods are not simply 'experience' goods which must be consumed in order to be evaluated; rather, these goods must be experienced in communities which direct us on how to evaluate them." Throughout our lives we rely on the wisdom and experience of others to help us make good choices. In addition to testifying to their personal certainty about otherworldly rewards, people often enumerate miracles—how they recovered from cancer, how they overcame alcoholism or drug abuse, how they became reliable and faithful spouses, how they survived a catastrophic accident, how their prayers for a dying child were answered, or how victory was snatched from defeat. Thus do people demonstrate that a religion "works," that its promises come true. Sometimes they also testify about their own mystical experiences as proof that religious explanations are valid. In the case of groups that engage in various forms of collective "ecstatic" experiences, they offer one another direct *demonstrations* of the existence of a God or Gods (Poloma, 1987). Testimonials are especially effective when they come from a trusted source. Thus friends are more persuasive than acquaintances, and the testimonials even of acquaintances are more persuasive than those of strangers.

Participation in ritual and prayer are also sources of confidence in religious expectations. I do not suggest that this is the primary reason that people engage in these religious activities—I think they do them mainly because they are believed to be proper forms of exchange with the divine. But neither do I suggest that the confidence these activities provide is an unconscious "function" that escapes individual notice. It is very common for people to pray for strengthened faith—"Lord, I believe; help thou mine unbelief" (Mark 9:30)—and the "peace of mind" gained through these activities is widely remarked, hence the principle: Confidence in religious explanations concerning otherworldly rewards increases to the extent that people *participate* in religious *rituals*.

It is quite astonishing, but although "ritual" is one of the most-used terms in social scientific writing on religion, it is a concept badly lacking in definitional efforts. Durkheim, for example, regarded ritual as *the* elementary form of the religious life, and claimed to know what it does, but never said what it *is*. Nor did Malinowski. A collection of outstanding anthropological studies was published under the title *Gods and Rituals* (Middleton, 1967), but "ritual" does not appear in its index (although there are eleven entries under the heading "chickens, sacrifice of"). My definition was influenced by Randall Collins' (1998) discussion of "interaction rituals."

Rituals are *collective ceremonies having a common focus and mood*. I define *ceremonies* as *formal* acts, usually based on *custom*, having a *preset pattern* or script. Finally, *religious* rituals are part of a specific religious culture.

By limiting ritual to *collective* ceremonies, I have excluded private, personal "rituals," as when a Catholic says the Rosary alone, but I include groups of Catholics saying the Rosary. By designating some rituals as *religious*, I exclude rituals associated with magic or nonreligious ceremonies, such as Nazi Party rallies. I have also omitted any claims that religious rituals are conducted in pursuit of divine favor, because while such motives are always at least implicit, they are not always explicit. That is, rituals may be experienced primarily as celebrations and festive occasions, not as a time for submitting petitions. For example, among the Dinka of the southern Sudan, even when "the occasion for a sacrifice may be a sad one . . . the ceremony itself is regarded by the Dinka as essentially a happy one, and they behave at such ceremonies as though they enjoyed themselves, and indeed attend in order to do so. Every sacrifice has a festive atmosphere" (Lienhardt, 1961:281). Another instance: Christmas services held in most Christian churches celebrate the birth of Jesus without reference to the blessings of faith. Similarly, the feast upon the breaking of the fast of Ramadan is an occasion of joy and thanksgiving in Muslim communities, as is the Passover seder among Jews.

However the term is defined, social scientists are unanimous that participation in rituals builds faith—"Ritual actions . . . [give] the members of a society confidence" is how George Homans (1941:172) put it in his youthful days as a functionalist. And Kingsley Davis (1949:534) advised that "[r]itual helps to remind the individual of the holy realm, to revivify and strengthen his faith in this realm." Even Durkheim (1915:226) admitted that the "*apparent* function [of ritual] is to strengthen the bonds attaching the believer to his god." Of course, he quickly added that what ritual "*really*" does "is strengthen the bonds attaching the individual to society, since god is only a figurative expression of society" (my italics).

I am entirely willing to give Durkheim and the functionalists their due on the observation that social rituals do generate group solidarity and, in that sense, social integration. However, as I have demonstrated elsewhere (Stark, in press), ritual participation does not contribute to conformity to group norms unless such conformity is explicitly linked to their conception of God. Thus a crucial element of solidarity is commitment to the central ideas and ideals of the group. And what religious social rituals produce is agreement about the value of religious ideas and ideals. For example, Christmas services assert the truth of all Christian teachings by affirming that Jesus was born the "son of God." In that sense, affirmation becomes integration.

However, to entertain functionalist assertions about how religious rituals contribute to group solidarity is hardly to accept their extraordinary claim that rituals not only confirm but *produce* religious beliefs. Radcliffe-Brown (1952:155) rejected the notion that religion is "primarily a matter of belief" as hopelessly Eurocentric and backward.[1] He argued that beliefs arise after the fact to explain rites and rituals: "[I]t is sometimes held that funeral and mourning rites are the result of a belief in a soul surviving death . . . I would rather hold the view that belief in a surviving soul is not the cause but the effect of the rites." Radcliffe-Brown then quoted Robertson Smith (1907), who rejected the "modern habit [of looking] at religion from the side of belief rather than that of practice" because many participants in a given ritual will explain it "in different ways."

No doubt many people in all societies are hazy about the doctrines of their religion. And it is certainly true that many people do learn the doctrines from participating in rituals *once the system is in place*. But it is absurd to argue that a group first staged the ritual and then originated the beliefs that give meaning and purpose to the ritual. Thus no doubt many Christians learn the Apostles' Creed by reciting it during worship services, but this is not to suppose that the religious explanations summed up by the creed were developed after the fact to explain why services are held. Can we really imagine that the Hopi learned from *doing* their rain-dance ritual that there is a rain God?

There can be no doubt, however, that the Hopi gained confidence in the existence of a rain God by dancing. In his work on the sociology of the world's philosophical schools, Randall Collins (1998) asks what makes particular ideas and texts sacred. He answers, not in terms of contents or meanings, but in terms of the rituals in which these ideas or texts are embodied. Indeed, a given individual's sense of a text's sacredness is usually far less intense during solitary reading than when it is read or recited as part of a social ritual.

Prayer is a *communication* addressed to a God or Gods, and a major consequence of prayer is to *build bonds* of affection and confidence between humans and the Gods.

Prayers may be silent or spoken out loud, impromptu or regular, formulaic or spontaneous, mandatory or voluntary, and they may express need, praise, hope, joy, or even despair. People may pray in private, in small groups (formal, as in the case of the Jewish minyan, or informal, as in the case of the family devotion), or as part of a collective ceremony. But in all cases prayers are meant to be *heard*. As Firth (1996:169) put it, "prayer is ostensibly a manifestation of a personal tie with the transcendent . . . [and] constitutes an act of faith or hope that it will reach its mark." As in

Forms of Prayer. The immense difference between praying to
an "essence" and to a "God" is revealed by these photographs.
The upper photo shows prayers written on paper and wrapped
around the wires of a fence next to a Shinto shrine in Kyoto, Japan;
the destination of these pleas is quite vague (© John T. Young/
CORBIS). But the British women kneeling in Westminster Cathedral,
shown in the lower photo, know to whom they are praying and
assume that their pleas for peace (in 1939) will be heard
(© Hulton-Deutsch Collection/CORBIS).

the case of ritual, people do not always pray *for* something; often prayer is an experience of sharing and emotional exchange much like that between humans having a long, intimate relationship, for in fact many people have come to regard their prayer relationship as long and loving (Poloma and Gallup, 1991). This is entirely to be expected. Homans (1974) law of liking reads that the longer people interact, the more they will come to like one another. Prayer, then, can have many purposes, but an important result is to reassure humans that religious phenomena are real.

Granted, we may not assume that prayer really is interactive, that there really is a second party. But that doesn't matter *if* the human experiences prayer as a two-party affair, if the divine seems to hear and to care. Thus when the Nuer address their God as *"madh,"* "a word which has for them the sense of intimate friendship" (Evans-Pritchard, 1956:8–9), this reflects a relationship established and experienced through prayer. Likewise, when Christians speak of "knowing the love of Christ," they do so not as a figure of speech but as an accurate description of their devotional life.

Confidence in prayer is increased by participation in *group* prayer; thus does prayer become ritual. When a group of Muslim men gather for prayer, form lines facing Mecca, and press their foreheads to the ground, each is reinforced by the actions of the others.

Participation in religious rituals builds group *solidarity.* It is well known that it requires months of constant drill and practice maneuvers to produce reliable and effective military units. Drill not only accustoms troops to acting together in immediate response to orders; more important, it affords the circumstances for linking the individual soldiers to one another by strong bonds of trust and friendship. It is these bonds, not idealism, that enable soldiers to face death—the role of idealism is to shape the expectations they impose in judging one another. In his masterpiece on military command, S.L.A. Marshall ([1954] 1978:153) noted that because fear affects everyone in battle, training should be designed to foster friendships among the ranks: "When a soldier is unknown to the men who are around him, he . . . has relatively little reason to fear losing the one thing he is likely to value more highly than life—his reputation as a man among other men." Marshall went on to point out that "it is the man who . . . is well known to his fellows" who will stand fast.

Participation in religious rituals is a form of drill that is well suited to foster strong bonds. Moreover, the bonds formed among participants include bonds to the divine being toward whom the rituals are oriented. Just as drill may not be important for troops who will never be sent into battle, so too participation in religious "drills" may not be needed to sustain uncontested faiths. But they are vital for the persistence of embattled minorities.

This entire discussion of prayer and ritual can be summed up: Religious persistence is a function of the *frequency* and *exclusivity* of participation in religious rituals.

In polytheistic cultures, ritual participation is typically rather infrequent, usually being limited to special occasions. Furthermore, these ritual events are spread among many rites and Gods. In contrast, an observant Muslim male prays to Allah five times a day (usually in unison with others), and an observant Jewish male joins nine others to form a minyan each morning. Participation in occasional rituals to various Gods may result in some generalized sense of commonality but does not build strong bonds to specific coreligionists and therefore cannot generate the truly intense solidarity that results when people frequently worship the same God in the company of the same people. Of course, for the latter to occur, there must exist a community of believers.

I have defined religious persistence in terms of a minority religious *group* subject to pressures and temptations to assimilate. Both factors lie mainly outside a group's control. For all that a religious minority may be provocative, it remains the option of the majority whether to exert pressures on the group to conform or to make it easy and rewarding to assimilate. The irony is that, short of genocide, the pressures imposed by the majority tend to increase solidarity among the minority. Indeed, religious persistence is facilitated by the social encapsulation of the group.

Social encapsulation means that members of the group are *concentrated* in specific locations and are *impeded* from having normal associations with outsiders. Quite aside from increasing the cohesive capacity of the group, encapsulation may prevent a group from disappearing via assimilation by making it nearly impossible. The barriers to association between Jews and Christians in medieval Europe or between the Muslim majority and the Jewish and Christian minorities were sketched in Chapters 2 and 3. Most of these restrictions were intended by the majorities to coerce conversion, while preventing contamination. But by excluding the minority from network ties to the majority, encapsulation effectively prevents assimilation. Because members of the minority are often aware of this fact, encapsulation is sometimes a two-way street. For example, just as the majority may prohibit conversion to the minority faith or intermarriage, the minority may impose similar prohibitions. The result is mutually exclusive networks that preclude the spread of faith.

The effectiveness of social encapsulation is greatly increased by group *visibility*, by *physical* and/or *cultural markers* that make individuals identifiable as members of the minority group. I have already mentioned the items of dress and demeanor that made Christians and Jews highly visible in Muslim societies and which identified Jews in Christian societies, to which must be added linguistic differences. Cultural markers such as these can, at least in principle, be shed or disguised, but marked physical differences are another matter. No doubt racial differences greatly contributed to the encapsulation of Jews and European Christians in Asia.

Finally, it seems not to be a coincidence that Judaism, Christianity, and Islam are religions "of the Book." Religious persistence requires relatively accurate and complete cultural transmission, and while humans have displayed remarkable capacities for oral transmission of culture, there is far less drift and accretion when the religious culture is written (Miller, 1994). As has often been remarked, the ancient Jews were unique not only for their monotheism but for their commitment to male literacy—required for proper participation in rituals. I am unwilling to claim that *literacy* is a requirement for persistence, but it is a very significant contributing factor. Literacy is, in this context, the ability to read and write in the language in which a group's sacred texts are written, and which is used in rituals and ceremonies. As will be seen, once the Chinese Jews had lost their Hebrew, they were illiterate even though they read and wrote Chinese—for they had no translations of their scriptures.

In the remainder of the chapter, I utilize this theory to illuminate the persistence of the Jews.

Jewish Persistence and Assimilation

In what follows I first briefly sketch the rather extraordinary extent and duration of the Jewish diaspora, showing how well this aspect of Jewish history fits the theory. Then I devote considerably more attention to Jewish assimilation in order to apply the principle of reversibility to the theory. That is, if I have correctly identified the factors that sustain the Jewish faith, then it ought to follow that when and where these factors shift, there should be a substantial decline in the ability of the Jews to resist assimilation. Briefly, as their conception of God shifts from that of a conscious, all-powerful being to an essence, as Jews cease to participate regularly in rituals and religious ceremonies, as they shed the cultural markers and practices that encapsulate them, all of this in combination with their growing acceptability in the surrounding societies, then high rates of Jewish assimilation should ensue.

Many groups migrated far and wide in ancient times, but, lacking a durable cultural mark, they left few traces and no identifiable descendants. In contrast, as Jews migrated all across Europe and to many parts of Asia, they established distinctive and enduring settlements, many of which remain. Had the Jews been polytheists like everyone else in ancient times, they would be just another barely remembered people, far less important but just as extinct as the Babylonians, Hittites, and Parthians. They remain only because they worshiped the One True God and sustained elaborate practices and cultural norms predicated on that belief. So long as this was true, they did not blend.

Elements of Jewish Persistence

In all parts of the diaspora the Jews were a relatively encapsulated group. In the West they were set apart by the antagonism of their neighbors and the discriminatory laws imposed on them by their host societies. In the East, the levels of conflict were far lower, and the external aspects of encapsulation were primarily a response to racial and cultural differences. But everywhere the Jews also tended to be encapsulated by their own religious and social exclusiveness.

It is absurd to claim that Christians originated anti-Semitism, as many scholars do (e.g., Gager, 1983; Isaac, 1964, 1971; Ruether, 1974). Of course, religious conflict tends to be far less intense when only one of the participants is particularistic (and when this group is much less powerful than the others), but anti-Semitism[2] was fully developed in the Greco-Roman world well before the birth of Jesus (Schäfer, 1997; Smallwood, 1981). Indeed, classical anti-Semitism was sufficiently intense to cause Jews to be expelled repeatedly. It was not an early Christian writer but Seneca, the distinguished Roman, who denounced the Jews as an "accursed race" and condemned their influence. It was the great Roman historian Tacitus who railed against the Jews because they "despise the gods." It was Roman law that prohibited the conversion of non-Jewish slaves and servants. And it was in pre-Christian Rome that from time to time converts to Judaism, even members of the upper class, risked expropriation, banishment, and even death. Moreover, as seen in the previous chapter, anti-Semitism is not lacking in Islam. Rather, beginning with Muhammad himself, Muslims have imposed severe restrictions on Jews and periodically have done their share of "ethnic cleansing."

It is equally absurd to propose that encapsulation was a one-way street—that Jews respected religious differences and, aside from the sorrow and pain they felt because of their mistreatment, generally sustained benign feelings toward gentiles. Such a portrait of Jews places polemical opportunities above common sense. Jews are human beings, not crash-test dummies. When subjected to hatred and contempt, Jews tend to respond in kind. In fact, as true monotheists, Jews despised the pagan Gods, looked down on those who honored them, and were not reluctant to say so. As for relations with Christianity, during the first several centuries Jewish attacks on Jesus were as lurid as those associated with the more extreme members of the current Jesus Seminar: he was depicted as a magician, a bastard, son of a harlot, a criminal rebel, and an associate of Satan (Stow, 1992). Indeed, a phrase calling for the destruction of Christianity was introduced into the daily prayers said in the synagogue (Horbury, 1982; Katz, 1984; Stow, 1992). And why not? If one rejects that Jesus was the Messiah, then from the Jewish perspective he willfully committed extraordinary blasphemy. Nor did the Jews' attitudes toward Christianity mellow as they settled into the life of a stigmatized, and reviled, subculture within Christian lands. Writing in about 1140, the Jewish chronicler Solomon bar Samson described the crusaders as going "to seek the grave of their disgrace[d] one," called the cross "a foul sign," and referred to Christian churches as "abomination[s]" (Stow, 1992:102–3, 108). Indeed, at about this same time Maimonides dismissed Jesus as one who "imagined that he would be the Messiah." He went on to charge that Jesus fulfilled the prophesy of Daniel that "men of violence among your own people shall lift themselves up in order to fulfill the vision; but they shall fail." Maimonides added, "Is there then a greater failure than this?" (in Vital, 1999:104). To which David Vital (ibid.) added, "No Jew in Christian Europe who ventured to reflect on the subject thought otherwise." It would truly have been a miracle had Jews not expressed such opinions of Christianity among themselves. The same is true of Jewish attitudes toward Islam—indeed, Maimonides was anxiously posing as a Muslim when he wrote these comments about Jesus (see Chapter 3).

Contemptuous views of outsiders are necessary for the survival of a stigmatized group. It is only by teaching their children to look down on outsiders that groups like the Amish are able to retain group loyalty and thereby to persist in a world that looks down on them. Amish who defect are shunned—their family and friends never speak to them again. The same was true of Jews in ancient and medieval days—and remains so for very Orthodox Jews today. It is quite impossible for groups to keep their attitudes toward outsiders secret. *All* groups have defectors. In addition to having defectors reveal their secrets, groups will reveal their attitudes toward outsiders by their reaction to those who join the majority. Thus when a group holds a funeral for someone who has assimilated, their views are clear. In this way, encapsulation is continuously reinforced from both sides.

The same applies to visibility. Both Muslim and Christian societies often required that Jewish identity be visible—that Jews wear something distinctive such as a badge or hat to reveal their group membership. But stigmatized groups often *choose* to be visible too—consider the Amish or the Hare Krishnas. As will be discussed, following the political emancipation of Jews in Europe, many Jewish communities became very concerned about the temptations to assimilate and therefore adopted the dress codes that are now associated with the ultra-Orthodox. Few realize that Jews only recently began to wear side-curls, black hats and clothing, and the like. These were not traditional: in ancient and medieval times Jews dressed and groomed like everyone else, apart from items required of them by law. Those responsible for the voluntary new visibility of Jews were quite candid about wishing to increase consciousness of kind.

However, many traditional Jewish practices also serve to encapsulate them. Keeping kosher not only limits where Jews may shop but greatly restricts their social relations with gentiles. Strict rules of Sabbath observance also make Jews very visible, and these (such as the prohibition against riding to the synagogue), as well as the limited availability of kosher food, impose a need to live in Jewish neighborhoods.

Viewed as a whole, the extent, duration, and militance of Jewish persistence is breathtaking. Masada was hardly a unique event. In York, England, in 1189, faced with mob violence, the Jewish community consisting of from 150 to 200 people committed mass suicide rather than convert to Christianity. Then in 1349, during the attacks on Jews as the Black Death raged, the Jewish communities in at least nine German cities chose suicide, although conversion would probably have caused the mobs to spare them (see Figure 3.1).

Again and again, Jews were ordered to convert or leave Christian or Muslim areas, whereupon the vast majority abandoned most of their possessions and all of their property, although they had no attractive destinations. As celebrated rabbi Leo Baeck noted in 1930, Jewish migrations "have been virtually always migrations for the sake of faith. The Jew could have stayed if he had departed from his religion, but he departed because he was determined to stay with his religion" (in Morganthau, 1967:47). Moreover, many Jews who did comply in order to stay made only sham conversions and secretly remained steadfast. As mentioned in the previous chapter, large numbers of Jews in Spain, including the Maimonides family, were willing to risk death by continuing to practice their religion in secret while pretending to be Muslims or Christians, and these communities of "crypto-Jews" endured for centuries (Alroy, 1975; Gitlitz, 1996; Netanyahu, 1999). Keep in mind that these Jews were not content merely to secretly retain Jewish beliefs, or even to silently reject their pretended conversion. They continued to actively practice their faith through group rituals and surreptitious observance of the Law. Often they were found out because their observance of the Sabbath and unwillingness to eat pork were noticed by Christian neighbors. But it was only by maintaining an active religious life that these communities endured.

It seems unnecessary to describe Jewish persistence in greater detail. Instead, considerably more can be learned about their persistence through a close analysis of instances when Jewish communities failed to withstand the pressures and temptations to assimilate.

The Successful Christian Mission to the Jews

Well before the start of the Christian era, the Jews in the Hellenic parts of the diaspora had adjusted to local lifestyles in ways that set them apart from Judaism as practiced in Jerusalem. Jews had been residents of cities such as Alexandria, Antioch, Sardis, and Corinth for centuries, and they had grown wealthy and acculturated. As early as the third century B.C.E. their Hebrew had decayed to the point that very few could read the Torah. Indeed, Jews in these communities were so Hellenized that most had Greek names, and the more educated among them were well trained in Greek philosophy. In an effort to overcome the language barrier, the Torah was translated into Greek—the Septuagint. In the process, not only Greek words but Hellenic ideas crept into the text. For example, Exod. 22:28 was rendered "You shall not revile *the gods*," which Calvin Roetzel (1985) interpreted as a gesture of accommodation toward pagans. Indeed, the most revered Jewish leader and writer of the time devoted most of his efforts to accommodating Judaism to Greek philosophy. Thus Philo of Alexandria (*ca. 20* B.C.E.–50) described God in ways that Plato would have found familiar: "the perfectly pure and unsullied Mind of the universe, transcending virtue, transcending knowledge, transcending the good itself and the beautiful itself" (in Corrigan et al., 1998:88). Philo was also very concerned to justify the Law on the basis of rational explanations. It was not sufficient for him that God had forbidden Jews to eat the flesh of birds of prey or of carnivorous mammals. The *reason* he had done so was to emphasize the virtue of peace. What Philo could not rationalize, he recast as allegories having no literal application to real life. As John Collins (1983:9) put it, "The allegorical interpretation of scripture by Philo and others is an evident method for reducing the dissonance between Jewish scriptures and philosophical religion." W.H.C. Frend made the same point, arguing that Philo attempted to interpret the Law "exclusively through the mirror of Greek philosophy" (1984:35). As a result, the clear religious and historical meaning of much of the Torah was "lost among the spiritual and moral sentiments whereby Philo sought to demonstrate the harmony and rationality of the universe" (ibid.). Philo's was not a lonely voice. His was perhaps the most celebrated Jewish voice of the time, and his views clearly reflected the concerns of many. Thus did the image of God sustained by the Hellenist Jews shift from that of the authoritative Yahweh to a rather remote, abstract Absolute Being.

To sum up: As their image of God became increasingly vague, the basis for their traditional particularism eroded, and the Hellenist Jews became increasingly tolerant of paganism. This greatly reduced religiously based antagonism toward them, since this was mainly a pagan response to Jewish particularism. In tandem with these religious trends, the Jews of the diaspora (especially in the eastern part of the empire) became very acculturated and only slightly encapsulated. They spoke and thought in Greek. They associated with Greeks and were uncomfortable with the more visible and limiting aspects of the Law; hence most of them seem to have been only superficially observant. Moreover, many (perhaps most) of these Hellenist Jews found it degrading to live among Greeks and embrace Greek culture and yet to remain "enclosed in a spiritual Ghetto and be reckoned among the 'barbarians'" (Tcherikover, 1958:81). Put another way, as the "pull" of Jewish solidarity was greatly reduced, so was the "push" of pagan ill-feelings.

Nonetheless, for all their respect for Greek philosophy and culture and their relative lack of particularism, the Jews of the diaspora did not embrace paganism. Even though many of them were quite uncomfortable with the ethnic aspects inherent in Judaism, they clung to some semblance of their faith as, indeed, the synagogue continued to attract many pagan "God-fearers" (see Chapter 2). Pantheons of small Gods are never a match for a God of unlimited power and scope, not even one who has been somewhat depersonalized. So, despite wishing to be fully accepted into the Greco-Roman world, the Jews were not ready to convert in order to assimilate. However, when presented with a vivid monotheistic option stripped of all Jewish ethnicity, many of them took it, thus swelling the ranks of the new Christian movement.

In *The Rise of Christianity* I attempted to show that theory, common sense, and the bulk of surviving evidence strongly suggest that the mission to the Jews did not fail, and that, rather than ceasing late in the first or by the middle of the second century, substantial rates of Jewish conversion to Christianity probably continued well into the fifth century. As I noted then, there were enough Jews in the diaspora to have provided an ample flow of converts for a very long time—historians estimate that Jews made up about 10 percent of the population of the empire during the early days of Christianity (Georgi, 1986; Meeks, 1983). When I wrote that book, I was unaware that historians now estimate that Jews constituted no more than 1 percent of the population of Europe in the Middle

Ages (Baron, 1952; Stow, 1992). Granted, in Roman times the Jewish population was larger in areas subsequently ruled by Islam. Thus it would be quite misleading to propose that the Jewish population had shrunk by a factor of 10 during the centuries and to attribute that to conversion. Nevertheless, these figures suggest a considerable decline in the Jewish population before the end of the "tranquil time" in Christian-Jewish relations, and such a decline is consistent with a substantial rate of conversion. Nor should this be surprising in light of the religious and social situation of the Hellenist Jews during the rise of Christianity. Here was a faith that was presented as the next step in God's plan for Jews, and which imposed no ethnic encumbrances.

However, even though Christianity attracted large numbers of Jewish converts, its impact on the remaining Jews was to revive and transform their Judaism. As Israel Yuval (in Boyarin, 1999:2) noted, it is a distortion of history to suppose that being the older faith, Judaism influenced Christianity, but not the reverse. Rather, "early Christianity and the Judaism of the Mishna are, in a manner of speaking, sister religions that were crystallized in the same period . . . having arisen more or less together historically." For all that the Mishna variety of Judaism emphasized rabbinical thought and authority, there was nothing tepid or accommodating about its views, and thus was the power to persist fully restored. The synagogues that survived the Christian mission to the Jews had become fully encapsulated bastions of opposition wherein God was no Absolute Being but was once again the God of Abraham, noting each and every thought and action, and about whose Laws there was nothing allegorical. Thus did Western Judaism rebound from its first era of substantial assimilation.

Assimilation of the Chinese Jews

Historians don't know when Jews first reached China, or when they established a durable community there (Abraham, 1999; Baron, 1952; Eber, 1999; Goldstein, 1999; Kublin, 1971; Leslie, 1972; Perlmann, 1909; Plaks, 1999; Pollak, 1998; Rhee, 1973;

Matteo Ricci (1552–1610). The illustrious Jesuit scholar
and missionary to China is shown in Chinese clothing. He
reported the existence of a sizable Jewish community in
China. © Archivo Iconografico, S.A./CORBIS.

Ross, 1982). A good case can be made that this occurred in the
first century, probably subsequent to the Roman destruction of Jerusalem (Leslie, 1972). What is clear is that Jewish communities
were well established in China by the ninth century, when their
presence was reported by Arab travelers and geographers, and
Marco Polo encountered Jews in Khanbaliq (Beijing) in 1286. Jewish communities are also mentioned in official Chinese documents
written in the fourteenth century. Of these Jewish communities,
only the one in Kaifeng survived to be discovered by the famous

Jesuit missionary Matteo Ricci in 1605. Inscriptions indicate that the first synagogue was built in Kaifeng (then the imperial capital of China) in 1163 and was subsequently reconstructed several times.

At its peak in about 1500, the Jewish community in Kaifeng probably included more than ten thousand members. A century later when Father Ricci arrived, membership was down to perhaps a thousand (Leslie, 1972). By early in the nineteenth century the Kaifeng synagogue lacked a rabbi, and knowledge of their faith was quite defective among the few who still regarded themselves as Jews (Eber, 1999). Following his visit in 1867, the Anglican bishop Samuel Schereschewsky reported: "They have entirely lost their religion and are scarcely distinguishable in any way from the Chinese. They have idols in their houses, and ancestral tablets . . . They intermarry . . . and have ceased to practice circumcision. In features, dress, habits, religion, they are essentially Chinese . . . They cannot read the Law, although the manuscripts are still in their possession" (in Muller 1937:69–73). By the twentieth century, the "Jews" of Kaifeng—the handful of people who recollected that their ancestors had been Jewish—were mere curiosities who granted interviews to a series of Western academics (Abraham, 1999).

The Jewish experience in China is an extraordinary example of religious persistence—authentic, orthodox Jewish enclaves endured for many centuries. But then they assimilated, retaining only vague notions about their Jewish past. What happened? First, their conception of God became increasingly vague, and their religious practices grew progressively syncretized—an amalgamation of Chinese and Hebrew concepts and customs. Second, the various bases for their encapsulation attenuated. Third, they were highly rewarded in secular careers that required mastery of Confucian philosophy.

Our knowledge of the theological ideas and religious practices of the Jews in China is based on several very lengthy inscriptions (dated 1489, 1512, 1663, and 1679) found in the courtyard of the synagogue at Kaifeng, and on reports written by Jesuit visitors during the seventeenth century. The synagogue inscriptions were written in Chinese, not Hebrew, and according to Donald Daniel

Leslie, the preeminent authority on the Kaifeng Jews, they clearly reveal that Chinese ideas had "crept into the beliefs and attitudes of the [Jews]. Confucian and Taoists influences are undoubtedly present in the . . . inscriptions, and many quotations from the Confucian classics are used. The terms for God and for the Law are those used by the educated Chinese for his own religious beliefs, and some of the mysticism is clothed in Taoist terminology" (1972:7). Thus the 1489 inscription noted:

> Truly in the matter of honouring Heaven, if a man did not venerate his ancestors he could not then properly offer sacrifices to the forefathers.
> Thus in the spring and autumn [as] sacrifices to the ancestors . . . he offered oxen and sheep, and seasonal food, and did not fail to honour the ancestors. (Ibid.:87)

Writing in 1704, the Jesuit missionary Jean-Paul Gozani noted that the Jews of Kaifeng honored the dead in their "Hall of Ancestors, with the same ceremonies as are employed [generally] in China." But he added that they did so without tablets commemorating the dead, as these constituted "images" and therefore were prohibited (ibid.:88). Moreover, they still circumcised male infants, observed the Sabbath, did not eat pork, celebrated Passover, and gathered to recite orthodox prayers. However, they also referred to the Law as the Tao, or the Way, burned incense to their ancestors, and, as noted on the 1663 inscription, "In matters concerning capping [a ceremony marking the passage into adulthood], marriage, deaths, and funerals, the Chinese custom is followed" (ibid.:102). As to God, the inscriptions do not acknowledge a "God who punishes or makes promises . . . The inscriptions imply that the God of the Jews and the [Way of] Heaven of the Chinese [the Tao] are one and the same" (Eber, 1999:32). Indeed, as noted on the 1663 inscription:

> Although there are some minor discrepancies between Confucian doctrine and our own, in their main focus of ideas and established practices both are exclusively concerned with honoring the Way of Heaven, venerating ancestors, valuing the relations of ruler and

subject, obedience to parents, harmony with families, correct ordering of social hierarchies, and good fellowship among friends: nothing
more than the "five cardinal relations" of mankind. (In Plaks,
1999:38)

It is impossible to catch any glimpse of Yahweh here.

As the inscriptions also report, as late as the fifteenth century
many of the Jews of Kaifeng could still read Hebrew. However, by
the eighteenth century, Jesuit visitors found that very little knowledge of Hebrew still survived: the community was illiterate insofar
as their sacred texts were concerned.

China has had periods of extreme xenophobia. Hence one of the
very earliest references to Jews in China is an account of a rebellion
in 879 that resulted in the destruction of Canton after a long siege
and the massacre of its inhabitants. Based on Chinese tax records,
the dead are reported to have included thousands of Muslim, Jewish, and Christian merchants (Leslie, 1972). But for most of the
existence of the synagogue at Kaifeng, relations between Jews and
other local Chinese seem to have been quite amicable. With the
establishment of the Ming dynasty (1368–1644) policies were instituted to minimize foreign influences. Thenceforth, foreigners were
required to marry native Chinese. Religious groups such as the
Jews and Muslims were regarded as foreigners, although they had
been residents for countless generations. It is not clear, however,
that these new policies had much impact on the Jews of Kaifeng,
since they had often intermarried from early days. In any event, by
the end of the sixteenth century intermarriage was pretty much the
rule (ibid.).

Intermarriage not only attenuated Jewish encapsulation by linking Jews to whole networks of Chinese in-laws, it also changed
how they looked! And, in addition to no longer being racially visible, they had adopted Chinese names (ibid.). However, the clearest
indication that Jewish encapsulation had broken down is that
members of the Kaifeng community began to have illustrious careers as government officials.

Song Nai Rhee (1973) attributed the assimilation of the Chinese
Jews to their very successful entry into the Chinese imperial civil

service. For many centuries, China staffed its state administration on the basis of merit, as established by performance on examinations devoted entirely to knowledge and understanding of the Confucian classics. Candidates devoted many years to intensive study, transforming themselves into Confucian scholars. Those with the highest grades were admitted to the ranks of the mandarins, who administered all state functions.

As it happened, Chinese Jews excelled at Confucian scholarship, and "beginning in the fourteenth century a large number of Jews from K'ai-feng did join the scholar-official class in increasing numbers as years went by" (Rhee, 1973:120). Thenceforth the community's "most brilliant and ambitious" young men spent long years in "Confucian indoctrination," to the detriment of their orthodoxy (Pollak, 1998:341). These were the young men from whose ranks rabbis would have come. Instead, their devotion to Confucian study resulted in their ignorance of Hebrew, and in their being very inclined to reinterpret Judaism according to Confucian concepts. To make matters worse, even though they were barely Jewish, these mandarins did not sever their ties with the Kaifeng community. To the contrary, they transposed their high secular status into equally high status within their home community. It was they who paid for expanding or rebuilding the synagogue. It was they who commissioned the inscriptions. It was they who pressed syncretized Judaism on their fellows, and it was they who overcame local opposition to such heterodoxy (Plaks, 1999; Pollak, 1998; Rhee, 1973).

The similarities between the Hellenist Jews and the Jews of China are very striking. In both situations, changes in religious conceptions mitigated their particularism and paved the way for an end to encapsulation. Both groups lost their Hebrew, adopted the local language, and took local names; both groups began to shed their religious identity in pursuit of economic and social rewards. The Hellenist Jews, of course, already looked like their Greco-Roman neighbors, while it took many centuries before the Chinese Jews looked Chinese. But the key aspect in both instances was the demise of external pressures vis-à-vis encapsulation. The decline began as Jews modified their fundamental religious concepts, thereby reducing their opposition to external religions, removing a major basis of conflict with their surrounding societies. The result was an extreme increase in the ease and rewards of assimilation. Sad to say, the persistence of religious and cultural minorities seems to depend on hostility between them and outsiders—within limits, solidarity thrives on oppression.

This is hardly an original idea. At the turn of the twentieth century, the scholar-merchant S. M. Perlmann, having interviewed several Kaifeng Jews, proposed that the survival of Jewish communities was gravely threatened when outsiders did not treat them as pariahs. Hence Perlmann (in Kublin, 1971:200–211) saw the Chinese Jews as examples of what was happening wherever Jews were given the same regard and "privileges as the dominant people." In contrast, he wrote, Judaism remains strong "in those countries where the hostility to the Jews is still strong and effective, because they will fight there and conserve themselves." Perlmann's was not a lonely voice; his views were representative of one side in an immense dispute that broke out in Europe at the start of the nineteenth century, as to how Jews should deal with their rapidly improving circumstances.

Europe: Emancipation and Assimilation

On January 28, 1790, the French National Assembly extended "the rights of active citizens" to the Jews of southwestern France— approximately four thousand Jews of Spanish origins. Then, on September 27, 1791, the assembly emancipated all of the remaining Jews in France—numbering about thirty thousand, most of them living near the German border (Baron, 1969; Magnus, 1997; Mendes-Flohr and Reinharz, 1995; Vital, 1999; Winock, 1998).

Immediately following the second decree, the Jewish banker Berr Isaac Berr wrote to all the Jews of France:

> At length the day has come when the veil, by which we were kept in a state of humiliation, is rent; at length we recover those rights which have been taken from us more than eighteen centuries ago . . .

We are now, thanks to the Supreme Being, and to the sovereignty of the nation, not only Men and Citizens, but we are Frenchmen! (Complete text in Mendes-Flohr and Reinharz, 1995:118–21)

As it turned out, Berr's embrace of nationalism was a bit premature, for Napoleon soon reimposed severe limits on Jewish liberty. His decree of 1806 reiterated the traditional condemnation of the Jews for their involvement in usury. Thus it would be necessary to rehabilitate "sentiments of civic morality" among the Jews; Napoleon acknowledged that these sentiments "have been stifled . . . by the abject state in which they have long languished and which it is not our intention either to maintain or renew" (ibid.:123–24). Napoleon then summonsed an assembly of Jewish notables to advise him on many questions concerning Jewish doctrine and culture. Finally, on March 17, 1808, Napoleon issued a decree meant to "reform" Jewish life.

The Napoleonic decree began by ruling that no debts owed to Jews could be collected except under supervision of the French courts, subject to stringent restrictions. It then decreed that "thenceforth, no Jew shall be permitted to devote himself to any business, negotiation, or any type of commerce without having a specific license from the prefect of the department in which he resides," and this license would need to be renewed annually. "Any commercial action undertaken by an unlicensed Jew shall be null and void," including any mortgage or contract. Next, it was decreed that Jews were prohibited from further migration into the area along the Rhine River—the longtime hotbed of anti-Semitism. Nor would Jews be admitted to any other area unless they became farmers and avoided all commercial or business activities. Jews were also forbidden to hire someone to take their place in the military draft but must serve in person. Finally, the decree was to remain in effect for ten years and then be assessed in the hope that by then "there will no longer be differences between them [Jews] and other citizens" (ibid.: 139–40).

With the defeat of Napoleon, the original terms of emancipation were restored in France. However, the area along the Rhine reverted to Prussian control, and the decree remained in force while the Prussians sorted things out with local authorities. Actually, Prussia had granted its Jews "equal civil rights and liberties with Christians" in 1775. But this applied only to Jews of means (the *Schutzjuden*), while the great majority of Prussia's thirty-two thousand Jews remained in the "undesirable" or "useless" category and suffered under an array of repressive regulations (Vital, 1999). At the Congress of Vienna held in 1815 to redraw boundaries and impose peace terms on France and its allies following Napoleon's final defeat at Waterloo, the German Confederation (a unified German state did not yet exist) adopted a resolution directing the individual states to effect "an amelioration" of all those who confessed "the Jewish faith in Germany" (complete text in Mendes-Flohr and Reinharz, 1995:143). This was easier said than done. Indeed, Prussian plans to suspend the Napoleonic decree in the Rhineland faced intense local resistance.

In her fine study of Jewish emancipation in Cologne (1798–1871), Shulamit S. Magnus (1997) detailed the city's long battle with Prussia for local authority over the Jews. Recall that Cologne was the site of murderous attacks on the Jews during both the First and the Second Crusades and again in 1349 during the "Black Death." Then, in 1424 Cologne expelled its Jews, as did many of the other principal cities in the Rhineland—although some of the expelled Jews did not go very far, settling in the smaller towns and villages of the area. For nearly four centuries, only an occasional Jew was allowed a temporary stay in Cologne—Jews were not allowed even to pass through the city unless escorted by the police. In 1784 Jews petitioned the city council for permission to pass without police escort and were turned down. Ten years later, when the city fell to the army of the revolutionary French Republic, French laws went into effect, including the emancipation decree, and Jews began to move back into the city. But they were not welcome.

Napoleon seems to have taken this into account when he decreed that Jews could not move into the Rhine area. And that is precisely why local authorities demanded that the Napoleonic decree remain in effect, rather than the Prussian policy as expressed in a new Edict of Emancipation proclaimed in 1812.

The reintegration of the Rhine cities into Prussia posed many problems beyond those involving Jews. Hence the royal cabinet appointed an *Immediat Justiz Kommission* to oversee the process. The *Kommission* decided that French law should be retained in this region. However, because Napoleon's decree on the Jews was set to expire in 1818, agitation broke out for and against its renewal. The anti-Jewish side won, and the decree remained in effect until it was modified in 1845 and then abolished 1847 (Magnus, 1997; Vital, 1999).

Meanwhile, emancipation was proceeding in western Europe. "By the last decades of the nineteenth century the settled German, Austrian, Hungarian, French, Dutch, Italian, and British Jews had all achieved legal emancipation" (Vital, 1999:310). And only in the Rhineland had there been significant local protests and organized resistance. This surely is not to say that anti-Semitism was limited to the Rhineland at this or any other time. But probably nowhere else had it burned itself so deeply into the local culture as in the Rhineland, where the legacy of the "Jew-roasters" lived on. As David Vital (ibid.:125) put it, "The history of Rhineland Jewry had been a long and unhappy one, an exceptionally dismal chronicle of persecution, massacre, mob violence, expulsion, and extortion." Indeed, it was deputies from the (sometimes) French area along the Rhine who had been the primary opponents of emancipation when it was debated and passed by the French National Assembly (Kahler, 1967; Winock, 1998).

The Assimilation Crisis

Just as Berr Isaac Berr was delighted to be a Frenchman, many other European Jews were equally delighted finally to be English, Dutch, Austrians, or Prussians. Nevertheless, the question soon arose: Were the roles of citizen and Jew fully compatible?

The major issue was that in many ways orthodoxy encapsulated Jews as fully as did preemancipation restrictions. One simply could not fully observe the Law and participate fully in the external society. For example, strict observance of the Sabbath made it very difficult, if not impossible, to pursue many crafts and occupations, including farming and military service. Kosher excluded some of the most important social activities with gentiles. Moreover, many self-styled "Enlightened Jews" (*maskilim*), such as Moses Mendelssohn, found traditional Jewish doctrines and forms of worship intellectually isolating and proposed reforms that would "fit in" better with the dominant, Christian religious culture, and especially with "enlightened" modernity (Katz, 1961; Vital, 1999). In the words of Mendelssohn, "I recognize no eternal truths other than those that are not merely comprehensible to human reason, but can also be demonstrated and verified by human powers" (complete text in Mendes-Flohr and Reinharz, 1995:97). Although Mendelssohn was a deist, he managed to remain within the sphere of Berlin Judaism, even if he was hated by many of those of more traditional faith. However, most Jews who ignored religious restrictions on their behavior or expressed irreligious views faced swift retaliation: excommunication grew increasingly frequent, and with it came complete isolation from family and friends. What was wanted was a collective solution offering the shelter of a "Jewish" religious community, while granting the freedom to participate freely in secular life.

The Reform Movement

Out of this need came the Reform movement, which was first housed in a "private" synagogue opened in Berlin in 1814 (although the term "Reform" was not yet in use). Here, among other innovations, men and women were seated together, and hymns were sung and prayers said in German. While the more religious Jews of Berlin were scandalized by these goings-on, it was not they but King Frederick William III who ordered this synagogue closed—possibly because it was feared that it "might prove attractive to Christians" (Vital, 1999:114). Three years later a similar synagogue, now referred to by its members as a "temple," opened in Hamburg. Its written constitution noted "the ever decreasing knowledge of the language" in which Jewish worship had been conducted, and promised that sermons and songs would be in German. The temple soon made more than good on these promises by installing an organ and hiring a gentile to play it.

Not content to create a service that resembled those in German Christian churches, the reformers also made very significant modifications in doctrine (Katz, 1961). They deleted from the benedictions and prayers all references to a return to the Holy Land. As for references to the "Redeemer of Israel," in 1818 Eliezer Liebermann (who may eventually have become a Catholic) wrote in his popular treatise supporting the new Hamburg temple that "[w]hat is referred to here is not actual redemption, but merely our deliverance from the troubles of Exile" (in Mendes-Flohr and Reinharz, 1995:165). These were minor changes compared with the alterations to the fundamental conception of God and the authority of the Law wrought by the increasingly influential *maskilim*. Like their secular counterparts who were hostile to all religion, but were especially contemptuous of Judaism (Voltaire had dismissed it as "ignorant and barbarous"), the *maskilim* were determined to replace "legends and superstitions" with a "reasonable" and philosophically "respectable" creed and practice. Indeed, just as had Philo nearly two millennia before them, they sponsored a remote and abstract conception of God and proclaimed that "divine law" was subject to amendment. When a Reform temple was once again opened in Berlin, Samuel Holdheim was selected as its rabbi and proceeded to teach that the Law is entirely situational: "A law, even though divine, is potent only so long as the conditions and circumstances of life, to meet which it was enacted, continue; when these change, however, the law also must be abrogated, even though it have God for its author" (in Blau, 1964:137). Thus Rabbi Holdheim's "God" seems unable to anticipate the flow of history or to reveal amendments as needed—an inability to be expected of a divine essence, but not of a conscious, all-powerful being. That Holdheim believed religion to be the product of human reflection seems clear.

The Reform movement was soon exported to the United States, with results to be examined later. Here it is appropriate to note that in Europe in the nineteenth century, some Jews had no problem reconciling their religious and secular life because their ties to Jewish religion or to the Jewish community were very tenuous or non-existent. It was to people who were somewhat more "Jewish" and who also wished to enjoy emancipation fully that Reform Judaism appealed, having been stripped of all the theological and ethnic aspects that hindered free association with gentiles. But, as the theory of persistence would predict, this solution was not without considerable peril.

Assimilation and Conversion

The assimilation of Jews in Germany and other nations of western Europe progressed quite rapidly throughout the nineteenth century. Just as the Hellenist Jews took Greek names, and the Jews of Kaifeng took Chinese names, so too the Jews of western Europe began rapidly to give their children non-Jewish names. For example, in 1846 in Cologne, fifty-one of sixty-two Jewish children had non-Jewish first names including Moritz, Juliana, Sibilla, and Adolf—"a clear sign of acculturation and hopes for integration" (Magnus, 1997:172).

Far more important than changing their names, Jews responded to their new circumstances with rapidly rising rates of intermarriage (Ruppin, 1934). In Berlin, during the 1870s, 13.1 percent of all marriages involving a Jew were mixed marriages (15.7 percent for Jewish men and 12.0 percent for Jewish women). By 1929 this had risen to nearly a third (29.1 percent). For Germany as a whole the intermarriage rate was 22.8 percent in 1929. However, these rates were much lower in eastern Europe: a minuscule 0.8 percent in Galicia in 1929; 6.8 percent in European Russia and 4.6 percent in the Ukraine during 1924–1926. I return to these regional differences shortly.

Also like the Jews in the Greco-Roman diaspora and in China, the Jews of western Europe were rapidly forgetting Hebrew. Indeed, this is why the Reform movement shifted its service into the local languages: German, French, and English especially.

Given the tug between faith and assimilation that existed even for Reform Jews, whose Sabbath remained on the "wrong" day, whose holidays were quite unfashionable, and whose identity was still burdened with anti-Semitic stereotypes, many Jews simply opted out. As is well known and widely analyzed, substantial numbers of European Jews committed themselves to the antireligious Left, many of them even accepting the militant anti-Semitism that flourished there, including Karl Marx's ferocious anticipation of *A World without Jews*, to quote the title of his often excused or "overlooked"[3] but brutally anti-Semitic tract published in 1843.

Not all Jews wishing to assimilate turned to the Left. Substantial numbers did what the Hellenist Jews had done before them: they became Christians. Of course, it was the most assimilated and "enlightened" Jews who did so. Thus while Moses Mendelssohn remained a Jew, of his six children, four converted; and of his nine grandchildren, eight were Christians, including Felix, the composer (Barnavi, 1992:173).

In recent years, many scholars have collected and analyzed an enormous trove of information on Jewish conversion to Christianity (Endelman, 1987; Hertz, 1987, 1992; Honigmann, 1989; Riff, 1981; Rozenblit, 1983). These studies are possible because in many places it was necessary to register one's religious status with the local government, and also because conversions to Christianity required official admission to a specific Christian body and became part of local church records. Based on these data, very substantial rates of conversion to Christianity have been demonstrated for many areas. This research has offended some Jewish historians, who seem to find the very idea quite distasteful, and who tend to emphasize flaws in various data sources. But, given the religious and social conditions just described, and the very substantially improved prospects for advancement inherent in conversion, it would have been strange had a lot of conversions *not* occurred. That is, as the "holding power" of the Jewish community had grown relatively weak, the "pulling power" of the external societies had grown strong.

Whatever the actual magnitude of Jewish conversion rates, it is the existence of *geographical variations* in the rates of conversion that are most pertinent to the theory. As with intermarriage rates, probably the highest rates of all prevailed in Berlin, where about 1.3 percent of resident Jews converted *each year* during the period

1820 though 1840. Given that Berlin attracted the most ambitious and "emancipated" of each new generation of German Jews, this is no surprise (Honigmann, 1989). For similar reasons, during the period 1898 to 1907, about 0.5 percent of Vienna's Jews converted annually, as did more than 0.3 percent of those in Prague (Riff, 1981). Many scholars have claimed that the vast majority of these conversions were without religious motivation, that they were merely acts of opportunism (Endelman, 1987), and the same has been said about intermarriage (Hertz, 1987, 1992). But that, of course, is the point. Religious persistence is sustained by obstinacy, not opportunism.

In any event, like intermarriage rates, conversion rates were not high everywhere. In the Rhineland conversion was rare. In Cologne, for example, only twenty Jews converted between 1830 and 1850, for an annual conversion rate of less than 0.1 percent (Magnus, 1997).[4] Conversion was even less common in eastern Europe—the annual rate was perhaps 0.01 percent (Vital, 1999:124). That defection was so very low in eastern Europe where "about six million persecuted and miserable wretches remain steadfastly faithful" was, according to an English observer, a "miracle" (ibid.).

The lack of conversion in the Rhineland can be understood on grounds that although Jews in that area were probably rather eager to assimilate (recall their penchant for Christian names), their Christian neighbors were not prepared to welcome them. Nowhere in western Europe did anti-Semitism burn so brightly.

As for eastern Europe, both intermarriage and conversion were rare there because the religious factor retained its uncompromised vigor among Jews, and, if anything, Jewish encapsulation was even greater than in previous eras—not merely because intense persecution continued, but because Jews chose to remain a highly visible, closed subculture.

Eastern Encapsulation Reaffirmed

From the start, the more orthodox voices of Judaism had warned that the theological and social aspects of the Reform movement and all other forms of acculturation spelled disaster for the persistence of a Jewish community. This was more than a battle between liberals and conservatives; it was primarily a battle between eastern and western Europe.

The Jewish populations of western European nations were very small. At the end of the nineteenth century, there were only slightly more than 80,000 Jews in France, 35,000 in Italy, and about 200,000 in Great Britain (most of them in London). Even in Germany there were fewer than half a million Jews. In fact, by that time more Jews lived in New York City than in all the nations of western Europe combined. Most of Europe's Jews lived in the East. There were 5.2 million Jews in the Russian Empire (including what became Poland), and another 2 million resided in the Austro-Hungarian Empire, most of them in Galicia (which also became part of Poland). Thus assimilation was affecting only a small proportion of European Jewry, for the vast majority of those in the East heeded the unanimous rabbinical appeal to hold fast, and the rest headed west, most of them to America.

Angry denunciations of everything connected to Reform Judaism and any other manifestation of assimilation began as soon as the leading rabbinical scholars in eastern Europe heard what was taking place. Among the first to respond was the esteemed Moses Sofer (also known as "the Hatam Sofer"). Head of a Talmudic school in Hungary, Sofer warned, "Do not touch the books of [Moses] Mendelssohn . . . Be warned not to change your Jewish names, speech, clothing—God forbid." Sofer went on: "Never say: 'Times have changed!' We have an old Father—praised be His name—who has never changed and will never change." Sofer was appalled that Jews in Hamburg not only had discontinued the practice of morning prayers in the synagogue and revised the text of prayers, but that they were praying in German! Hebrew "is the language of the Holy One, Blessed be He, in which He gave us His Torah and it is inconceivable to speak before Him in our everyday language" (complete text in Mendes-Flohr and Reinharz, 1995:169–73).

Sofer's most famous student, Akiba Joseph Schlesinger, warned Jews against changing their names or their language. If a man's "first name is Aaron, he should not be called Adolf"; he reminded his readers of Sofer's assertion that one of the most important reasons "[o]ur ancestors were redeemed from Egypt" was that "they did not change their names." Schlesinger argued that Jews should not learn or use Western languages except as necessary for purposes of trading with outsiders, as all languages are prohibited except "Hebrew, Greek, Aramaic and Arabic" because "the Torah was given to Israel in these four languages." In addition, "Yiddish is, from the viewpoint of Jewish law, just like Hebrew." In this regard, Schlesinger noted that although it is forbidden to translate the Torah into the languages of other nations, this does not apply to Yiddish, since this is a language exclusive to Jews and not spoken in any other nation.[5] As for the Reform Jews, they will "descend to Gehenna and will be punished there for many generations" (complete text in Mendes-Flohr and Reinharz, 1995:202–5).

Orthodox spokesmen warned not only against non-Jewish languages but also against dressing in the current fashion of gentiles. Soon they began to advise that one should dress like a Jew and to condemn abandoning "Jewish dress." But, as noted earlier in this chapter, for most of history there was no Jewish dress (aside from identifying symbols required of Jews by gentile laws). What these rabbis were referring to, and what we take to be Jewish dress today, was entirely an artifact of the refusal to adopt modern styles. Once it was prohibited that Jews adopt modern fashions, Jewish clothing (and grooming) froze in place, and that style *became* the dated, "traditional" fashion now associated with the ultra-Orthodox. Hence the style we now associate with Jews is nothing more than the style of dress that was conventional two centuries ago in eastern Europe. Nevertheless, as this style became "Jewish dress" it served as a highly visible marker of identity.

To sum up: Jews persisted in the East because Jewish encapsulation persisted, even increased. And eastern Jews chose to remain a distinctive, socially isolated community because God ordained it.

Meanwhile, Judaism was lagging in the West. Although the membership rolls of the Reform temples grew rapidly, they asked very little of their members and received less. Attendance was poor, and members seldom *did* anything religious. The temples were not open for morning worship, so no minyans gathered. Seders were "out-of-date." It was akin to superstition to light candles on the eve of the Sabbath, and kosher was unnecessary. As for God, Jews in western Europe increasingly inclined toward an impersonal Higher Power.

The end of this story will never be known; the Nazis destroyed this entire world. East and West, from the most fully assimilated Jews to the most Orthodox, gone. Ironically, after nearly two thousand years of conflict with their Christian neighbors, when the Holocaust came, it wore a pagan face and spoke the language of race and *blut*, not faith.

The Condition of American Jews

As recently as 1820 the Jewish population of the United States was insignificant—numbering perhaps 4,000. Then, in 1840 began the first substantial wave of Jewish immigration, and by 1880 there were about 280,000 American Jews. Nearly all of these Jews came from German areas of Europe, and they brought the Reform movement with them. Indeed, by the 1870s "Reform Judaism was almost synonymous with American Judaism. Of almost two hundred congregations, fewer than a dozen were Orthodox" (Danzger, 1989:21).

Moreover, in America the Reform movement soon made an even more radical break with tradition than had occurred in Europe. In 1885 a conference of Reform rabbis met in Pittsburgh and adopted a remarkable eight-point platform, much of which could as well have been written by William Ernest Hocking (see Chapter 2).

It began, "We recognize in every religion an attempt to grasp the Infinite One," and then recommended the "God-idea" of Judaism as "developed and spiritualized by Jewish teachers in accordance with the moral and philosophical progress of their respective ages." Notice that the platform does not refer simply to God but to the "God-idea," a formulation that would have pleased any deist.

Turning to the Bible, the Reform rabbis noted that it, of course, reflects "the primitive ideas of its own age." As for Jewish forms of worship, we "reject all [ceremonies] as are not adapted to the views and habits of modern civilization."

As for the Law, the platform dismissed it as having "originated in ages and under the influence of ideas altogether foreign to our present mental and spiritual state . . . observance in our day is apt rather to obstruct than to further modern spiritual elevation." Next, the conference declared, "We consider ourselves no longer a nation but a religious community, and therefore [do not] expect . . . a return to Palestine." Indeed, Judaism is "a progressive religion, ever striving to be in accord with the postulates of reason." At the end, the platform rejected both "Hell and Paradise" as having no part in Judaism (complete text in Mendes-Flohr and Reinharz, 1995:468–69).

When several million Jews immigrated to the United States from eastern Europe late in the nineteenth and early in the twentieth century, this was the dominant form of Judaism they encountered—well established and much admired by Protestant intellectuals. Although the form of Judaism they had left behind was resolutely orthodox, it must also be understood that the most orthodox chose not to abandon the intensely Jewish enclaves of Russia and Poland. Leaving was, in and of itself, a modest form of assimilation.

Assimilation

Large numbers of these eastern newcomers were content with an entirely secular Judaism consisting only of associating with other Jews, reading Yiddish newspapers, and observing some Jewish customs, but without any involvement in organized religious expression. Others were devoted leftists, eager to put an end to all forms of religion. Indeed, Jewish-dominated "Socialist and labor groups at times held marches and balls on Yom Kippur, specifically choosing to desecrate to the utmost this holy day of fasting" (Danzger, 1989:21). As for those of more religious inclination, organized American Judaism continued to be dominated by the Reform movement as eastern Jews associated it with American ways. They had, after all, immigrated not only to escape poverty and anti-Semitism but in pursuit of "modernity." So the consensus soon arose that Orthodoxy had no future in America, being an anachronism doomed to die out in another generation or two (Danzger, 1989; Glazer, 1957; Sklare, 1971).

In apparent confirmation of this judgment, American Jews began to display very high rates of assimilation. Names changed. Seymour and Morton were in; Solomon and Moses were out (Lieberson, 2000). Rates of intermarriage soared. By the mid-1960s about one of every five Jews who married wed a non-Jew. This, along with the low fertility of American Jews, prompted Elihu Bergman (1977) to calculate that by the year 2076 there would be only 20 percent as many Jews in the United States as in 1976. Even secular journalists began to write stories about "the vanishing American Jew" (Wertheimer, 1993). Since then, the intermarriage rate has continued to rise, and the fertility rate has kept going down (Goldstein, 1981; Waxman, 2000).

Even the rise of Conservative Judaism, instituted as a more moderate alternative to the Reform movement and having enjoyed a considerable boom in the 1940s and early 1950s (Wertheimer, 1993), has done very little to stem the tide of decline—nor, indeed, has awareness of the Holocaust. The fact remains that today American Jews are not very "Jewish."

Table 4.1 is based on a large national survey of American Jews. It was conducted on the basis of an elaborate and effective method for locating everyone having a Jewish background, rather than relying on the more common, and very biased, method of sampling membership roles of synagogues and of Jewish organizations (Stark and Roberts, 2001). In constructing this table, I eliminated all persons who did not claim Jewish as their *current* religious preference. Even so, the data show that only 33.2 percent have *ever* belonged to a synagogue, and only one in ten attends weekly. Quite in keeping with Reform teachings, few Jews (14.2 percent) agree that the Bible is the actual word of God. Only 11.6 percent of American Jews keep kosher;[6] not many more (18.9 percent) usually light candles on Friday night. Granted, 68.8 percent usually light Hanukkah candles, but the religious significance of this seems somewhat offset by the fact that nearly a third (30.6 percent) put up a Christmas tree.

Table 4.1
How Jewish Are American Jews?

% who have *ever* belonged to a synagogue	33.2
% who usually attend synagogue weekly	10.0
% who agree the Bible is the actual word of God	14.2
% who keep kosher	11.6
% who usually light candles on Friday night	18.9
% who usually light Hanukkah candles	68.8
% who sometimes have a Christmas tree	30.6
% who sometimes attend a non-Jewish religious service	39.4

Source: The National Jewish Population Survey, 1990.

Note: Includes only those who gave Jewish as their current religious preference. N = 1,713.

It must not be thought that these findings merely reflect a generally "secularized" American culture. It is only the Jewish faith, not faith in general, that has eroded in the United States; American Christians are notable for their high levels of religiousness.

Conversion

Table 4.1 also shows that two of five American Jews acknowledge that they sometimes attend non-Jewish services. Students of new religious movements have long known that people from nonpracticing Jewish backgrounds are by far the best candidates for recruitment. For example, the sons and daughters of "secular" Jews are many times overrepresented in ISKCON (Hare Krishna), Scientology, Wicca (modern witchcraft), the Unification Church (Moonies), and a variety of Eastern groups such as Ananda and Satchidananda Ashram (Stark and Bainbridge, 1985). In her engaging book on the Rajneesh movement, which drew several thousand Americans to a communal village in central Oregon during the 1980s,

Marion S. Goldman (1999:231) reported that "Jews were stunningly overrepresented."

However, because these movements are very small, the total Jewish membership of all of them added together would not amount to any substantial number of Jewish defectors. Moreover, the common wisdom has been that American Jews seldom convert to Christianity—and certainly not Jews raised in secular homes. In fact, *only* Jews raised in secular homes or in a highly accommodated form of Judaism ever convert to anything. Studies of converts do not turn up persons from Orthodox Jewish backgrounds.

As for the claim that Jews rarely convert to Christianity, the results of the National Jewish Population Survey conducted in 1990 (and discussed above) show otherwise. American Jews currently exhibit a very high rate of conversion. Of the 6,840,000 Americans of Jewish parentage, only 61.5 percent (4,210,000) acknowledge their current religious preference as Jewish (an additional 185,000 American Jews are converts from another faith). Thus more than a third of born Jews have abandoned Judaism—16.4 percent have embraced irreligiousness, and 1,325,000 (or 19.4 percent) have converted to another faith, nearly all of them to Christianity (Kosmin et al., 1991).

Despite many unfounded and sometimes disingenuous efforts to arouse anxiety among American Jews about threats from the "Christian Right," not only has anti-Semitism become an insignificant aspect of American culture, evangelical Christians are those *least* given to prejudice against Jews and are the Americans most committed to supporting Israel (see Chapter 5). American Jews cannot depend upon bigots to provide them with solidarity.

Clearly, most American Jews have lost all religious basis for sustaining a distinctive identity, and the protective encapsulation once provided by their Jewishness has collapsed. Thus contemporary concerns over the persistence of a Jewish community would seem well founded—but only until one looks beyond the assimilated Jews, to the uncompromised world of Orthodoxy! Here are tightly knit, rapidly growing communities of Jews who wholeheartedly embrace the God of Israel, who carefully observe the Law, who wear "Jewish" dress, whose Hebrew is fluent, who do not intermarry, whose fertility is abundant, and who do not attend non-Jewish services, put up Christmas trees, or study Asian scriptures.

It is entirely plausible that the Orthodox will soon become the Jewish community by default, not only because of their high fertility and low rate of defection, but because they have begun to attract converts from the ranks of Jews raised in secularity (Danzger, 1989; Davidman, 1991). Thus does an authentic Judaism not only persist but prosper. In addition, there are signs of an authentic religious revival going on in non-Orthodox American Jewish circles (Wertheimer, 1993). Consider that Reform rabbis have begun to pray in Hebrew, and that the men in many of their congregations now wear *yarmulkes* within the synagogue, that some Reform congregations have installed *mikveh* baths, that many younger members are keeping kosher, and that it has become quite respectable to discuss God's will. Since I have written about this at some length recently (Stark and Finke, 2000), I shall not pursue it here, except to suggest that the insight seems to be going around that to be Jewish, one must be a Jew.

Conclusion

Religious persistence is possible only for those with a vivid conception of a God who calls upon them to endure. But is that enough? Must persistent religious groups also rely on conflict to maintain their solidarity? Is a harmonious, monotheistic pluralism impossible? We shall see.

Notes

1. "In European countries, and more particularly since the Reformation, religion has come to be considered as primarily a matter of belief. This is itself a phenomenon which needs to be explained, I think, in terms of social development. We are concerned here only with the effects on the thinking of anthropologists. Among many of them there is a tendency to treat belief as primary: rites are considered the results of beliefs" (Radcliffe-Brown, 1952:155).

2. Attempts to identify pre-Christian prejudice against Jews as "merely" anti-*Judaism* in order to *define* anti-Semitism as peculiar to Christians are polemics having no scholarly worth.

3. In a preface to the first "unexpurgated English" edition of *A World without Jews* (1960), Dagobert D. Runes noted in his forward "that most of Marx's anti-Semitic references, in his correspondence, his journalistic writings and his books, were entirely eliminated by his various editors." It seems appropriate that the full texts were made available by the State Publishing House in Moscow, whose editors shared the virulent anti-Semitism of the Soviet regime and therefore saw no reason to suppress Marx's views. Western leftists did not follow suit. Hence the British Marxist academic David McLellan devoted an entire book to reciting Marx's "critique" of religion without using the word Jew, let alone discussing Marx's anti-Semitism (McLellan, 1987).

4. My calculations, based on population data provided in Magnus, 1997.

5. Yiddish is a mixture of medieval German dialects developed in the Jewish ghettos of central Europe and was expanded by borrowings from Hebrew and Slavic. Subsequently, Yiddish was the source of many words used in American English, as amusingly documented by Leo Rosten in *The Joys of Yiddish* (1968).

6. A combination of two items, one on kosher meat, the other on kosher dishes and kitchen utensils.

"Buddies." Gravestones in the U.S. Army cemetery near Omaha Beach,
where many soldiers died during the landings at Normandy, mark Jewish graves
with the Star of David and those of Christian soldiers with a Cross.
© Tim Page/CORBIS.

. 5 .

God's *Grace*: Pluralism and Civility

In the name of God, the Merciful, the Compassionate
—The Qur'ān

Just as the United States proved that pluralism invigorates religion, it has demonstrated that particularistic faiths can observe norms of public civility. In this final chapter I explain how this is possible.

It is useful to begin with *the* social question: How can fundamentally selfish creatures be induced to live in harmony? Until quite recently the answer was always found in collective means of *repression*, typically the state. Thomas Hobbes (*1588–1679*) concluded that in the absence of a powerful state, human selfishness would result in a life that was "solitary, poor, nasty, brutish, and short" ([1651] 1968:186). To prevent this dismal state of affairs, Hobbes (ibid.:223) advised that it is necessary for humans to impose "a restraint upon themselves" in the form of "some Power . . . contrary to their natural Passions . . . the Commonwealth." In the context of the problem at hand, Hobbes advised that religious tranquillity required the state to thwart all outbursts of religious dissent—at least until such time as humans outgrew their "credulity" and "ignorance" and finally rejected all Gods as "creatures of their own fancy" (ibid.:167, 168). Meanwhile, there should be a single authoritative church wherein the "Civil Sovereign is the Supreme Pastor, to whose charge the whole flock of his Subjects is committed, and consequently it is by his authority, that all other Pastors are made, and have the power to teach, and perform all other Pastoral offices" (ibid.:569).[1]

David Hume (*1711–1776*) also saw social disruption and violence as inherent in religious diversity and believed that only where there is a monopoly religion can there be religious tranquillity. He reasoned that when there are many sects within a society, the leaders of each will express "the most violent abhorrence of all other sects," causing no end of trouble for the governing elite, and therefore wise politicians will support and sustain a single religious organization and will repress all challengers (1754, 3:30).

Hume's model was, of course, an idealized remembrance of the "Catholic centuries" during which relative religious tranquillity had prevailed as Church and State prevented any challenges to the Universal Faith. In fairness, it must be acknowledged that the Catholic Church probably demonstrated the highest degree to which a monopoly church can serve diverse demand. It achieved widespread appeal by offering a spectrum of religious options ranging from a very undemanding Christianized form of traditional polytheism to a very high-tension monastic option for those seeking maximum religious expression. In addition, by basing its parishes on geographic boundaries and by permitting substantial variation as to styles of worship and levels of intensity across nearby parishes, the Church accommodated a range of preferences, catering especially to niches rooted in class and ethnicity. Even in modern times, there are remarkable differences in the intensity and style of Catholic parishes in different parts of the same city (Finke and Stark, 1992).

Nevertheless, while religious conflict was often muffled by the Catholic monopoly, the potential for violent outbursts was ever present and often realized. Moreover, even when nonconformity was tolerated, this was done without civility. For example, the second half of the first millennium may have been a period of tranquillity in Christian-Jewish relations, but the era was still marked by virulent anti-Semitism. The same incivility existed wherever Islam was the monopoly faith.

By its very nature, the diversity of religious demand requires pluralism. Only specialized "firms" can adequately serve each of the niches inherent in any religious "market" because efforts directed toward a lower-tension niche always destroy credibility vis-à-vis higher-tension niches. For example, as described in Chapter 3, the laxity of the mass appeal of the Church of Power was seen as nothing less than sinful heresy from the perspective of the Church of Piety. In the absence of pluralism, unserved niches always foster dissent. But if pluralism is allowed to respond to demand, what then? Given the existence of many particularistic faiths, how is conflict to be managed and civility achieved? Here again, Adam Smith had an answer.

A Theory of Pluralism and Religious Civility

Adam Smith's great insight about social life is that cooperative and socially beneficial outcomes can result from each individual human's acting to maximize his or her selfish interests. "[Although the individual] intends only his own gain . . . he is . . . led by an invisible hand to promote an end which was no part of his intention . . . By pursuing his own interest he frequently promotes that of society more effectively than when he really intends to promote it" (Smith, [1776] 1981, 1:456). For example, as each person trying to sell a specific item seeks to maximize her or his gain, the result will be that buyers benefit from the lowest price sufficient to motivate others to produce and sell that item. This is because when faced with competition from other sellers, in order to make a sale each seller will reduce his or her price relative to others until the lowest price is reached. Or, to use Smith's metaphor, as each individual reaches out for gain, there is created a collective "invisible hand" of the marketplace forcing prices down. Of course, this requires an unregulated market wherein each seller is free to set a sale price, and each buyer is free to seek the lowest price. For this condition to exist—for there to be a "free market"—no seller can control so much of the supply of the item as to be able to influence its price. To the degree that the market is not free, buyers are prey to price-fixing—in the extreme situation there is only one supplier, who can demand the maximum price that buyers are able to pay. In very rare situations, monopolies can exist if there is but one potential source of supply of the item. Generally, however, monopolies require coercion to prevent competition. This is not the place to debate the virtues of Smith's economic theories. Instead, I will show that when applied to religious economies, his "invisible hand" principle explains how pluralism can generate civility.

As with most other kinds of firms, monopoly churches can exist only when backed by the coercive powers of the state, for there can be no limit to the ability to formulate and offer religious culture. Thus the "natural state" of the religious economy is for there to exist a large number of suppliers. Both Hobbes and Hume accepted this view, seeing the proliferation of religious bodies as incompatible with tranquillity, and concluding that it is therefore necessary for the state to sustain a monopoly church. But when Smith's notions about the "invisible hand" are applied to a free religious market, as each body pursues its selfish interest, religious civility is the likely result.

Responding to the conclusions of his friend Hume that religious tranquillity necessitated one church, Smith argued ([1776] 1981:793–94) that this was the most "dangerous and troublesome" situation, and that conflict can be avoided only

> where the society is divided into two or three hundred, or perhaps as many [as a] thousand small sects, of which no one could be considerable enough to disturb the publick tranquillity. The teachers of each sect, seeing themselves surrounded on all sides with more adversaries than friends, would be obliged to learn the candour and moderation which is so seldom to be found among the teachers of great sects . . . The teachers of each little sect, finding themselves almost alone, would be obliged to respect those of almost every other sect, and the concessions which they would mutually find it both convenient and agreeable to make to one another . . . [would result in] publick tranquillity.

That is, as each weak firm seeks to secure itself from attack, self-interest will lead to the collective observance of civility. Put more formally: Where there exist particularistic religions, *norms of religious civility* will develop to the extent that the religious economy achieves a *pluralistic equilibrium*. By norms of civility I mean *public behavior* governed by *mutual respect* among faiths, hence public moderation of particularism. A pluralistic equilibrium exists when *power* is sufficiently *diffused* among a set of competitors that conflict is not in anyone's interest.

Arithmetic of Pluralism

The question arises, How much pluralism is required to generate norms of civility? Clearly, Smith's prescription of hundreds of weak religious bodies will suffice. But it seems likely that a rather smaller number will suffice too—although it may well be that eventually unregulated religious economies will always generate Smith's "hundreds." Unfortunately, despite decades of mathematical analyses of coalitions, there is no firm theoretical basis for concluding how many independent religious bodies are needed to constitute a plural equilibrium. However, by combining some of the mathematical results with empirical examples, and mixing in some common sense, we may arrive at some arithmetic guidelines.

Consider the minimal case: the coexistence of *two* particularistic groups. To the extent that they perceive one another as equally matched, they will be reluctant to risk violent conflict, but relations will always be shaped by barely concealed hatred and contempt. In the absence of other restraints, whenever one side thinks it has sufficiently greater power, it can be expected to attack the other—even after centuries of "peace." Muslims and Hindus in India are an example, as are Muslims and Orthodox Catholics in the Balkans. Sometimes, when there is a great disparity in power, the weaker group may be tolerated for various specific reasons, as Jews were tolerated by Christians—but without any pretense of civility. It seems certain that two are too few to develop norms of civility.

Mathematical studies of triads as well as empirical examples suggest that sometimes as few as *three* groups may achieve an equilibrium wherein civility might arise (Axelrod, 1984; Caplow, 1968; De Swann, 1973). A necessary condition is that any combination of two groups be more powerful than the third group alone—otherwise, the strongest group will simply crush the others. No two will combine to eliminate the third, however, because that would leave the weaker survivor in subsequent peril. The result is a "standoff" or equilibrium. Should this continue for a sufficient time, it seems conceivable that the perception of mutual dependency would give rise to some semblance of public civility.

A second triadic possibility is that if two of the groups are so utterly weak as to pose no threat to the third, they might be tolerated. But as with the Jews and Christians within Islamic societies, this would not give rise to civility.

Whether or not three groups can achieve an equilibrium, that *four* can do so has been demonstrated by the events in the Netherlands (Bakvis, 1981; Barrett, 1982; Martin, 1978; Monsma and Soper, 1997; Tash, 1991). The London Conference of 1839 left the Netherlands divided between a dominant Protestant north and a sullen Catholic south, both sides being burdened with bitter memories of the religious wars. The Dutch Protestants were overwhelmingly of the Calvinist persuasion and used their domination of the government to establish themselves as the state church: the Netherlands Reformed Church (*Nederlandse Hervormde Kerk*, NHK). An emerging and politically very powerful third religious faction consisted of the most liberal elements within the NHK and a secular elite of irreligious intellectuals, most having a predilection for leftist politics. Finally, from the earliest days of the NHK, a fourth religious faction rapidly formed as conservative Protestants began to withdraw and organize a dissenting, more orthodox, Calvinist denomination, now known as the Reformed Church (*Gereformeede Kerken*, or GK). Thus the religious economy of the Netherlands comprises four major groups: the NHK, the Roman Catholics, the liberals, and the orthodox Calvinists.

Limited both by treaty and by more powerful Catholic neighbors, the NHK could not resort to violence to deal with either the Catholics or the dissenting Calvinists. So, in combination with the liberals, the NHK sought to eradicate dissent through the schools. Thus in 1878 the Dutch parliament passed a new school law that would in effect have shut down denominational schools, requiring all children to attend secular schools. It was no secret that the law was intended to erase religious sectarianism and disagreement by "liberating" the younger generation from "outmoded Christian beliefs" (Monsma and Soper, 1997:56). A prominent liberal and

NHK leader explained that in this way "opinionated and fanatical idiots" can be excluded from teaching, and "rural youth" can be freed from the "prejudices" that are "all too apparent in these days of civil dissension" (in Glenn, 1987:47).

Five days later, the impossible happened. The orthodox Calvinists and the Roman Catholics, having long histories of intense opposition, formed what liberal observers called a "monstrous alliance" to protect their schools (Monsma and Soper, 1997:57). This alliance soon controlled parliament and repealed the offensive legislation. Known today as the Christian Democratic Appeal, the Catholic-Calvinist coalition remains a major force in Dutch politics.

Obviously, when the two most particularistic religious groups in the Netherlands found it necessary to form a coalition to withstand liberal oppression, they could not continue to express hostile opinions of one another—at least not in public. Consequently, an admirable level of public religious civility prevails among religious groups in the Netherlands, albeit liberals and secularists often do not observe these courtesies—as is true of their American counterparts as well.

Pseudo-Pluralism

Not all societies having several religions are pluralistic. A society may appear to have multiple religions, even multiple particularistic religions, but because there is little or no interaction among members, the actual situation more closely resembles separate societies—each with its own religion—than a pluralistic society. Competition is the essential feature of true pluralism. Religious groups must missionize, and individuals must be free to shift faiths accordingly.

It is quite possible for a number of particularistic faiths to exist within a society, but where they are based on isolated social networks such as regions or castes, there may be no competition. For example, faith A may be based on a high-status caste and deny membership to anyone not also a member of the caste; faith B may impose similar rules on a lower-status caste, and so on. An example is India, where for many centuries Muslim rulers were distin-

225

guished from their Hindu subjects by ethnicity as well as religion. Or residents of one region may be members of faith A, while those in other regions may be members of faiths B, C, and D. This is not pluralism but analytically should be treated as an instance of neighboring societies, each with a different faith. An example is Indonesia, where Muslims, Hindus, Christians, Buddhists, and syncretistic variants of each are based on different areas (often islands) and ethnolinguistic groups. These are instances of pseudo-pluralism, wherein conflict tends to be muted by simple lack of contact and does not result in civility.

Faith and Civility

It is rather easy for nonexclusive faiths to live in peace. Similarly, within pluralistic societies, civility will come more easily to those having low levels of intensity and/or whose image of God has drifted toward deism. Recall from Chapter 2 that it was because he conceived of God not as a being but as an essence that William Hocking thought it was beyond the bounds of civility to missionize to non-Christians and unthinkable for Christians to compete with one another for members. Indeed, the idea that religious groups ought to respect one another seems obvious to those who believe that one religion is as unfounded as another. Thus it was not the Puritan fathers in Massachusetts, the Anglicans in New York, or even the Baptists in North Carolina who opposed religious establishment in the new American nation, or who advocated the free expression of religion; it was deists such as Thomas Jefferson who did so.

It follows that within pluralistic societies, norms of civility will develop *most rapidly* among the *least* religious and those who conceive of the supernatural as an *essence*. Consequently, as norms of civility develop, the most *intense* public religious *conflicts* will occur between the least and the most religious.

Recall that in the Netherlands it wasn't the case that the orthodox Calvinists tried to close Catholic schools; it was the secularists and religious liberals who attempted to use the schools to "reeducate" both the Calvinists and Catholics. Ever since, the major fault line separating Dutch religious factions has been between the religious and the irreligious or less religious. As will be seen, that is the primary division in contemporary America too.

Cleavages and Civility

As mentioned, true pluralism may not exist where different religions constitute very isolated social networks. Within truly pluralistic societies, conflicts among particularistic religions will be amplified to the degree that the lines of religious separation are *concurrent* with other significant *social cleavages* within the society, such as caste, ethnicity, or region. Conversely, civility will prevail to the degree that lines of religious separation crosscut other significant social cleavages within the society. By social cleavages, I mean recognized divisions within a society based on stratification, culture, and/or region.

Although I have introduced important qualifiers, the major theoretical point is that the conflict inherent in monotheism will be overcome by norms of civility when religious freedom results in the proliferation of religious groups to the extent that it is in the interest of each to support norms of civility. In light of this proposition, consider what might have happened had Constantine not given state preference to Christianity and had not supported those who demanded adherence to a universal orthodoxy. Most pagan temples would still have failed, although it would have taken far longer, and a few of them might even have survived by moving toward monotheism or by specializing in magic. But, regardless of the fate of paganism, religious pluralism would still have flourished. There already were several competing, well-organized "brands" of Christianity, and the normal process of sect formation would have continued to produce more. Judaism would have remained a significant factor, and it too would have generated new sects. Thus by perhaps the seventh century, the religious landscape of Italy might have resembled that of the United States today, and the religious climate might have been as civil as in the days when no temple claimed to worship the Only God. To pursue these matters, let us examine the American case in detail.

The Rise of American Religious Civility

Apparently unaware of Adam Smith's analysis, Robin M. Williams, Jr. (1951:320) attributed "the rise of religious freedom and toleration" in America to the fact that "there was no cleavage between two or only a few opposing religious groupings, but rather a fragmented diversity of numerous small sects"; hence "conflict could not be massive or unitary." Williams also pointed out that no attempt at establishment was possible because no religious group "had the opportunity to seize a dominant political position" (see Table 5.1). Thus did an array of exceedingly particularistic sects give rise to religious freedom and toleration, even though, as Williams (ibid.:321) recognized, "nobody intended it."

It is important to keep in mind that exclusive, particularistic religious groups do not learn tolerance by having been persecuted. Thus, for example, although they fled persecution in England and were barely tolerated during their stay in Holland, the Puritans gained insights not into the virtues of toleration but only about the need for power. The Massachusetts Bay Colony was, from the very start, committed to an exclusive religious establishment that persecuted any hint of nonconformity. For example, when Quakers were detected, even if they were merely in transit aboard a ship in Boston Harbor, they were subject to public whippings before being expelled from the colony. Between 1659 and 1661 four Quakers who had previously been whipped and driven out of Massachusetts were hanged for having returned.

When religious civility eventually came to Massachusetts, it did so more as the result of a drift into deism than as the product of civic enlightenment. By the middle of the eighteenth century, Unitarianism began to attract Massachusetts' clergy; by the end of the century Unitarians held many of the most influential and desirable Congregational pulpits, and Harvard was securely in their grasp. Despite various disingenuous claims to the contrary, this brand of Unitarianism was not simply a matter of having demoted Christ to mere humanity, or having dispensed with the concept of the Holy Spirit; it was a more significant matter of shifting the conception

Table 5.1
American Pluralism, 1776

Denomination	Number of Congregations
Congregational	668
Presbyterian[a]	588
Baptist[b]	497
Episcopal	495
Quakers	310
German Reformed	159
Lutheran[c]	150
Dutch Reformed	120
Methodist	65
Roman Catholic	56
Moravian	31
Separatist and Independent	27
Dunker	24
Mennonite	16
Huguenot	7
Sandemanian	6
Jewish	5
Total	3,228

Source: Finke and Stark, 1992.

[a]Includes all divisions, such as New Light, Old Light, Associate Reformed, etc.

[b]Includes all divisions, such as Separate, Six Principle, Seventh Day, Rogerene, etc.

[c]Includes all synods.

of God from an active being to an essence—the "Architect of the Universe," but a remote, if benign, power. The founding of an explicitly Unitarian Association did not produce a very impressive body (essences never do), and most Unitarians, especially among the clergy, chose to remain within the more influential denominations—especially the Congregationalists, Presbyterians, and Episcopalians. As for Harvard: "The divinity school which gradually took shape between 1811 and 1819 professed to be simply Christian; but its faculty and students were Unitarian and remained so with few exceptions during the entire nineteenth century . . . moreover, the entire university was pervaded by the spirit of the movement. Most of its presidents and faculty were Unitarians" (Ahlstrom, 1972, 1:483). Indeed, the first Darwinian on the Harvard faculty was not in the biology or geology department, but in the divinity school, announcing soon after his appointment in 1880 that he should not be referred to as a Christian (Finke and Stark, 1992).

Given the prevailing theological views, there was little reason for denominational conflicts in New England except, of course, with those "benighted souls" who still clung to traditional Christianity and needlessly stirred up the people. It was this latter concern that caused the clergy of Massachusetts and Connecticut to respond to George Whitefield's revival campaigns by causing their colonial legislatures to outlaw "Itinerant Preaching" (Finke and Stark, 1992). Similar concerns led the Presbyterians and Congregationalists to enter into the 1801 Plan of Union, under which they would sustain noncompeting missionary efforts to the western frontier areas. In addition, the Presbyterians vowed not to maintain churches north of the Connecticut border, and the Congregationalists ceded them everything to the south. In the end, this cartel arrangement resulted merely in the rapid decline of both denominations as evangelical Methodists and Baptists overwhelmed them (Finke and Stark, 1992). By doing so, however, the evangelicals deeply offended those committed to the new, noncompetitive, "nonjudgmental" liberalism. A Congregationalist clergyman sent to Arkansas wrote home to his superiors in 1846: "After a minute examination and mature and prayerful deliberation I have come to the settled conviction that it would be decidedly for the religious interests of Arkansas if every minister and preacher of the above denominations [Methodists and Baptists] were out of the State" (in Sweet, 1964:698).

But while they complained about incivility and made efforts toward ecumenicity, American intellectuals, religious and irreligious alike, limited their concerns to Protestantism. From the most liberal Congregationalists to the most traditional Baptists, anti-Catholicism was rife, particularly among clergy. Thus on Sunday, August 10, 1834, Lyman Beecher, one of the most prominent Congregational liberals of the day (and whose daughter wrote *Uncle Tom's Cabin*) gave three thunderous sermons in Boston churches during which he voiced the theme soon to appear in his tract *A Plea for the West*, in which he warned against a plot by the pope to seize the Mississippi valley. Freewill offerings taken after each sermon raised a total of four thousand dollars, a very sizable amount for that time, indicative of the fact that these were wealthy congregations (Finke and Stark, 1992).

Nevertheless, in Beecher's day anti-Catholicism lacked reality, consisting mainly of "tales from the Old Country" as the Reformation was replayed in Protestant sermons, and the grievances against the "Whore of Rome" were reiterated. Although most Americans accepted this view of Catholicism, most tended to regard these as European issues, having no greater relevance to them than disputes over royal succession. Given the small number of American Catholics, charges about Vatican plots against the United States lacked plausibility. Later in the nineteenth century this began to change as millions of Catholic immigrants arrived from Ireland, Italy, and eastern Europe and soon took political control of many large cities. It was in response to this new, threatening reality that serious "nativist" movements arose to preserve America as a Protestant nation. It was only *then* that signs reading "No Popery" appeared in shop windows across the nation (if not in the Catholic-dominated cities).

As for Jews, partly owing to their very small numbers and their full assimilation into the nonreligious culture, anti-Semitism was relatively latent, and "the prevailing temper [toward Jews] was

"City of Brotherly Love." An anti-Catholic mob of Philadelphians rioted in 1844. When the militia fired into the crowd, the rioters fired back—first with handguns and then with a cannon—and mob rule prevailed in the city for the next three days, during which the two largest Catholic churches were burned to the ground. © Bettmann/CORBIS.

overwhelmingly tolerant" during most of the nineteenth century (Handlin, 1951:541). Jews posed no threat to Christian dominance, nor was there any substantial Catholic threat to cause any collateral intolerance. Anti-Semitism became a significant aspect of American life late in the century when the arrival of millions of Catholic immigrants did arouse Protestant anxieties, which were exacerbated by the arrival at that same time of waves of immigrant, eastern European Jews. The nativist groups soon opposed the admission of both Catholics and Jews. By 1922, even the Unitarians of Harvard found it appropriate to impose strict quotas on Jewish enrollment—as did all of the Ivy League schools. These quotas remained in force until the 1960s, as both anti-Semitism and anti-Catholicism proved to be long-lived.

As recently as the 1950s, Paul Blanshard's *American Freedom and Catholic Power,* which sought to rouse the nation against the inextricable link between Roman Catholicism and political dictatorship, was a best-seller. In 1960, during his presidential campaign, John F. Kennedy had to swear that if elected he would not obey orders from the pope. When I began my career, religious prejudice was still sufficiently prevalent to prompt massive research efforts, and none of my teachers or peers would have thought it possible that within a few years our graduate students would be puzzled by these concerns. Not only have anti-Semitic, anti-Catholic, and anti-Protestant attitudes become uncommon, but their public expression by anyone respectable is unthinkable (of course, it remains fashionable to vilify "fundamentalists" and "cultists"). But if the triumph of religious civility took my generation by surprise, it was still a long time coming.

Civility was imposed on particularistic faiths by the extensive pluralism of America and the correspondingly high costs inherent in conflict. Not only were there literally hundreds of Protestant denominations; even the large Protestant bodies were separated by theology and enthusiasm into disputatious camps. In addition, by the end of the nineteenth century, Roman Catholics had become a major factor in American diversity. Jews had also become a significant factor because, despite their small numbers, they were concentrated in a few influential cities—indeed, by early in the twentieth century Jews outnumbered both Protestants and Catholics in New York City. In these days, too, America abounded with secular intellectuals—rationalists, freethinkers, and village atheists—who also claimed a place in the negotiations over religious relations. Of all these religious groups, the Catholics had the most difficult theological problems to solve in order to proceed along the road to civility. However, it turned out to be the secular intellectuals who proved least able to achieve civility—then and now.

Taming Catholic Particularism

The first step toward civility faced by American Catholicism involved acceptance of the principle of the separation of Church and State. For many centuries the Church had taken the position that, because it was the One True Church, governments were required

233

to sustain the Church and scatter its enemies. In Europe, even early in the twentieth century, this remained the official Catholic view, but it was entirely discordant not only with the political circumstances of the American Church but with the philosophical outlook of Catholics reared in this truly pluralistic setting. Thus toward the end of the nineteenth century, many prominent Catholics, including James Cardinal Gibbons and Archbishop John Ireland, emphasized and affirmed the wisdom of the First Amendment, arguing that state involvement in religious affairs was ill suited for the American situation. Their views were both misunderstood and misrepresented in Europe and eventually led to the condemnation of "Americanism" in an apostolic letter from Pope Leo XIII to Cardinal Gibbons in January, 1899 (Ahlstrom, 1972; Hennesey, 1981; Maynard, 1941).

The pope's letter actually said little or nothing about separation of Church and State but attacked notions about leaving decisions concerning spiritual choices in the hands of the individual, guided by the Holy Spirit rather than by the authority of the Church. Since no influential American Catholic ever had expressed such an antiinstitutional view, the condemnation was irrelevant. In fact, however, the anger over the loss or potential loss of a favored relationship with the state in some European nations lay behind the condemnation, and this remained a cause of concern for many Catholic leaders for several decades. However, both Cardinal Gibbons and Archbishop Ireland knew that the Church-State question was minor compared with the problem presented by the fundamental Catholic principle: Outside the Church there is no salvation (*extra ecclesiam nulla salus*). Thus even the most worshipful Protestants, let alone Jews, were bound for Hell.

On this rested the entire edifice of Catholic legitimacy, and it was not to be compromised to the slightest extent, as evidenced by centuries of militant attempts to suppress all heretics and schismatics. Applied to the American circumstance, this doctrine outlawed virtually all overt acts of civility. Indeed, Catholics (clergy as well as laity) were forbidden even to enter non-Catholic religious structures. This practice dated back to the days of Christian martyrs who died rather than enter pagan shrines or participate in any pagan rite, entirely in keeping with the belief that there is but One True Church in service to the One True God. But in the American situation this rule was painfully divisive. For example, when Protestants died, their Catholic friends and even relatives could not, in good conscience, attend the funeral, although Protestants could attend the funerals of their Catholic friends and relatives. This may have been a trivial matter in Europe, but in America large numbers of Catholics had Protestant friends and relatives, and the problem was especially acute in small towns, where absences from funerals and weddings were obvious.

For generations, therefore, Catholic efforts at religious civility foundered on the rock of Peter as various attempts were made to sail around it. Perhaps the first modestly successful effort was made in 1942 by the immensely influential Jesuit John Courtney Murray. Writing in *Theological Studies*, he suggested transforming the negative form, "no salvation outside the church," into a positive version: "It is by the Church alone that salvation has come to humanity, and by the Church alone it comes to the individual." Murray believed that this rewording could be justified in the interests of "practical tact" and as constituting an act of "courteous charity." And, in fact, many leading liberal Protestant theologians did notice and welcome the tactfulness intended by this formulation.

However, even such a minor shift in emphasis upset many Catholics, who saw it as a first step in the surrender of Catholic exclusivity. The most important of these critics was the well-known Jesuit poet Leonard Feeney, who had been serving as director of the Catholic student center at Harvard since 1941. Father Feeney believed that the issue here was a matter not of courteous expression but of honesty: one must either tell the truth, which is that salvation comes only through the Church, and thereby be discourteous, or deny one of the most central tenets of the faith in the interests of harmony. Opting for truth, Feeney began to thunder the traditional formula in sermons and in the periodical he founded in 1946 for the purpose of attacking his liberal Catholic opponents. Feeney's efforts soon began to attract considerable attention in the secular press, which embarrassed the Catholic academic and ecclesiastical establishments, including the archbishop of Boston, all of whom urged him to adopt a tactful silence. "I am not overtactful in taking into account what non-Catholics will think," Father Feeney admitted (in Clarke, 1950:177).

Unbeknownst to him, or apparently to his American opponents, Father Feeney's campaign had been lost even before it got going. Agonizing over what he was being told about the onset of the Nazi death camps, in June 1943 Pope Pius XII issued an encyclical that, in attempting to mitigate the spirit of exclusivity, opened the door to the acceptance of pluralism. In *Mystici Corpus Christi* (On the Mystical Body of Christ), Pius reasserted the Catholic claim to be the "true Church of Jesus Christ," the "One, Holy, Catholic, Apostolic Roman Church," but at the end he introduced a subtle point, relating it to the position taken by the Council of Trent (*1545–1563*) that God's mercy would extend to persons of implicit faith (*fides in voto*) among peoples to whom the gospel message had not yet been brought. The pope went a step beyond, extending the doctrine to those who had heard but were unable to accept because of sincere error. As he put it, some people outside the Church may still be within its sphere of salvation because they display an "unconscious yearning and desire" to genuine faith and therefore are Catholics, although they are unaware of it.

This statement, which came eventually to be referred to as the doctrine of the "unconscious Catholic," offended some non-Catholics, but it set the Church on a course that eventually made it impossible not to extend some degree of respect to any sincerely religious person. It also sealed the fate of Father Feeney. In August 1949 the Holy Office (also known as the Inquisition) wrote a letter to the archbishop of Boston that spelled out the full implications of the doctrine:

> Therefore, that one may obtain eternal salvation, it is not always required that he be incorporated into the Church *actually* as a member, but it is necessary that at least he be united to her by *desire* and *longing*. However, this desire need not always be explicit, as it is in catechumens; but when a person is involved in invincible ignorance, God accepts also an implicit desire, so called because it is included in that good disposition of soul whereby a person wishes his will to be conformed to the will of God.

Ecumenism. Pope John Paul II and Rabbi Meir Lau
confer during the pope's visit to Israel in 2000.
© AFP/CORBIS.

As for Father Feeney, the letter announced that for his conscious unwillingness to submit to the Church (to be quiet after having been told by his bishop to desist), Feeney was excommunicated.

Twenty years later, Vatican II took ecumenism further. It ceased all reference to Protestants as heretics or to the Orthodox as schismatics, substituting the phrase "separated brethren." In the "Decree on Ecumenism" issued in November 1964, the council reasserted the primacy of the Church but acknowledged that many elements of truth "can exist outside the visible boundaries of the Catholic church" (Baum, 1966:184). "The brethren divided from us also carry out many liturgical actions of the Christian religion

237

. . . [and] these most certainly can truly engender a life of grace, and, one must say, can aptly give access to the communion of salvation" (ibid.). But perhaps the greatest concession made by this decree was the official withdrawal of prohibitions against entering non-Catholic churches or participating in some religious ceremonies with non-Catholics. This permission was not "to be used indiscriminately," but judgments on these matters were consigned to local authorities (ibid., 192–93). Almost immediately, all across America Catholics began to attend non-Catholic funerals and weddings, and soon after that Catholic and Protestant pentecostals began to hold joint prayer sessions.

Protestant Approaches

Theologically, at least, Protestants had less difficulty accommodating Catholics, having already begun to accommodate one another. That is, as various denominations began to admit the fundamental Christianity of other denominations (even if their theology was flawed), this necessarily included Catholics—however grudgingly. Thus in 1813 the president of Harvard remarked in a public lecture that members of his generation had overcome "much of that abhorrence of papists which our fathers felt themselves obliged to maintain," and admitted that "it may be thought lawful for us to believe in the compatibility of the Romish faith with a capacity for salvation and admit the possible, nay more, the presumptive Christianity of a virtuous and devout Roman Catholic" (in Hennesey, 1981:117).

Thus it was that nineteenth-century American anti-Catholicism was based far less on religious differences than on political issues, particularly on issues concerning democracy and the separation of Church and State. As he warned against "Romanism," as mentioned previously, Lyman Beecher thundered in 1834: "The Catholic Church holds now in darkness and bondage nearly half of the civilized world . . . It is the skillful, powerful, dreadful system of corruption to those who wield it, and of slavery and debasement to those who live under it" (1835:36).

And, of course, it was attempts to lay such charges to rest that led to the American heresy. But as time passed and Catholic political machines controlling the large eastern cities did not infringe on anyone's liberties, the political suspicions of Catholicism began to wane—albeit to a lesser degree in those parts of the nation having no local experience to guide them. Even so, Al Smith's Catholicism *may* have cost him the 1928 presidential election, but it did not prevent him from being the Democratic nominee or from receiving the votes of millions of Protestants and carrying six states in the southern "Bible Belt."

Jews and Civility

But if Protestants had no serious theological inhibitions concerning Catholics as Christians, both had problems concerning the salvation of the Jews. The doctrine of the unconscious Catholic had initially been prompted by Pope Pius XII's concerns about Europe's Jews and was widely interpreted in that light. Concerns about anti-Semitism also prompted the Vatican II Council to condemn the idea that the Jews were responsible for the Crucifixion (*Nostra Aetate*, October 1965). The Vatican has continued to issue statements recognizing the religious legitimacy of Judaism. In June 1986 Pope John Paul II made an official visit to the main synagogue in Rome, where he participated in an eighty-minute service. During his address, the pope said that his visit was "meant to make a decisive contribution to the consolidation of the good relations between our two communities in imitation of the example of so many men and women who have worked and are still working today on both sides to overcome old prejudices and to secure an ever wider and fuller recognition of that 'bond' and that 'common spiritual patrimony' that exists between Jews and Christians" (Foy and Avato, 1987:37).

It is important to recognize that the Roman Catholic Church has not renounced its claim to exclusivity. The "Decree on Ecumenism" quoted above clearly asserted Catholic primacy as the "one and only Church of God" (Baum, 1966:183), asserting that "it is through Christ's Catholic Church alone, which is the all-embracing means of salvation, that the fullness of the means of salvation can be obtained" (ibid.:185). And when the pope spoke in the synagogue, he noted the common origins that bind Christianity and Judaism but did not even imply that the two faiths are equally valid—an "unconscious Catholicism" is not the equivalent of the conscious variety. Thus when Catholics emphasize common bonds and allow that some other faiths have elements of truth, they display civility, not accommodation. In matters of sincere faith, no more can be asked.

Lacking a doctrine of the "unconscious Christian," Protestants faced a long struggle to deal with the question of Jewish salvation. In addition, concerns about centuries of anti-Semitism must not obscure the fact that Jews also have several theological problems concerning the religious legitimacy of Christians. The first involves Jesus. As Martin Buber summed up, "To the Christian, the Jew is a stubborn fellow who is still waiting for the Messiah; to the Jew, the Christian is a heedless fellow who in an unredeemed world declares that redemption has somehow or other taken place" (in Niebuhr, 1958:98). The second problem involves the question of just *who are* God's Chosen people. These matters became especially pressing in New York City, and it was there that they were eventually dealt with.

New York Pluralism

One of the first moments of true public religious civility occurred in 1904 at St. Mark's German Evangelical Lutheran Church in Manhattan, following the drowning of more than a thousand of its Sunday school students, teachers, and choir members when their tour boat caught fire and sank only several miles off shore. During the huge memorial service held at St. Mark's, a message was read from the Catholic archbishop of New York: "May the Giver of all strength comfort you and yours in this dreadful hour of your sorrow." And at the end, several hundred Lutheran, Methodist, Episcopal, and Presbyterian clergy joined with a number of Jewish rabbis to sing (in German) "Who knows how near my end may be?" (Bainbridge, 1997).

240

A Forgotten Tragedy. On June 15, 1904, the paddle-wheel excursion boat *General Slocum* took the Sunday school students and teachers of New York City's St. Mark's German Evangelical Lutheran Church on a harbor tour. The ship burst into flames and sank, killing 1,021 persons—many church families lost all of their children. The aftermath produced the first interfaith service in the city's history. © Bettmann/CORBIS.

Notice that Catholic priests did not actually attend the memorial service at St. Mark's for the drowned Lutheran children. Possibly they might have done so had it been held in a secular building such as a sports arena. But, as already noted, in those days, Catholics were forbidden to enter non-Catholic religious structures. Moreover, some Catholics (especially prelates in Europe) might have been quite offended that the archbishop of New York had referred merely to the "Giver of all strength," rather than to Almighty God or to Jesus Christ, suspecting that his vague reference was meant to conciliate Jews and liberals. If so, this was the very *essence of civility*—which is *to not fully say what one truly believes, but to modify one's remarks out of deference to what others present truly believe.*

That this event occurred in New York City is no surprise; efforts at public religious civility ought to have first appeared where there

Table 5.2
Religious Membership in New York City, 1926

Unchurched[a]	34.2%
Jewish	28.5%
Roman Catholic	28.0%
Protestant	8.7%
Liberal	7.9%
Conservative	0.8%
Eastern Orthodox	0.4%
New Religions[b]	0.2%

[a]Not enrolled as members of any local congregation.
[b]Christian Science, Spiritualist, Theosophy, Ethical Culture, Mormon, etc.

was the most extensive pluralism. Indeed, New York's religious composition was (and remains) unique. Like many American cities, by the end of the nineteenth century, New York had a very high percentage of Catholics. But unlike any other American city it had an equally high percentage of Jews. Protestants have long been extremely underrepresented in New York, and evangelical Protestants are hardly to be found. Table 5.2 shows the religious composition of New York City according to the United States Census of Religious Bodies for 1926—at the time when local religious leaders had begun serious efforts to present a united front on public occasions.

These membership statistics were compiled by the census from forms submitted by each individual parish and congregation in the nation, each reporting its total membership as well as many other significant facts (such as the languages in which services were conducted). Therefore, in order to be counted as a church member, an individual had to be listed on the membership rolls of a specific congregation or parish.

As was true everywhere in America, the largest group (34.2 percent) consisted of those who were not on a local church roll and thus are classified as "unchurched," even though most would have stated a religious preference if asked. Jews (28.5 percent) made up the second largest group, and Roman Catholics (28.0 percent) the third largest. New York's Protestant population was small, amounting to fewer than one in ten, and virtually none of them belonged to more conservative, evangelical denominations. I have not counted Baptists (0.4 percent) or Methodists (0.9 percent) among the conservatives because all of the white Baptists were affiliated with the Northern Baptist Convention, which was by then quite liberal, as was the Methodist Church (Finke and Stark, 1992). Indicative of the liberalism of New York City Protestants at this time is that the Unitarians outnumbered every conservative body except for the Missouri Lutherans. As for nonconformity, there were twice as many Spiritualists as Unitarians. By comparison, in the nation as a whole, in 1926 the Roman Catholics made up only 16 percent of the population, Jews made up 3.6 percent, 36 percent were Protestants (about 40 percent of them belonging to conservative denominations), and 44 percent were unchurched—most of the "unchurched" thought of themselves as Protestants (Finke and Stark, 1992).

In weighing the religious factions in New York City, we must note that although greatly outnumbered, the Protestants were the most powerful group—their local social and economic dominance was enhanced by their huge numerical advantage in the nation. Thus the search for civility in New York City was negotiated among four major factions: liberal Protestants, Roman Catholics, Jews, and secular intellectuals—some of whom presumed to speak on behalf of the unchurched. And the most prominent early Protestant sponsors of civility were of the deistic persuasion.

Recall from Chapter 2 that beginning in the 1920s liberal Christians disavowed missionizing. Along with Harvard's William Ernest Hocking, Daniel Johnson Fleming (1925) of New York's Union Seminary asserted that Christianity has no claim to any special truth beyond that contained in all of the world's major faiths. Consequently, when they denounced all efforts to convert others as "a humiliating mistake," this included missions to the Jews, which were a significant part of the Christian mission efforts of the late nineteenth and early twentieth centuries. By 1900 there were more than 850 full-time American and British Protestant missionaries "to the Jews" worldwide, 78 of them devoted to Jewish immigrants in New York City (Beach, 1903). About the same number were at work in 1920 (Robinson, 1923).

Hocking and his friends were not alone; many liberal Protestants called for the end of such missionizing, identifying it as an intolerable affront to Jews. Not surprisingly, many Jewish leaders agreed. This led to the formation in 1923 of the Commission on Good Will Between Jews and Christians—with headquarters in New York City. In 1928 this group was replaced by the National Conference of Christians and Jews, for the purpose of promoting "justice, amity, understanding, and cooperation among Protestants, Catholics, and Jews." In 1934 this organization established Brotherhood Week in February, and by the 1950s New York City had an official Interfaith Day, featuring public ceremonies involving Protestant, Catholic, and Jewish clergy. Soon, Thanksgiving Day became another annual occasion for interfaith ceremonies in New York (Herberg, [1955] 1960).

However, even if the issues of the divinity of Jesus and of the salvation of the Jews were irrelevant to leading Protestant liberals, these were still matters of great concern to more conventional Christians and Jews. For them, the goal was civility—to find a basis for courtesy and respect that did not depend on rejecting the core of their respective faiths. And it came to pass that by taking part in public expressions of faith, New Yorkers helped to evolve something that eventually came to be known as the American *civil religion*.

Civil Religion and Religious Civility

In the 1930s a new school of social theory began to develop among social scientists at Harvard, under the leadership of Talcott Parsons. Calling themselves *structural-functionalists*, they dominated sociology and anthropology in America (and to a lessor extent elsewhere) through the 1960s.

The distinctive structural-functionalist viewpoint was to regard societies as highly integrated social systems, and to attempt to explain the presence of any major social structure or item of culture on the basis of its contribution (function) to the effective maintenance of the social system (structure). In postulating the basic requirements of all social systems, these social scientists proposed the need for moral integration—that in order for a society to hold together, members must share a common set of values, a conception of morality and moral purpose. This aspect of structural-functionalism derived from Emile Durkheim, for whom religious beliefs were but the reflection of society itself, with religious ritual being the means by which group solidarity was reinforced, and faith in the moral order reaffirmed. It was for this reason that Parsons ([1937] 1949:427) interpreted Durkheim as saying not merely that "religion is a social phenomenon," but that "society is a religious phenomenon." Hence the basic structural-functionalist axiom: *Religion functions to integrate social systems*. From there it was but a tiny step to the conclusion that in order to function, *societies require "religion."* As Robin M. Williams, Jr. (1951:312), one of Parsons' most accomplished students, expressed it: "Every functioning society has to an important degree a *common* religion. The possession of a common set of ideas, rituals, and symbols can supply an overarching sense of unity even in a society riddled with conflicts."

Peter Berger captured this overarching function of religion in the title of his book *The Sacred Canopy* (1969). Berger argued that the "sacred" (religion) stands in opposition to chaos, to the collapse of social order: "The sacred cosmos emerges out of chaos and continues to confront the latter as its terrible contrary" (ibid.:26). Lodged within a religious institution, the sacred cosmos serves as a "sacred canopy" that gives meaning, plausibility, and legitimacy to the norms and social arrangements within the society "beneath" its shelter. That is, "the classical task of religion" is to construct "a common world within which all of social life receives ultimate meaning binding on everybody" (ibid.:133–34).

This claim that societies must have religion in order to be integrated is no longer credible in light of the evidence that in many societies there is no link between religion and morality (Stark, in press). Of course, through the many years when functionalists (structural or otherwise) were unaware of this, the proposition was affirmed with confidence, and, to be sure, religion *may* integrate monotheistic societies having a monopoly or at least very dominant religious organization (if it doesn't prompt religious rebellions). In any case, it was obvious from the start that the United States presented a difficult challenge: *pluralism.* How can a society be morally integrated if the population is splintered into many competing faiths with diverse moral visions, and having a long history of mutual antagonism? Berger was doubtful about the long-term capacity of any such society to survive because religious plausibility structures are "inherently precarious" and "hang . . . on a thin thread" (ibid.: 17). Therefore, religions lose credibility when they must compete (ibid.:50–51). Berger concluded that religion was essentially doomed by pluralism, and that to survive, modern societies would have to develop new, secular, canopies.

However, Berger's pessimism was dismissed by more orthodox structural-functionalists, who claimed that when a society holds together despite internal religious conflicts, as American society has done, its "sacred canopy" must not be associated with *any* specific religious faction but must transcend and overarch them all, thereby being immune from mutual contradiction. Thus Will Herberg attributed the moral integration of the United States to "the American Way of Life." In his immensely influential *Protestant—Catholic—Jew* ([1955] 1960:75) he wrote: "It is the American Way of Life that supplies American society with an 'overarching sense of unity' amid conflict . . . The American Way of Life is, at bottom, a spiritual structure, a system of ideas and ideals, of aspirations and values, of beliefs and standards; it synthesizes all that commends itself to the American as the right, the good, and the true in actual life."

Others acknowledged the existence of common sacred values in rather more invidious terms—Martin E. Marty (1958:78) decried American "state Shinto." Finally, Parsons' disciple Robert Bellah identified *civil religion* as the basis for the moral integration of pluralist America.

Bellah (1967:3–4) argued that one can identify "common elements of religious orientation that the great majority of Americans share." These "provide a religious dimension for the whole fabric of American life." Moreover, this is a "public religious dimension"; hence he called it the "American civil religion." In the body of his essay, Bellah drew excerpts from many American presidential speeches to isolate the principle elements of the civil religion as expressed on such ceremonial occasions as inaugurations or at moments of great social stress—"references to God are almost invariably to be found in the pronouncements of American presidents on solemn occasions" (ibid.:2). John F. Kennedy concluded his inauguration address: "With good conscience our only rewards, with history the final judge of our deeds, let us go forth to lead the land we love, asking His blessing and His help, but knowing that here on earth God's work must truly be our own." Bellah pointed out that Kennedy "did not refer to Jesus Christ, or to Moses, or to the Christian church . . . his only reference was to God, a word which almost all Americans can accept but which means" different things to different people (ibid.:3). It is this civil religion that Bellah proposed as fulfillment of the functionalist religious imperative.

As the concept of civil religion matured, it has come to stand for far more than the religious beliefs and sentiments most Americans hold in common. Many authors have suggested that what might otherwise be regarded as secular aspects of American culture, such as the Constitution and the Declaration of Independence, the flag, and various historical stories, have been infused with sacredness and therefore are components of the civil religion. With Phillip Hammond (1989), I suggest that this is much too broad a definition and neglects the fact that to the extent that it is useful to propose the sacred status of these aspects of culture, they are *made sacred* only by association with things seen as intrinsically sacred—religious things. Hence I limit discussion to civil *religion*.

No doubt civil religion often serves the national unity. At times of great peril or symbolic importance, it seems appropriate to most Americans that their leaders and opinion-makers invoke God and ask for everyone's prayers, and no doubt this produces a far more powerful appeal than does one limited to secular values. However, it is important to recognize that what Bellah called civil religion is largely the product of religious civility, as John Murray Cuddihy (1978) very perceptively pointed out. That is, the religion invoked on public occasions is expected to conform to the minimum standards of civility—to say nothing more than that to which all (or nearly all) can assent. For example, one is expected to invoke God, not Jesus Christ. Better yet, one should follow the example of the archbishop of New York and refer to "the Giver of all strength."

Recognize that, being constrained by norms of civility, the civil religion is the religion of virtually *no one* beyond a few deists. Rather, it holds the power to move people because it triggers a response in each individual based on his or her own far more vital and distinctive faith. Put another way, different people hear quite different things when the civil religion is invoked. This gives it universal appeal, but the civil religion is not *itself* a sacred canopy. It might better be described as a rhetorical weather bulletin that causes individuals to unfurl their own "sacred umbrellas"—to invoke Christian Smith's (1998:106) wonderful image. Smith continued:

> Canopies are expansive, immobile, and held up by props beyond the reach of those covered. Umbrellas, on the other hand, are small, handheld, and portable—like the faith-sustaining religious worlds that modern people construct for themselves ... In the pluralistic, modern world, people don't need macro-encompassing sacred cosmoses to maintain their religious beliefs. They only need "sacred umbrellas" ... religious reference groups ... "under" which their beliefs can make complete sense.

I cannot overstate the importance of the realization that people can *both* make common cause within the conventions of religious civility *and* retain full commitment to a particularistic umbrella. But while most people seem able to enjoy the shelter of their own umbrella, confident that it is superior to all others, and still not be offended by other umbrellas, many intellectuals seem to find this impossible—Reinhold Niebuhr being a classic instance. The famous Protestant theologian struggled for years to find a way to reconcile his admiration of Judaism and his vigorous Zionism with his equally vigorous Christianity, eventually modifying the latter by concluding that Jews are exempt from the need to accept Christ (Niebuhr, 1958). Irving Kristol (1949) suggested that Niebuhr's failure to "keep the faith" lay in his inability to separate the need for inhibitions on public religious expression from the need to fully express one's private convictions. That is, Niebuhr felt it indecent only to treat other faiths *as if* they were legitimate. Rather, honesty required that he first accept them as equally inspired. In this regard, Niebuhr reflected (and probably was influenced by) a celebrated essay on prejudice written by the most influential American liberal pundit of the first half of the twentieth century. In *A Preface to Morals* ([1929] 1964:70–71), Walter Lippmann wrote:

> As a consequence . . . of religious freedom the churches find themselves in an anomalous position. Inwardly, to their communicants, they continue to assert that they possess the only complete version of truth. But outwardly, in their civic relation with other churches and with civil power, they preach and practice toleration . . . [This] involves deep psychological difficulty for members of the congregation. As communicants they are expected to believe without reservation that their church is the only true means of salvation . . . But as citizens they are expected to maintain a neutral indifference to the claims of all sects. This is the best compromise that human wisdom has yet devised, but it has one inevitable consequence which the superficial advocates of toleration often overlook . . . The human soul is not so divided in compartments that man can be indifferent in one part of his soul and firmly believing in another . . . The existence of many churches in one community weakens the foundations of them all.

Fifty years later, having quoted this section of Lippmann's discussion at far greater length than I have done, John Murray Cuddihy (1978) pursued this tension between public and private convictions to explain why Niebuhr and so many other advocates of civility balanced their psychological accounts by modifying their faith, and to condemn them for having done so. But Cuddihy seemed to express even greater contempt for people of faith who are civil despite their fundamental differences. To Cuddihy (ibid.:210–11) this was mere "formalism," a "fiction of civility." Warming more fully to his critique, Cuddihy demanded more than that people should merely "show respect for." They must somehow truly embrace and achieve unreserved solidarity, and this without betraying their faith. Then, in his brief closing paragraph, Cuddihy laid the final blame: "The Protestant ethic deferred consumption. The Protestant esthetic defers ostentation. The Protestant etiquette—or, bourgeois civility—defers community." No mere civility here, at least.

Lippmann's analysis probably captures the inner life of intellectuals and, in this case, especially of theologians. They *are* given to seeking "cognitive balance." But most people don't intellectualize their faith, and, in my experience, religious Americans are fully able not merely to respect but to genuinely like others of a different faith, while remaining confident that theirs is the Best of All Umbrellas. Contrary to Cuddihy (ibid.:210), such civility is far more than "a solidarity of the surface." It is, in fact, the most sophisticated solidarity of all: to live in respectful harmony while maintaining profoundly conflicting faiths.

Southern "Incivility"

The emergence of vocal religious liberals and of a highly secular mass media has exposed the American South to considerable abuse concerning religious incivility. The complaint is that the civil religion does not prevail in the southern "Bible Belt," not even on public occasions. Instead, unabashed references to Christ and to Christianity as the key to salvation are made openly—even in the press and on local radio and television. Condemnation of this state of affairs takes two forms. First, southerners are characterized as uneducated fundamentalists, so ignorant that they *believe* in Christian particularism. Of this, more in a moment. The second stresses that southerners are bigots who don't have the civility not to *say* these things.

Efforts to discover the "Bible Belt" on the basis of individual behavior have always failed! Survey studies invariably show that people in the South do not pray more often or go to church more often, nor are they more apt to hold basic religious beliefs than are people in many other parts of the nation (Stark and Bainbridge, 1985). But it is true that when one is driving through the South, it does seem like a much more religious area of the nation because religious expression is frequent, open, and seemingly uninhibited by norms of civility. Why? Because, lacking significant pluralism, southerners have not had to worry about offending Catholics or Jews, or even liberal Protestants, for that matter. The reason the South lacks Catholics and Jews has to do with patterns of immigration. When the major waves of Catholic and Jewish immigrants arrived, there was nothing in the South to attract them—they were not interested in exchanging a life of poverty in Europe for life in a South smashed by the Civil War and mired in extreme poverty. Thus, to a considerable extent, the South has remained the "Protestant society" that once included the rest of the nation. Hence an "interfaith" public ceremony in much of the South will usually involve the presence of seven varieties of Baptists, five species of Methodists, four brands of Presbyterians, nine kinds of Pentecostals, and sometimes an Episcopalian. On such an occasion, local norms of civility insist that nothing be said concerning such controversial matters as infant versus adult baptism, or about the merits of full immersion, and certainly there will be no discussion of gifts of the spirit. But everyone will talk about "Our Lord and Savior Jesus Christ." If that sounds like a Bible Belt, it's because Americans elsewhere are constrained to limit such talk to the privacy of their own services. As for southerners as ignorant fundamentalists, that brings me to the worst current offenders of norms of civility: secularists, both churched and unchurched.

Secular Incivility

Recently, the local media expressed approval when the chief of police of Seattle prohibited his officers from wearing their uniforms to take part in a "March for Jesus." The media were equally agreeable when, the *next day*, the chief wore his uniform to march in the "Lesbian Gay Bisexual Transgender Parade." In similar fashion, protest vigils against capital punishment held outside prisons when an execution is scheduled are invariably treated with respect, but vigils outside abortion clinics are not. When animal rights activists berate and abuse women in public for wearing furs, their media treatment is favorable in comparison to that given demonstrations against clubs featuring women wearing nothing. When 1960s leftists are caught after years of living underground in order to avoid punishment for planting bombs or killing policemen, the press encourages and condones very mild or even suspended sentences for such "youthful idealism." But there is no hint of sympathy for those who have bombed an abortion clinic or shot an abortionist. Every Christmas the media help to uncover some "tasteless" public school chorus director who included "sectarian" carols in a concert, meanwhile expressing outrage that religious "fanatics" protest against the use of government funds to subsidize or display virulently antireligious "art" such as Serrano's *Piss Christ*, consisting of a crucifix in a tube of urine. The clear standard used by most of the media is that moral engagement is wonderful so long as it is entirely secular. As for religious morality, or indeed any deeply felt religious expression, nothing could be more misguided or even dangerous. Indeed, the media could not even report the death of Mother Teresa without providing "balance" by soliciting nasty attacks on her sincerity and merit from various professional atheists.[2]

Amazingly enough, it is deists within the churches—most of them clergy—who are the most vociferous opponents of public expressions of traditional Judeo-Christian values, typically on grounds of "fundamentalism." Moreover, this is nothing new. Recall how the liberal churchmen in New England in the eighteenth century responded to George Whitefield's revivals by outlawing them, or how Congregational and Presbyterian clerics condemned the enthusiasm of Baptists and Methodists in the nineteenth century—how dare they pray in "language of unbecoming familiarity with God?" thundered the eminent Congregationalist divine Asahel Nettleton (Beecher and Nettleton, 1828:91).

Ironically, by the start of the twentieth century it was the Methodists, now become dignified liberals, who expelled many clergy (and congregations) because they supported the Holiness Movement. But it was during the 1920s that truly vicious attacks by the liberal clergy on "sectarians" came into full blossom, particularly in New York City and at the Ivy League divinity schools. For example, the collection of nonpracticing clergy on the staff of the Institute of Social and Religious Research, funded by Rockefeller money and located in New York City, were without any restraint in their published condemnations of evangelical Protestants as "a poor class of mixed blood and moronic intelligence," "a backwash of sectarianism . . . in . . . the more backward sections of the nation," the product of "inferior minds"; they asserted that sound religious practice would require that the administration of country churches be taken "out of the hand of the weak brother and the silly sister" (Finke and Stark, 1992:234).

In 1959, upon completion of his term as president of the National Council of Churches (headquartered on Riverside Drive in New York City), the Reverend Eugene Carson Blake lamented that church unity was prevented by the "cultural crudities" of evangelical Protestant beliefs (1959:76). Then, in what he seems to have thought was a conciliatory tone, he urged his colleagues to help "to bring these sincere men out of theological isolation and personal provincialism."

In an essay initially published in the Jesuit magazine *America*, Father Patrick M. Arnold of St. Louis University denounced "fundamentalism" (including the Catholic variety) as a form of "religious disease" (1990:174) marked by "extreme fanaticism" and "fear of, and outright hostility to, modern values and thought" (ibid.:181). This so impressed the very liberal Notre Dame theologian Father Richard P. O'Brien that he reprinted excerpts from Arnold's essay in one of his weekly newspaper columns.

One must, of course, cite John Shelby Spong, until recently the Episcopalian bishop of Newark, not only because of his extraordinary incivility, but because he gets to express it so frequently on television—the media can't resist an actual bishop who says God is not conscious and Christ did not rise, and who is willing to attack those who do believe these "myths" as captives of "irrational religious anger," and of beliefs used only "to bolster deeply insecure and fearful people" (1992:4–5). Another member of the choir is the Reverend Peter J. Gomes, professor of Christian morals at Harvard Divinity, who edified readers of *Harvard Magazine* (the alumni periodical) to the effect that the grip of evangelical Protantism lies in "paranoia more than a policy" (1996:36). Not to be outdone by his Christian colleagues, Mortimer Ostow (1990:113), psychoanalyst and faculty member of the Jewish Theological Seminary of America, diagnosed "the fundamentalist [as] regressing to the state of the mind of the child who resists differentiation from its mother. The messiah and the group itself represent the returning mother."

Little wonder, then, that writers in the secular press offer similar libels. Writing in the *Washington Post*, Michael Weisskopf (1993:A10) characterized evangelical Protestants as "poor, uneducated and easy to command."[3] "Fashionable" opinion "knows" that traditional believers, and especially those who conceive of God as an active, all-seeing being who actually hears prayers, are stupid, crazy, ignorant, and dangerous. But competent social scientists know that these are lies, entirely equivalent to fantasies concerning Jewish conspiracies or orgies in Catholic convents. Nor are these beliefs about evangelicals to be excused on grounds of "ignorance." I have too often acquainted reporters with the facts, only to find no trace of them in the final article or film segment. Once again, let it be noted that there is an immense body of research refuting these efforts to denigrate religious people. It even turns out that religious people are rather superior in terms of their mental and physical health. Since I have contributed to and summarized this literature extensively in other work, I shall not repeat it here (Stark and Finke, 2000).

As things now stand, secularists campaign even against the civil religion—*no* religious expression is inclusive, all being an affront to the nonbeliever. Therefore, it is urged, all public expressions of religion should be suppressed—no prayers of any sort, no matter how interreligious, should even be uttered at public events—and all "religious" holidays should be sanitized into secularity: "Jingle Bells," yes; "Silent Night," no. That this is an affront to the majority seems to count for nothing. That this conflict is between secularity and religion, rather than among religions, is apparent in the fact that most religious Jews do not support protests against Christmas holiday displays, for example, but merely ask for an equal opportunity for Hanukkah displays.

Success and Civility

A primary reason for the constant effort to associate faith with ignorance and poverty is to convince the public that not only may "these people" differ from them on religious grounds but they are located on the far side of other significant social cleavages. Thus current media images of ignorant "rednecks" marching to the beat of the Religious Right add class cleavages to imputed ideological shortcomings in precisely the same way as was done with Catholics back in the 1840s: "Irishmen fresh from the bogs of Ireland are led up to vote like dumb brutes . . . to vote down intelligent, honest, native Americans" (in Hennesey, 1981:119). Indeed, a major factor in the demise of anti-Catholicism was their upward mobility—when it became obvious that Catholics matched Protestants in terms of income and education, their acceptance was ensured.

Since television news now dominates, it is worth mention that a major method of imputing shortcomings to religious people (or to anyone with whom they disagree) is the ability of the media to select whom to show doing what. Ever since the invention of the camera, newspeople have biased their presentations by picking un-flattering photos of their opponents and flattering photos of their friends. In coverage of social movements, it long has been their practice to bias reports by selecting which persons to offer as repre-sentative of a group. Old-time news photographers used to brag that they had never taken a picture of an attractive prohibitionist or of a goofy or sinister-looking "wet." The lesson was not lost on contemporary photo and TV journalists—compare film of pro-choice and pro-life demonstrators sometime, and discover that usu-ally the women representing the latter outweigh their opponents by an average of a hundred pounds.

A great irony is that in recent times, while the media have been very concerned to falsely identify evangelical Christians as poor, uneducated, and southerners, they have been equally concerned to present them as lily-white (hence racists)—this is especially true of coverage given to groups such as the Promise Keepers. In fact, the Promise Keepers and many similar Christian organizations, most

Pentecostal groups, and the Jehovah's Witnesses are unusually interracial (Everton, 1999; Stark and Iannaccone, 1997). But one seldom sees that on television or reads about it in the press, since most media people "know" that these groups are racist—no matter who shows up. Thus the *Village Voice* (in Leo, 1997) denounced the Promise Keepers for their "policy of racial diversity so overt that it reeks of insincerity."

Of course, committed Christians sometimes respond in kind. Remarkably, however, for all that the Christian Right preoccupies secularist publications, secularists, in turn, are rarely even mentioned in evangelical publications. When they are, the responses are usually soberly issue-oriented or consist of complaints about the falsity or inappropriateness of the condemnations. Seldom, however, do these responses violate norms of religious civility. Indeed, there is far greater emphasis on interfaith ties and on ecumenical conversations and cooperation in publications such as *Charisma*, *Christianity Today*, or *First Things* than in liberal periodicals such as *Christian Century* or *America*. And, as even the *New York Times* has acknowledged, it is the Reverend Jerry Falwell, not Bishop John Shelby Spong or the Reverend Martin E. Marty, who has been decorated by the government of Israel. This is entirely consistent with the results of national surveys, which show that evangelical Christians, including persons who identify themselves as supporters of the Religious Right, are substantially more favorable toward Israel, and somewhat more favorable toward Jews in general, than are liberal Christians or the irreligious (see, e.g., Smith, 1999)—despite the fact that evangelicals continue to support missions to convert Jews to Christianity! Moreover, a new study has demonstrated that the *only* significant form of religious prejudice in America is "Anti-Fundamentalism," and it is concentrated among highly educated people without an active religious affiliation (Bolce and DeMaio, 1999).

The Globalization of Civility?

However, even at its worst, American religious incivility is tepid compared with what prevails in most of the rest of the world. During the past decade Muslims have killed more than a million Christians in the Sudan, and the mounting death toll in Indonesia shows no signs of abating. Religious violence occurs daily in India. In Mexico, Protestant converts still risk being murdered in the more remote villages. Recently, the Russian Orthodox Church has prevailed in the passage of repressive laws against "foreign faiths," which apply even to some of the more traditional factions within Orthodoxy. In Lithuania it is the Roman Catholic hierarchy who have prompted government repression of Protestants. Meanwhile, as they have for many centuries, Orthodox Catholics, Roman Catholics, and Muslims in the Balkans continue to kill one another. Of course, missionizing by "unbelievers" still carries the death penalty in most Islamic nations. In contrast, the Chinese government is quite evenhanded, murdering, torturing, and imprisoning everyone having *any* form of serious religious commitment.

Even in western Europe there is a constant stream of virulent, official condemnations of nonconforming religious groups, accompanied by policies of open harassment and repression of all competitors to the recognized, and usually subsidized, churches. In principle, most nations of western Europe assert freedom of worship, but in reality they permit almost unlimited discretion to bureaucrats and parliaments concerning specific policies and decisions to impose sanctions on minority religions. I have recently published a substantial account of how most European governments are using their powers to repress religious pluralism, often very severely (Stark and Finke, 2000). Here it is sufficient to note that these are democratic nations which claim to respect human rights. If even they remain intolerant and repressive of religious nonconformity, can we ever expect brutal religious repression to stop in nations making no pretense about respecting human rights?

Since so much religion has diffused around the world, isn't it possible that one day norms of religious civility will diffuse too? According to many enthusiastic proponents of "globalization theory," travel, trade, and the mass media expose people in many nations to one another's culture, and the expected result is a substantial degree of sociocultural amalgamation (Beyer, 1994; Meyer, 1980; Robertson, 1985, 1992; Robertson and Garrett, 1991; Simpson, 1996; Wallerstein, 1974, 1984). Some presume that globalization will end religious conflict because it will destroy or simply bypass all traditional religions (Lechner, 1991a, 1991b; Wallerstein, 1974, 1984), leaving, at most, a "universalistic" residue wherein all religions are regarded as the same (Turner, 1991). This is, of course, merely the old secularization thesis in new clothes, and equally unfounded (Stark, 1999c). But a rather more moderate claim is that the globalization of religious norms more compatible with modernity and tolerance will be speeded by the fact that so many religious institutions already are international. Thus, for example, it can be argued that given the presence of the Roman Catholic Church in so many nations, and given that recent popes have taken significant steps toward religious civility, that church can serve as a vehicle for the spread of legal toleration and norms of civility (Roberts, 1995).

This is hardly the place to register my skepticism concerning globalization. It seems sufficient to register my doubts that religious intolerance and incivility will be overcome by the diffusion or globalization of liberal enlightenment. An esteemed Irish-American politician loved to explain that "all politics is local," and I think this truth fully applies to the "politics" of religious civility. Hence while presenting a model of civility in the United States, locally in various parts of Europe the Roman Catholic Church has encouraged the repression and persecution of "dissenting" religious groups. If Pope John Paul II has several times directed quite conciliatory remarks toward Jews, he has also consistently attacked local Protestant "sects and new religious groups who sow confusion" in every Latin American nation he has visited (Sywulka, 1996:94).

What I think this shows is that norms of civility depend on local conditions. Societies will not exhibit religious civility unless, or until, they develop a truly pluralistic religious situation of their own—like Americans before them, other societies will not develop religious civility until they must. Thus before there will be religious civility in Europe, for example, there must first be significant pluralism, which may, in fact, soon exist because of two current trends. First, rising levels of immigration are bringing substantial numbers of Roman and Orthodox Catholics as well as Muslims to nations having Protestant state churches (Hamberg, 1995, 1999). Second, the immense American-based mission to "Christianize" Europe portends a diversity of evangelical Protestant groups, as outlined in Chapter 2. *If* these trends do produce pluralism, *then* we may observe the appearance of religious civility in European nations.[4]

As for the rest of the world, it seems very unlikely that people will learn the lessons of tolerance merely by observing events abroad.

Conclusion

For generations, the prevailing social scientific orthodoxy about religious pluralism has been strangely contradictory. On the one hand, with Adam Smith as the unrecognized dissenter, *everyone* has believed that pluralism weakens all faiths as each undercuts the plausibility of all of the others. On the other hand, it has been regarded as equally certain that these implausible and waning faiths will nevertheless be able to generate such intense partisanship as to cause deadly conflicts. Not only were these views contradictory, but each is clearly wrong. Nowhere does religious apathy and alienation prevail so widely, and nowhere is there a greater potential for violent religious conflict, than in societies where one religious body attempts to maintain a monopoly. The key to high levels of local religious commitment *and* of religious civility, is not fewer religions, but more.

Notes

1. I have imposed modern spelling.

2. See the incredible piece by Germaine Greer in *Newsweek*, September 8, 1997.

3. Presented with overwhelming evidence to the contrary, the editors of the *Post* published a retraction concerning poverty and education, letting "easy to command" stand.

4. In keeping with the theory, religious civility already seems well on its way in several Latin American nations such as Chile, where Protestant groups have gained large memberships.

Abraham, Wendy R. 1999. "Memories of Kaifeng's Jewish Descendents Today: Historical Significance in Light of Observations by Westerners Since 1605." In *The Jews of China*, vol. 1, *Historical and Comparative Perspectives*, edited by Jonathan Goldstein, 71–86. Armonk, NY: M. E. Sharpe.

Ahlstrom, Sidney E. 1972. *A Religious History of the American People*. 2 vols. New Haven: Yale University Press.

Albright, William Foxwell. 1957. *From the Stone Age to Christianity: Monotheism and the Historical Process*. 2d ed. Garden City, NY: Doubleday.

Aldred, Cyril. 1988. *Akhenaten: King of Egypt*. London: Thames and Hudson.

Allen, Charlotte. 1998. *The Human Christ: The Search for the Historical Jesus*. New York: The Free Press.

———. 1996. "Is Nothing Sacred?: Casting Out the Gods from Religious Studies." *Lingua Franca*, November, 31–40.

Allen, Wayne. 1999. "Case Study on Dependency: When the Mission Pays the Pastor." *Mission Frontiers* 21 (January–February): 38–41.

Alroy, Gil Carl. 1975. *Behind the Middle East Conflict: The Real Impasse between Arab and Jew*. New York: G. P. Putnam's Sons.

Anderson, Gary M. 1988. "Mr. Smith and the Preachers: The Economics of Religion in the Wealth of Nations." *Journal of Political Economy* 96:1066–88.

Anderson, John. 1994. *Religion, State and Politics in the Soviet Union and Successor States*. Cambridge: Cambridge University Press.

Armstrong, Karen. 1993. *Muhammad: A Biography of the Prophet*. San Francisco: Harper.

Arnold, Patrick M., S.J. 1990. "The Reemergence of Fundamentalism in the Catholic Church." In *The Fundamentalist Phenomenon*, edited by Norman J. Cohen, 172–91. Grand Rapids, MI: Eerdmans.

Arnold, T. W. 1896. *The Preaching of Islam: A History of the Propagation of the Muslim Faith*. Lahore (India): Sh. Muhammad Ashraf.

Arrington, Leonard J. 1985. *Brigham Young: American Moses*. New York: Alfred A. Knopf.

Arrington, Leonard J., and Davis Bitton. 1979. *The Mormon Experience: A History of the Latter-day Saints*. New York: Alfred A. Knopf.

Ashtor, Eliyahu. 1973. *The Jews of Moslem Spain*. Philadelphia: Jewish Publication Society of America.

Assis, Yom Tov. 1997. *The Golden Age of Aragonese Jewry*. London: The Littman Library of Jewish Civilization.

Assis, Yom Tov, in association with Adam Gruzman. 1978. *History of the Jews in Aragon*. Jerusalem: The Magnes Press, Hebrew University.

Athyal, Saphir. 1998. "Agencies Work Together in Romania." *Marc Newsletter* 98, no. 3:1, 6.

Atiya, Aziz S. [1938] 1965. *The Crusade in the Later Middle Ages*. New York: Kraus Reprint Corportation.

Axelrod, Robert. 1984. *The Evolution of Cooperation*. New York: Basic Books.

Ayerst, David, and A.S.T. Fisher. 1971. *Records of Christianity*. Vol 1. Oxford: Basil Blackwell.

Backman, Milton V., Jr. 1988. "Lo, Here! Lo, There! Early in the Spring of 1820." In *The Prophet Joseph: Essays on the Life and Mission of Joseph Smith*, edited by Larry C. Porter and Susan Easton Black, 19–35. Salt Lake City: Deseret Book Company.

———. 1982. *The Heavens Resound: A History of the Latter-day Saints in Ohio, 1830–1838*. Salt Lake City: Deseret Books.

Baer, Yitzhak. 1961. *A History of the Jews in Christian Spain*. 2 vols. Philadelphia: The Jewish Publication Society of America.

Bagnall, Roger S. 1993. *Egypt in Late Antiquity*. Princeton, NJ: Princeton University Press.

Bainbridge, William F. 1882. *Around the World Tour of Christian Missions: A Universal Survey*. New York: C. R. Blackall and Company.

Bainbridge, William Sims. 1997. *The Sociology of Religious Movements*. New York: Routledge.

Bainbridge, William Sims, and Rodney Stark. 1979. "Cult Formation: Three Compatible Models." *Sociological Analysis* 40:283–95.

Bakvis, Herman. 1981. *Catholic Power in the Netherlands*. Kingston, Ontario: McGill-Queen's University Press.

Bamberger, Bernard J. 1939. *Proselytism in the Talmudic Period*. New York: Hebrew Union College Press.

Barker, Eileen. 1984. *The Making of a Moonie: Brainwashing or Choice?* Oxford: Basil Blackwell.

Barkun, Michael. 1986. *Crucible of the Millennium*. Syracuse, NY: Syracuse University Press.

Barnavi, Eli, ed. 1992. *A Historical Atlas of the Jewish People*. New York: Schocken Books.

Baron, Salo Wittmayer. 1969. *A Social and Religious History of the Jews*. Vols. 13 and 14. New York: Columbia University Press.

———. 1967. *A Social and Religious History of the Jews*. Vol. 11. New York: Columbia University Press.

———. 1965. *A Social and Religious History of the Jews*. Vols. 9 and 10. New York: Columbia University Press.

———. 1957. *A Social and Religious History of the Jews*. Vols. 3, 4, and 5. New York: Columbia University Press.

———. 1952. *A Social and Religious History of the Jews*. Vols. 1 and 2. New York: Columbia University Press.

Barrett, David B. 1998. Personal communication.

———. 1982. *World Christian Encyclopedia*. Oxford: Oxford University Press.

———. 1968. *Schism and Renewal in Africa*. Nairobi, Kenya: Oxford University Press.

Barrow, John D., and Frank J. Tipler. 1988. *The Anthropic Cosmological Principle*. Oxford: Oxford University Press.

Barton, Ralph. 1946. "The Religion of the Ifugaos." *American Anthropologist* 40:4.

Bastide, Roger. 1978. *African Religions in Brazil*. Baltimore: Johns Hopkins University Press.

Bat Ye'or. 1985. *The Dhimmi: Jews and Christians under Islam*. Rutherford, NJ: Fairleigh Dickinson University Press.

Bauckham, Richard. 1990. *Jude and the Relatives of Jesus in the Early Church*. Edinburgh: T & T Clark.

Baum, Gregory, ed. 1966. *The Teachings of the Second Vatican Council: Complete Texts of the Constitutions, Decrees, and Declarations*. Westminster, MD: The Newman Press.

Baumer, Franklin L. 1960. *Religion and the Rise of Scepticism*. New York: Harcourt Brace.

Baumgarten, Albert I. 1997. *The Flourishing of Jewish Sects in the Maccabean Era: An Interpretation*. Leiden: Brill.

Beach, Harlan P. 1903. *A Geography and Atlas of Protestant Missions*. Vol. 2, *Statistics and Atlas*. New York: Student Volunteer Movement for Foreign Missions.

Beach, Harlan P., and Charles H. Fahs. 1925. *World Missionary Atlas*. New York: Institute of Social and Religious Research.

Beard, Mary, John North, and Simon Price. 1998. *Religions of Rome*. Vol. 1, *A History*. Cambridge: Cambridge University Press.

Becker, C. H. 1913. "The Expansion of the Saracens, Africa and Europe." Chapter 12 in *The Cambridge Medieval History*. Cambridge: Cambridge University Press.

Becker, Gary S. 1964. *Human Capital: A Theoretical and Empirical Analysis*. New York: Columbia University Press.

Beecher, Lyman. 1835. *A Plea for the West*. 2d ed. New York: Leavitt, Lord & Co.

Beecher, Lyman, and Asahel Nettleton. 1828. *Letters of the Rev. Dr. Beecher and Rev. Mr. Nettleton of the "New Measures" in Conducting Revivals of Religion*. New York: G. & C. Carvill.

Bellah, Robert N. 1967. "Civil Religion in America." *Daedalus* 96:1–21.

———. 1964. "Religious Evolution." *American Sociological Review* 29:358–74.

Bendiner, Elmer. 1983. *The Rise and Fall of Paradise*. New York: G. P. Putnam's Sons.

Benedict, Ruth. 1938. "Religion." In *General Anthropology*, edited by Franz Boas, 627–65. New York: C. D. Heath.

Berger, Peter. 1969. *The Sacred Canopy*. New York: Doubleday.

———, ed. 1981. *The Other Side of God*. Garden City, NY: Doubleday.

Bergman, Elihu. 1977. "The American Jewish Population Erosion." *Midstream*, October, 9–19.

Betts, George Herbert. 1929. *The Beliefs of 700 Ministers*. New York: Abingdon Press.

Beyer, Peter. 1994. *Religion and Globalization*. London: Sage.

Biddle, Martin. 1999. *The Tomb of Christ*. Phoenix Mill, Gloucestershire: Sutton.

Bienert, Wolfgang A. 1991. "The Relatives of Jesus." *New Testament Apocrypha*, rev. ed., edited by Wilhelm Schneemelcher, translated from German by R. McL. Wilson, 470–88. Louisville: Westminster/John Knox Press.

Blake, Eugene Carson. 1959. "The American Churches and Ecumenical Mission." In *The Ecumenical Era in Church and Society*, edited by Edward J. Juri, 75–91. New York: Macmillan Co.

Blanshard, Paul. 1958. *American Freedom and Catholic Power*. 2d ed. Boston: Beacon Press.

Blau, Joseph L. 1964. *Modern Varieties of Judaism*. New York: Columbia University Press.

Bloch, Marc. [1940] 1961. *Feudal Society*. Vol. 1. Chicago: University of Chicago Press.

Boak, Arthur E. R. 1955a. "The Populations of Roman and Byzantine Karanis." *Historia* 4:157–62.

———. 1955b. *Manpower Shortage and the Fall of the Roman Empire in the West.* Ann Arbor: University of Michigan Press.

———. 1947. *A History of Rome to 565 <ft6>A.<ft6>D.* 3d ed. New York: Macmillan.

Bobrovnikov, Vladimir. 1996. "The Islamic Revival and the National Question in Post-Soviet Dagestan." *Religion, State and Society* 24:233–38.

Bolce, Louis, and Gerald DeMaio. 1999. "Religious Outlook, Culture War Politics, and Antipathy toward Christian Fundamentalists." *Public Opinion Quarterly.* 63:29–61.

Bossy, John. 1985. *Christianity in the West 1400–1700.* New York: Oxford University Press.

Bowker, John, ed. 1997. *The Oxford Dictionary of World Religions.* Oxford: Oxford University Press.

Boyarin, Daniel. 1999. *Dying for God: Martyrdom and the Making of Christianity and Judaism.* Stanford, CA: Stanford University Press.

Brier, Bob. 1998. *The Murder of Tutankhamen: A True Story.* New York: G. P. Putnam's Sons.

Brodie, Fawn W. 1945. *No Man Knows My History: The Life of Joseph Smith.* New York: Alfred A. Knopf.

Brøndsted, Johannes. 1965. *The Vikings.* Baltimore: Penguin Books.

Brown, Peter. 1988. *The Body and Society: Men, Women and Sexual Renunciation in Early Christianity.* New York: Columbia Unversity Press.

Brown, R. E. 1966. *The Gospel According to John.* 2 vols. Garden City, NY: Anchor Books.

Buckley, Michael J. 1987. *At the Origins of Modern Atheism.* New Haven: Yale University Press.

Bulliet, Richard W. 1979. *Conversion to Islam in the Medieval Period: An Essay in Quantitative History.* Cambridge: Harvard University Press.

Burckardt, Jacob. [1860] 1949. *The Age of Constantine the Great.* New York: Pantheon Books.

Burn, A. R. 1953. "Hic breve vivitur." *Past and Present* 4:2–31.

Burns, Robert I. 1984. *Muslims, Christians, and Jews in the Crusader Kingdom of Valencia.* Cambridge: Cambridge University Press.

Bushman, Richard L. 1988. "Joseph Smith's Family Background." In *The Prophet Joseph: Essays on the Life and Mission of Joseph Smith*, edited by Larry C. Porter and Susan Easton Black, 1–18. Salt Lake City: Deseret Book Company.

Bushman, Richard L. 1984. *Joseph Smith and the Beginnings of Mormonism*. Urbana: University of Illinois Press.

Butler, Jon. 1982. "Enthusiasm Described and Decried: The Great Awakenings as Interpretative Fiction." *Journal of American History* 69:305–25.

Bynum, Caroline Walker. 1982. *Jesus as Mother: Studies in the Spirituality of the High Middle Ages*. Berkeley and Los Angeles: University of California Press.

Caird, Edward. 1899. *The Evolution of Religion*. 3d ed. 2 vols. Glasgow: James Maclehose and Sons.

Calvin, John. [1559] 1989. *Institutes of the Christian Religion*. Grand Rapids, MI: Eerdmans.

———. [1555] 1980. *John Calvin's Sermons on the Ten Commandments*. Grand Rapids, MI: Baker Book House.

Caplow, Theodore. 1968. *Two Against One: Coalitions in Triads*. Englewood Cliffs, NJ: Prentice-Hall.

Capps, Donald, and Michael Carroll. 1988. "Interview." *Journal for the Scientific Study of Religion* 27:429–41.

Carden, Paul. 1998. "Cults and New Religious Movements in the Former Soviet Union." *East-West Church and Ministry Report*. 6 (Summer): 1–5).

Carroll, Michael P. 1987. "Praying the Rosary: The Anal-Erotic Origins of a Popular Catholic Devotion." *Journal for the Scientific Study of Religion* 26:486–98.

Cartwright, Frederick F. 1972. *Disease and History*. New York: Dorset Press.

Chatterjee, Sunil Kumar. 1984. *William Carey and Serampore*. Calcutta: Gosh Publishing Concern.

Chazan, Robert. 2000. *God, Humanity, and History: The Hebrew First Crusade Narratives*. Berkeley and Los Angeles: University of California Press.

———. 1996. *In the Year 1096: The First Crusade and the Jews*. Philadelphia: The Jewish Publication Society.

———. 1989. *Daggers of Faith: Thirteenth Century Christian Missionizing and Jewish Response*. Berkeley and Los Angeles: University of California Press.

———. 1986. *European Jewry and the First Crusade*. Berkeley and Los Angeles: University of California Press.

———, ed. 1980. *Church, State, and Jew in the Middle Ages* (a collection of original sources). West Orange, NJ: Behrman House.

Chee-Beng, Tan. 1994. "Chinese Religion: Continuity, Transformation, and Identity with Special Reference to Malaysia." In *Religions Sans Frontières?*, edited by Roberto Cipriani, 257–89. Rome: Dipartimento per L'Informazione e Editoria.

Cheetham, Nicolas. 1983. *Keepers of the Keys: A History of Popes from St. Peter to John Paul II*. New York: Scribner's.

Chen, Hsinchih. 1995. "The Development of Taiwanese Folk Religion, 1683–1945." Ph.D. diss., Department of Sociology, University of Washington.

Ch'en, Kenneth K. S. 1964. *Buddhism in China: A Historical Survey*. Princeton, NJ: Princeton University Press.

Christiansen, Eric. 1980. *The Northern Crusades: The Baltic and the Catholic Frontier, 1100–1525*. Minneapolis: University of Minnesota Press.

Clarke, Catherine Goddard. 1950. *The Loyolas and the Cabots: The Story of the Boston Heresy*. Boston: Ravengate Press.

Clarke, Peter B. 1999. "'Pop Star' Priests and the Catholic Response to the 'Explosion' of Evangelical Protestantism in Brazil: The Beginning of the End of the 'Walkout'?" *Journal of Contemporary Religion* 14:203–16.

Clendenin, Daniel B., ed. 1995. *Eastern Orthodox Theology: A Contemporary Reader*. Grand Rapids, MI: Baker Books.

Clough, Bradley S. 1997. "Buddhism." In *God*, edited by Jacob Neusner, 56–84. Cleveland: The Pilgrim Press.

Cohen, Gershon D. 1967. "Messianic Postures of Ashkenazim and Sephardim (Pior to Sabbatai Zevi)." In *Studies of the Leo Baeck Institute*, edited by Max Kreutzberger, 117–56. New York.

Cohen, Mark. 1996. "Islam and the Jews: Myth, Counter-Myth, History." In *Jews among Muslims: Communities in the Precolonial Middle East*, edited by Shlomo Deshen and Walter P. Zenner, 50–63. London: Macmillan.

———. 1994. *Under Crescent and Cross: The Jews in the Middle Ages*. Princeton, NJ: Princeton University Press.

Cohen, Shaye J. D. 1992. "Was Judaism in Antiquity a Missionary Religion?" In *Studies in Jewish Civilization—2*, edited by Menachem Mor, 14–23. New York: University Press of America.

———. 1990. "Religion, Ethnicity, and 'Hellenism' in the Emergence of Jewish Identity in Maccabean Palestine." In *Religion and Religious Practice in the Seleucid Kingdon*, edited by Per Bilde, Troels Engberg-

Pedersen, Lise Hannestad, and Jan Zahle, 205–23. Aarhus (Denmark): Aarhus University Press.

———. 1987. *From the Maccabees to the Mishnah*. Philadelphia: The Westminster Press.

Cohn, Norman. 1961. *The Pursuit of the Millennium*. 2d ed. New York: Harper Torchbooks.

Coleman, James S. 1990. *Foundations of Social Theory*. Cambridge: Harvard University Press, Belknap Press.

———. 1956. "Social Cleavage and Religious Conflict." *Journal of Social Issues* 12:44–56.

Collins, John J. 1983. *Between Athens and Jerusalem: Jewish Identity in the Hellenistic Diaspora*. New York: Crossroad.

Collins, Randall. 1998. *A Sociology of Philosophies: A Global Theory of Intellectual Change*. Cambridge: Harvard University Press.

Comte, Auguste. [1830] 1896. *The Positive Philosophy*. Translated and edited by Harriet Martineau. London: George Bell and Sons.

Cooley, John K. 1965. *Baal, Christ, and Mohammed: Religion and Revolution in North Africa*. New York: Holt, Rinehart and Winston.

Corrigan, John A., Carlos M. N. Eire, Frederick M. Denny, and Martin S. Jaffee. 1998. *Readings in Judaism, Christianity, and Islam*. Upper Saddle River, NJ: Prentice-Hall.

Costen, Michael. 1997. *The Cathars and the Albigensian Crusade*. Manchester: Manchester University Press.

Cowling, T. G. 1977. *Isaac Newton and Astrology: The Eighteenth Selig Brodestsky Memorial Lecture*. Leeds: Leeds University Press.

Cox, Harvey. 1983. "Interview." In *Hare Krishna, Hare Krishna*, edited by Steven J. Gelberg, 21–60. New York: Grove Press.

Coxill, H. Wakelin, and Sir Kenneth Grubb. 1967. *World Christian Handbook*. London: Lutterworth Press.

Cragg, Gerald R. 1964. *Reason and Authority in the Eighteenth Century*. Cambridge: Cambridge University Press.

Creasy, Edward Shepherd. [1852] 1987. *Fifteen Decisive Battles of the World*. New York: Dorset Press.

Cuddihy, John Murray. 1978. *No Offense: Civil Religion and Protestant Taste*. New York: Seabury Press.

Cumont, Franz. [1912] 1960. *Astrology and Religion among the Greeks and Romans*. New York: Dover Publications.

———. [1911] 1956. *Oriental Religions in Roman Paganism*. New York: Dover Publications.

Daiber, Karl-Fritz. 1996. "Religion and Modernity in Germany." *Social Compass* 43:411–23.

Danzger, M. Herbert. 1989. *Returning to Tradition: The Contemporary Revival of Orthodox Judaism*. New Haven: Yale University Press.

Davidman, Lynn. 1991. *Tradition in a Rootless World: Women Turn to Orthodox Judaism*. Berkeley and Los Angeles: University of California Press.

Davie, Grace. 1994. *Religion in Britain since 1945: Believing without Belonging*. Oxford: Blackwell.

Davies, Norman. 1996. *Europe: A History*. Oxford: Oxford University Press.

Davis, Kingsley. 1949. *Human Society*. New York: Macmillan.

Delumeau, Jean. 1977a. *Christianisme va-t-il mourir?* Paris: Hachette.

———. 1977b. *Catholicism between Luther and Voltaire*. Philadelphia: Westminster Press.

Denny, Frederick M. 1993. "Islam and the Muslim Community." In *Religious Traditions of the World*, edited by H. Byron Earhart, 605–712. San Franciso: HarperSanFrancisco.

De Rue, Martine. 1998. "The Missionaries: The First Contact between Paganism and Christianity." In *The Pagan Middle Ages*, edited by Ludo J. R. Milis, 13–37. Rochester, NY: The Boydell Press.

Derwacter, Frederick Milton. 1930. *Preparing the Way for Paul: The Proselyte Movement in Later Judaism*. New York: Macmillan.

Deshen, Shlomo, and Walter P. Zenner, eds. 1996. *Jews among Muslims: Communities in the Precolonial Middle East*. London: Macmillan.

De Swann, Abram. 1973. *Coalition Theories and Cabinet Formations*. Amsterdam: Elsevier Scientific Publishing Co.

Dimont, Max I. [1962] 1994. *Jews, God and History*. New York: Mentor.

Dixon, Tomas. 1997. "Are Minority Churches Targets for Discrimination?" *Christianity Today* 41, no. 8:74.

Dodd, C. H. 1963. *Historical Tradition in the Fourth Gospel*. Cambridge: Cambridge University Press.

Dorn, Harold. 1991. *The Geography of Science*. Baltimore: Johns Hopkins University Press.

Douglas, Mary. 1975. *Implicit Meanings: Essays in Anthropology*. London: Routledge & Kegan Paul.

Drake, H. A. 2000. *Constantine and the Bishops: The Politics of Intolerance*. Baltimore: Johns Hopkins University Press.

Drummond, Richard Henry. 1971. *A History of Christianity in Japan*. Grand Rapids, MI: Eerdmans.

Dubnov, S. M. 1920. *History of the Jews in Russia and Poland: From Earliest Times until the Present Day*. 2 vols. Philadelphia: The Jewish Publication Society of America.

Duffy, Eamon. 1997. *Saints and Sinners: A History of Popes*. New Haven: Yale University Press.

Dulles, Avery, S.J. 1992. *Models of Revelation*. Maryknoll, NY: Orbis Books.

Durant, Will and Ariel. 1967. *Rousseau and Revolution*. New York: Simon and Schuster.

Durkheim, Emile. 1915. *The Elementary Forms of the Religious Life*. London: George Allen and Unwin.

———. [1915] 1995. *The Elementary Forms of the Religious Life*. Translated by Karen E. Fields. New York: The Free Press.

———. [1886] 1994. "Review of Part VI of the *Principles of Sociology* by Herbert Spencer." *Revue philosophique de la France et de l'étranger* 21:61–69. Translated and published by W.S.F. Pickering, *Durkheim on Religion*. Atlanta: Scholars Press, 13–23.

Dutt, Sukumar. 1962. *Buddhist Monks and Monasteries of India*. London: Allen and Unwin.

Earhart, H. Byron. 1993. "Religions of Japan: Many Traditions, One Sacred Way." In *Religious Traditions of the World*, edited by H. Byron Earhart, 1077–1187. San Francisco: HarperSanFrancisco.

———. 1984. *Religions of Japan*. San Francisco: HarperSanFrancisco.

Eber, Irene. 1999. "Kaifeng Jews: The Sinification of Identity." In *The Jews of China*, vol. 1, *Historical and Comparative Perspectives*, edited by Jonathan Goldstein, 22–35. Armonk, NY: M. E. Sharpe.

Edbury, Peter. 1999. "Warfare in the Latin East." In *Medieval Warfare: A History*, edited by Maurice Keen, 89–112. Oxford: Oxford University Press.

Eddy, Sherwood. 1945. *Pathfinders of the World Missionary Crusade*. New York: Abingdon-Cokesbury Press.

Edelman, Diana Vikander, ed. 1996. *The Triumph of Elohim: From Yahwisms to Judaisms*. Grand Rapids, MI: Eerdmans.

Eichhorn, Werner. 1959. "Taoism." In *The Concise Encyclopaedia of Living Faiths*, edited by R. C. Zaehner, 385–401. Boston: Beacon.

Eidelberg, Shlomo. 1977. *The Jews and the Crusaders: The Hebrew Chronicles of the First and Second Crusades*. Madison: University of Wisconsin Press.

Eisenman, Robert. 1997. *James the Brother of Jesus*. New York: Viking.

Ellwood, Robert S. 1993. "A Japanese Mythic Trickster Figure: Susa-no-o." In *Mythical Trickster Figures: Contours, Contexts, and Criticisms,* edited by William J. Hynes and William G. Doty, 141–58. Tuscaloosa: University of Alabama Press.

Endelman, Todd M. 1987. *Jewish Apostasy in the Modern World.* New York: Holmes & Meier.

Eusebius. 1965. *The History of the Church.* Translated by G. A. Williamson. Harmondsworth, Middlesex: Penguin Books.

Evans-Pritchard, Sir Edward. 1967. *The Zande Trickster.* Oxford: Clarendon Press.

———. 1956. *Nuer Religion.* Oxford: Oxford University Press.

Everton, Sean. 1999. "The Promise Keepers: Religious Revival or Third Wave of the Religious Right." M.A. thesis, Department of Sociology, San Jose State University.

Farah, Caesar E. 1994. *Islam: Beliefs and Observances.* 5th ed. Hauppauge, NY: Barron's.

Feldman, Louis. 1993. *Jew and Gentile in the Ancient World: Attitudes and Interaction from Alexander to Justinian.* Princeton, NJ: Princeton University Press.

Ferrell, Arthur. 1986. *The Fall of the Roman Empire: The Military Explanation.* London: Thames and Hudson.

Feuerbach, Ludwig von. [1841] 1957. *The Essence of Christianity.* New York: Harper Torchbooks.

Filatov, Sergei. 1994. "On Paradoxes of the Post-Communist Russian Orthodox Church." In *Religions Sans Frontières?,* edited by Roberto Cipriani, 117–25. Rome: Dipartimento per L'Informazione e Editoria.

Finegan, Jack. 1992. *The Archeology of the New Testament.* Rev. ed. Princeton, NJ: Princeton University Press.

Finke, Roger, Avery M. Guest, and Rodney Stark. 1996. "Pluralism and Religious Participation: New York, 1855–1865." *American Sociological Review* 61:203–18.

Finke, Roger, and Rodney Stark. 1992. *The Churching of America, 1776–1990: Winners and Losers in Our Religious Economy.* New Brunswick, NJ: Rutgers University Press.

———. 1988. "Religious Economies and Sacred Canopies: Religious Mobilization in American Cities, 1906." *American Sociological Review* 53:41–49.

Firth, Raymond. 1996. *Religion: A Humanist Interpretation.* London: Routledge.

Fischel, W. J. 1969. *Jews in the Economic and Political Life of Mediaeval Islam*. New York: Ktav Publishing House.

Flannery, Edward H. 1985. *The Anguish of the Jews: Twenty-Three Centuries of Antisemistism*. Rev. ed. Mahwah, NJ: Paulist Press.

Fleming, Daniel Johnson. 1925. *Whither Bound in Missions?* New York: Association Press.

Fletcher, Richard. 1997. *The Barbarian Conversion: From Paganism to Christianity*. New York: Henry Holt.

———. 1992. *Moorish Spain*. Berkeley and Los Angeles: University of California Press.

Fortune, Reo F. 1935. "Manus Religion." *Memoirs of the American Philosophical Society* 3.

Fowler, Jeaneane. 1997. *Hinduism: Beliefs and Practices*. Brighton: Sussex Academica Press.

Fox, Robin Lane. 1987. *Pagans and Christians*. New York: Knopf.

Foy, Felician A., and Rose M. Avato, eds. 1987. *1987 Catholic Almanac*. Huntington, IN: Our Sunday Visitor Publishing Co.

Frazer, Sir James George. 1927. *Man, God and Immortality: Thoughts on Human Progress*. New York: Macmillan.

———. 1922. *The Golden Bough*. New York: Macmillan.

Freedom House. 1995. *Freedom in the World*. New York: Freedom House.

Frend, W.H.C. 1984. *The Rise of Christianity*. Philadelphia: Fortress Press.

———. 1965. *Martyrdom and Persecution in the Early Church*. Oxford: Basil Blackwell.

Freud, Sigmund. [1939] 1957. *Moses and Monotheism*. New York: Vantage Books.

———. [1927] 1961. *The Future of an Illusion*. Garden City, NY: Doubleday.

Fück, J. [1936] 1981. "The Originality of the Prophet." Translated from German in *Studies in Islam*, edited by Merlin L. Swartz, 86–98. New York: Oxford University Press.

Gager, John G. 1983. *The Origins of Anti-Semitism: Attitudes towards Judaism in Pagan and Christian Antiquity*. New York: Oxford University Press.

Gallup International. 1984. *Human Values and Beliefs*. London: Scholarly Resources.

Gaskoin, C.J.B. [1904] 1966. *Alcuin: His Life and His Work*. New York: Russell and Russell.

Geertz, Clifford. 1960. *The Religion of Java*. Glencoe, IL: The Free Press.

———. 1956. *The Development of the Japanese Economy*. Boston: Center for International Studies, MIT.

Geertz, Hildred. 1963. "Indonesian Cultures and Communities." In *Indonesia*, edited by Ruth T. McVey, 24–96. New Haven, CT: HRAF Press.

Genovese, Eugene. 1965. *The Political Economy of Slavery: Studies in the Economy and Society of the Slave South*. New York: Pantheon.

Georgi, Dieter. 1995. "The Early Church; Internal Migration of New Religion." *Harvard Theological Review* 88:35–68.

———. 1986. *The Opponents of Paul in Second Corinthians*. Philadelphia: Fortress.

Gibbon, Edward. [1788] 1994. *The History of the Decline and Fall of the Roman Empire*. 3 vols. London: Allen Lane, The Penguin Press.

Gidal, Nachum T. 1988. *Jews in Germany: From Roman Times to the Weimar Republic*. Cologne: Könemann.

Gifford, Paul. 1998. *African Christianity: Its Public Role*. Bloomington: Indiana University Press.

Gill, Anthony. 1999. "The Struggle to Be Soul Provider: Catholic Responses to Protestant Growth in Latin America." In *Latin American Religion in Motion*, edited by Christian Smith, 1–31. New York: Routeldge.

———. 1998. *Rendering unto Caesar: The Roman Catholic Church and the State in Latin America*. Chicago: University of Chicago Press.

Gilliam, J. F. 1961. "The Plague under Marcus Aurelius." *American Journal of Philology* 94:243–55.

Gillingham, John. 1999. "An Age of Expansion: c.1020–1204." In *Medieval Warfare: A History*, edited by Maurice Keen, 59–88. Oxford: Oxford University Press.

Gillman, Neil. 1997. *The Death of Death: Resurrection and Immortality in Jewish Thought*. Woodstock, VT: Jewish Lights Publishing.

Ginzberg, Louis. [1911] 1939. *The Legends of the Jews*. Vols. 2 and 3. Philadelphia: The Jewish Publication Society.

Gitlitz, David M. 1996. *Secrecy and Deceit: The Religion of the Crypto-Jews*. Philadelphia: The Jewish Publication Society.

Glazer, Nathan. 1957. *American Judaism*. Chicago: University of Chicago Press.

Glenn, Charles L., Jr. 1987. *The Myth of the Common School*. Amherst: University of Massachusetts Press.

Glock, Charles Y. 1959. "The Religious Revival in America." In *Religion and the Face of America*, edited by Jane Zahn, 25–42. Berkeley and Los Angeles: University of California Press.

Glock, Charles Y., and Rodney Stark. 1966. *Christian Beliefs and Anti-Semitism*. New York: Harper and Row.

Glock, Charles Y., and Robert Wuthnow. 1979. "Departures from Conventional Religion." In *The Religious Dimension*, edited by Robert Wuthnow, 47–68. New York: Academic Press.

Goiten, S.D. 1964. *Jews and Arabs: Their Contact through the Ages*. New York: Schocken Books.

Goldman, Marion S. 1999. *Passionate Journeys: Why Successful Women Joined a Cult*. Ann Arbor: University of Michigan Press.

Goldstein, David B. 1999. Paper on the Cohen genetic signature among the Lemba. Read at a conference on human evolution, Cold Springs Harbor Laboratory, Long Island, New York.

Goldstein, Jonathan, ed. 1999. *The Jews of China*. Vol. 1, *Historical and Comparative Perspectives*. Armonk, NY: M. E. Sharpe.

Goldstein, Sidney. 1981. "Jews in the United States: Perspectives from Demography." *American Jewish Yearbook* 81:3–60.

Gombrich, Richard F. 1971. *Precept and Practice: Traditional Buddhism in the Rural Highlands of Ceylon*. Oxord: Clarendon Press.

Gomes, Peter J. 1996. "The New Liberation Theology." *Harvard Magazine* 99, no. 2:34–36.

Goodman, Martin. 1994. *Mission and Conversion: Proselytizing in the Religious History of the Roman Empire*. Oxford: Clarendon Press.

Gordon-McCutchan, R. C. 1983. "Great Awakenings." *Sociological Analysis* 44:83–95.

Graetz, Heinrich Hirsh. 1895. *History of the Jews*. Vol. 5. Philadelphia: The Jewish Publication Society of America.

———. 1894a. *History of the Jews*. Vol. 4. Philadelphia: The Jewish Publication Society of America.

———. 1894b. *History of the Jews*. Vol. 3. Philadelphia: The Jewish Publication Society of America.

Grant, Michael. 1981. *Dawn of the Middle Ages*. New York: McGraw-Hill.

———. 1978. *History of Rome*. London: Faber and Faber.

———. 1973. *The Jews in the Roman World*. New York: Charles Scribner's Sons.

Grant, Robert M. 1977. *Early Christianity and Society: Seven Studies.* San Francisco: Harper and Row.

Greeley, Andrew M. 1995. *Religion as Poetry.* New Brunswick, NJ: Transaction.

———. 1989. *Myths of Religion.* New York: Warner Books.

———. 1988. "Evidence That a Maternal Image of God Correlates with Liberal Politics." *Sociology and Social Research* 72:150–54.

———. 1983. "Religious Imagination Questions in the GSS—A Note for Interested Parties." *National Opinion Research Center Report.* Chicago: NORC.

———. 1975. *Sociology of the Paranormal: A Reconnaissance.* Beverly Hills: Sage.

Green, Ronald M. 1988. *Religion and Moral Reason: A New Method for Comparative Study.* New York: Oxford University Press.

Griffiths, Nicholas. 1996. *The Cross and the Serpent: Religious Repression and Resurgence in Colonial Peru.* Norman: University of Oklahoma Press.

Grosser, Paul E., and Edwin G. Halpern. 1983. *Anti-Semitism: Causes and Effects. An Analysis and Chronology of Nineteen Hundred Years of Anti-Semitic Attitudes and Practices.* New York: The Philosophical Library.

Grubb, Kenneth G., and E. J. Bingle, eds. 1949. *World Christian Handbook.* London: World Dominion Press.

Guthrie, Stewart Elliott. 1996. "Religion: What Is It?" *Journal for the Scientific Study of Religion* 35:412–19.

Hamberg, Eva M. 1999. "Migration and Religious Change." In *Religion and Social Transitions* (publication 95), edited by Elia Helander. Helsinki: University of Helsinki Department of Practical Theology.

———. 1995. "World-views and Value Systems among Immigrants: Long-term Stability or Change? A Study of Hungarian Immigrants in Sweden." *Sociale Wetenschappen* 38, no. 4:85–108

Hamilton, Bernard. 1981. *The Medieval Inquisition.* New York: Holmes and Meier.

Hammond, Phillip E. 1989. "Constitutional Faith, Legitimating Myth, Civil Religion." *Law and Social Inquiry* 14:377–91.

Handlin, Oscar. 1951. "How U.S. Anti-Semitism Really Began." *Commentary* 11 (June): 541.

Handy, Lowell K. 1996. "The Appearance of Pantheon in Judah." In *The Triumph of Elohim: From Yahwisms to Judaisms*, edited by Diana Vikander Edelman, 27–43. Grand Rapids, MI: Eerdmans.

Hannah, Ian C. 1924. *Christian Monasticism: A Great Force in History*. London: George Allen & Unwin.

Hanson, J. W., ed. 1894. *The World's Parliament of Religions*. Chicago: International Publishing Co.

Harnack, Adolph von. [1908] 1962. *The Mission and Expansion of Christianity in the First Three Centuries*. Translated by James Moffatt. 2 vols. New York: G. P. Putnam's Sons.

Hechter, Michael, and Satoshi Kanazawa. 1997. "Sociological Rational Choice Theory." *Annual Review of Sociology* 23:191–214.

Hennesey, James, S.J. 1981. *American Catholics: A History of the Roman Catholic Community in the United States*. New York: Oxford University Press.

Herberg, Will. [1955] 1960. *Protestant—Catholic—Jew: An Essay in American Religious Sociology*. Garden City, NY: Doubleday.

Herodotus. [Ca. 450 B.C.E.] 1987. *The History*. Translated by David Grene. Chicago: University of Chicago Press.

Hertz, Deborah. 1992. "Women at the Edge of Judaism: Female Converts in Germany, 1600–1750." In *Jewish Assimilation, Acculturation, and Accommodation*, edited by Menachem Mor, 87–109. Lanham, MD: University Press of America.

———. 1987. "Seductive Conversion in Berlin, 1770–1809." In *Jewish Apostasy in the Modern World*, edited by Todd M. Endleman, 48–82. New York: Holmes & Meier.

Hertzberg, Arthur. 1968. *The French Enlightenment and the Jews*. New York: Columbia University Press.

Hickey, Anne Ewing. 1987. *Women of the Roman Aristocracy as Christian Monastics*. Ann Arbon, MI: UMI Research Press.

Hillgarth, J. N., ed. 1986. *Christianity and Paganism 350–750: The Conversion of Western Europe*. Philadelphia: University of Pennsylvania Press.

Hiney, Tom. 2000. *On the Missionary Trail*. New York: Atlantic Monthly Press.

Hobbes, Thomas. [1651] 1968. *Leviathan*. London: Penguin.

Hocking, William Ernest. 1932. *Re-thinking Missions: A Layman's Inquiry after One Hundred Years* (report of the Commission of Appraisal, Laymen's Foreign Missions Inquiry). New York: Harper & Brothers.

———. 1912. *The Meaning of God in Human Experience: A Philosophic Study of Religion*. New Haven: Yale University Press.

Hodgson, Marshall G. S. 1974. *The Venture of Islam*. Vols. 1 and 2. Chicago: University of Chicago Press.

Holborn, Hajo. 1982. *A History of Modern Germany: The Reformation*. Princeton, NJ: Princeton University Press.

Homans, George. 1974. *Social Behavior: Its Elementary Forms*. Rev. ed. New York: Harcourt Brace Jovanovich.

———. 1941. "Anxiety and Ritual: The Theories of Malinowski and Radcliffe-Brown." *American Anthropologist* 43:164–72.

Honigmann, Peter. 1989. "Jewish Conversions—A Measure of Assimilation? A Discussion of the Berlin Secession Statistics of 1770–1940." *Leo Baeck Institute Yearbook*, 34:3–45. London: Secker & Warburg.

Hood, Ralph W., Jr. 1997. "The Empirical Study of Mysticism." In *The Psychology of Religion: Theoretical Approaches*, edited by Bernard Spilka and Daniel N. McIntosh, 222–32. Boulder, CO: Westview Press.

———. 1985. "Mysticism." In *The Sacred in a Secular Age*, edited by Phillip E. Hammond, 285–97. Berkeley and Los Angeles: University of California Press.

Hopkins, Mark. 1861. "Semi-Centennial Discourse." In *Memorial Volume of the First Fifty Years of the American Board of Commissioners for Foreign Missions*, 11–36. Boston: Missionary House.

Horbury, William. 1982. "The Benediction of the NINIM and Early Jewish-Christian Controversy." *Journal of Theological Studies* 20:245–64.

Horsley, Richard A. 1989. *Sociology and the Jesus Movement*. New York: Crossroad.

Housley, Norman. 1992. *The Later Crusades, 1274–1580: From Lyons to Alcazar*. Oxford: Oxford University Press.

Howell, Julia Day. 1997. "ASC Induction Techniques, Spiritual Experiences, and Commitment to New Religious Movements." *Sociology of Religion* 58:141–64.

Hume, David. 1754. *The History of England*. 6 vols. London: A. Millar.

———. [1748] 1962. *Inquiry Concerning Human Understanding*. New York: Macmillan.

Hutchison, Ralph Cooper. 1927. "Christianity and Proselytism." *Atlantic Monthly* 140 (November): 620–25.

Hutchison, William R. 1987. *Errand to the World: American Protestant Thought and Foreign Missions*. Chicago: University of Chicago Press.

Hynes, William J., and William G. Doty, eds. 1993. *Mythical Trickster Figures: Contours, Contexts, and Criticisms*. Tuscaloosa: University of Alabama Press.

Iannaccone, Laurence R. 1995. "Risk, Rationality, and Religious Portfolios." *Economic Inquiry* 33:285–95.

———. 1990. "Religious Practice: A Human Capital Approach." *Journal for the Scientific Study of Religion* 29:297–314.

———. 1988. "A Formal Model of Church and Sect." *American Journal of Sociology* 94 (supplement): S241–S268.

Inglehart, Ronald. 1997. *Modernization and Postmodernization: Cultural, Economic, and Political Change in Forty-Three Societies*. Princeton, NJ: Princeton University Press.

Introvigne, Massimo. 1997. "Religious Liberty in Western Europe." *ISKCON Communications Journal 5*, no. 2:37–48.

Isaac, Jules. 1971. *Jesus and Israel*. New York: Holt, Rinehart, and Winston.

———. 1964. *The Teaching of Contempt: Christian Roots of Anti-Semitism*. New York: Holt, Rinehart, and Winston.

James, E. O. 1960. *The Ancient Gods: The History and Diffusion of Religion in the Ancient Near East and the Eastern Meditarranean*. New York: G. P. Putnam's Sons.

James, Edward. 1988. *The Franks*. Oxford: Basil Blackwell.

Johansen, Alf. 1983. "The Russian Orthodox Church as Reflected in Orthodox and Atheist Publications in the Soviet Union." *Occasional Papers on Religion in Eastern Europe* 3, no. 2:1–26.

Johnson, Benton. 1963. "On Church and Sect." *American Sociological Review* 28:539–49.

Johnson, Patrick. 1993. *Operation World*. Grand Rapids, MI: Zondervan Publishing House.

Johnson, Paul. 1976. *A History of Christianity*. New York: Atheneum.

Johnstone, Patrick. 1993. *Operation World*. Carlisle, PA: OM Publishing.

Jolly, Karen Louise. 1996. *Popular Religion in Late Saxon England*. Chapel Hill: University of North Carolina Press.

Jones, Gwyn. 1968. *A History of the Vikings*. London: Oxford University Press.

Judah, J. Stillson. 1974. *Hare Krishna and the Counterculture*. New York: Wiley.

Kaelber, Lutz. 1998. *Schools of Asceticism: Ideology and Organization in Medieval Religious Communities*. University Park: Pennsylvania State University Press.

Kahler, Erich. 1967. "The Jews and the Germans." In *Studies of the Leo Baeck Institute*, edited by Max Kreutzberger, 19–43. New York: Frederick Ungar Publishing Co.

Kane, J. Herbert. 1971. *A Global View of Christian Missions from Pentecost to the Present.* Grand Rapids, MI: Baker Book House.

Kane, P. V. 1953. *History of Dharmasastra.* Vol. 3. Poona: Bhandarkar Oriental Research Institute.

Kant, Immanuel. 1929. *Kant Selections.* Edited by Theodore Meyer Greene. New York: Charles Scribner's Sons.

Kaplan, Steven, Tudor Parfitt, and Emanuela Trevisan Semi, eds. 1995. *Beteween Africa and Zion.* Jerusalem: Ben-Zvi Institute.

Karmiris, John. 1973. "Concerning the Sacraments." In *Eastern Orthodox Theology: A Contemporary Reader,* edited by Daniel B. Clendenin, 21–31. Grand Rapids, MI: Baker Books, 1995.

Katz, Jacob. 1961. *Tradition and Crisis: Jewish Society at the End of the Middle Ages.* New York: The Free Press.

Katz, Steven T. 1994. *The Holocaust in Historical Context.* Vol. 1. New York: Oxford University Press.

———. 1984. "Issues in the Separation of Judaism and Christianity after 70 C.E.: A Reconsideration." *Journal of Biblical Literature* 103:43–76.

Kaufmann, Yehezkel. 1960. *The Religion of Israel.* Chicago: University of Chicago Press.

Kayser, Rudolf. 1949. *The Life and Times of Jehudah Halevi.* New York: Philosophical Library.

Keith, Graham. 1997. *Hated without a Cause? A Survey of Anti-Semitism.* Carlisle (UK): Paternoster Press.

Kelley, Dean M. 1972. *Why Conservative Churches Are Growing.* New York: Harper and Row.

Khomiakov, Aleksei. 1895. "The Church Is One." In *Russia and the English Church in the Last Fifty Years,* edited by W. J. Birbeck, 201–37. London: Rivington.

Kieckhefer, Richard. 1989. *Magic in the Middle Ages.* Cambridge: Cambridge University Press.

Klugel, James L. 1997. *The Bible As It Was.* Cambridge: Harvard University Press.

Knipe, David. M. 1993. "Hinduism: Experiments in the Sacred." In *Religious Traditions of the World,* edited by H. Byron Earhart, 713–840. San Francisco: HarperSanFrancisco.

Knowles, David. 1969. *Christian Monasticism.* New York: McGraw-Hill.

Koester, Helmut. 1982. *History and Literature of Early Christianity.* Vol. 2 of *Introduction to the New Testament.* New York: Walter de Gruyter.

Kokosalakis, Nikos. 1994. "The Historical Continuity of Cultural Specificity of Eastern Orthodox Christianity." In *Religions Sans Frontières?,* edited by Roberto Cipriani, 126–43. Rome: Dipartimento per L'Informazione e Editoria.

Kosmin, Barry A., Sidney Goldstein, Joseph Waksberg, Nava Lerer, Ariella Keysar, and Jeffrey Scheckner. 1991. *Highlights of the CJF 1990 National Jewish Population Survey.* New York: The Council of Jewish Federations.

Krindatch, A. D. 1995. "Geography of Religions in Russia." Paper presented at the meetings of the Society for the Scientific Study of Religion.

Kristol, Irving. 1949. "Review." *Commentary* 8 (July): 101.

Kublin, Hyman, ed. 1971. *Jews in Old China: Some Western Views.* New York: Paragon.

Kuhn, Thomas S. 1962. *The Structure of Scientific Revolutions.* Chicago: University of Chicago Press.

La Barre, Weston. 1969. *They Shall Take Up Serpents.* New York: Schocken.

Lambert, Frank. 1990. "'Peddlar in Divinity': George Whitefield and the Great Awakening, 1737–1745." *Journal of American History* 77:812–37.

Lambert, Malcolm. 1992. *Medieval Heresy.* Oxford: Basil Blackwell.

Lamotte, Etienne. 1988. *History of Indian Buddhism.* Louvain: Publications Universitaires.

Lang, Andrew. 1901. *Myth, Ritual and Religion.* London: Longmans, Green & Co.

———. 1899. *Magic and Religion.* London: Longmans, Green & Co.

———. 1898. *The Making of Religion.* London: Longmans, Green & Co.

Lang, Graeme, and Lars Ragvold. 1993. *The Rise of a Refugee God: Hong Kong's Wong Tai Sin.* Oxford: Oxford University Press.

Lawrence, Peter. 1964. *Road Belong Cargo: A Study of the Cargo Movement in South Madang District, New Guinea.* Manchester: Manchester University Press.

Lea, H. C. 1967. *A History of the Inquisition in Spain.* New York: Macmillan.

Lechner, Frank J. 1991a. "The Case against Secularization; A Rebuttal." *Social Forces* 69:1103–19.

———. 1991b. "Religion, Law, and Global Order." In *Religion and the Global Order,* edited by Roland Robertson and William R. Garrett, 263–80. New York: Paragon.

Lee, Richard Wayne. 1995. "Strained Bedfellows: Pagans, New Agers, and 'Starchy Humanists' in Unitarian Universalism." *Sociology of Religion* 56:379–96.

Legge, J. D. 1965. *Indonesia*. Englewood Cliffs, NJ: Prentice-Hall.

Lenowitz, Harris. 1998. *The Jewish Messiahs: From Galilee to Crown Heights*. New York: Oxford University Press.

Leo, John. 1997. "Cultural Left Draws a Bead on Promise Keepers." *US News and World Report*, July 28, 18.

Leon, Harry J. [1960] 1995. *The Jews of Ancient Rome*. Peabody, MA: Hendrickson Publishers.

Leslie, Donald Daniel. 1972. *The Survival of the Chinese Jews*. Leiden: E. J. Brill.

Lester, Robert C. 1993. "Buddhism: The Path to Nirvana." In *Religious Traditions of the World*, edited by H. Byron Earhart, 847–971. San Francisco: HarperSanFrancisco.

Lewis, Bernard. 1984. *The Jews of Islam*. Princeton, NJ: Princeton University Press.

Lewis, C. S. [1949] 1980. *The Weight of Glory*. New York: Simon & Schuster.

Lichtheim, Miriam. 1976. *Ancient Egyptian Literature: A Book of Readings*. Berkeley and Los Angeles: University of California Press.

Lieberson, Stanley. 2000. *A Matter of Taste: How Names, Fashions, and Culture Change*. New Haven: Yale University Press.

Liederman, Lina Molokotos. 1995. "The Headscarf Affair: A Case Study of Religion, Society and Mass Media in Contemporary France." Thesis, Ecole Pratique des Hautes Etudes, Sorbonne.

Lienhardt, Godfrey. 1961. *Divinity and Experience: The Religion of the Dinka*. Oxford: Oxford University Press.

Linton, Ralph. 1936. *The Study of Man: An Introduction*. Englewood Cliffs, NJ: Prentice-Hall.

Lippmann, Walter. [1929] 1964. *A Preface to Morals*. New York: Time Incorporated.

Lixfeld, Hannjost. 1994. *Folklore and Facism*. Bloomington: Indiana University Press.

Lofland, John, and Rodney Stark. 1965. "Becoming a World-Saver: A Theory of Conversion to a Deviant Perspective." *American Sociological Review* 30:862–75.

Long, Emil J. 1953. *Two Thousand Years: A History of Anti-Semitism*. New York: Exposition Press.

Lourie, Elena. 1990. *Crusade and Colonisation: Muslims, Christians and Jews in Medieval Aragon*. Aldershot (UK): Variorum.

Luttwak, Edward N. 1976. *The Grand Strategy of the Roman Empire*. Baltimore: Johns Hopkins University Press.

Mack, Burton L. 1996. *Who Wrote the New Testament?: The Making of the Christian Myth*. San Francisco: HarperSanFrancisco.

MacKenzie, F. A. 1930. *The Russian Crufixion: The Full Story of the Persecution of Religion under Bolshevism*. London: Jarrolds.

MacMullen, Ramsay. 1984. *Christianizing the Roman Empire*. New Haven: Yale University Press.

———. 1981. *Paganism in the Roman Empire*. New Haven: Yale University Press.

Magnus, Shulamit S. 1997. *Jewish Emancipation in a German City, Cologne, 1798–1871*. Stanford, CA: Stanford University Press.

Maier, Christoph. 1994. *Preaching the Crusades: Mendicant Friars and the Cross in the Thirteenth Century*. Cambridge: Cambridge University Press.

Majumder, R. C. 1963. *Hindu Colonies in the Far East*. Calcutta: Mukhopadhyay.

Malinowski, Bronislaw. 1935. *The Foundations of Faith and Morals*. Oxford: Oxford University Press.

Mann, Vivian B. 1992. "Preface." In *Convivencia: Jews, Muslims, and Christians in Medieval Spain*, edited by Vivian B. Mann, Thomas G. Glock, and Jerrilyn D. Dodds. New York: George Braziller.

Marcus, Jacob R. 1969. *The Jew in the Medieval World*. New York: Atheneum.

Marshall, S.L.A. [1954] 1978. *Men against Fire: The Problem of Battle Command in Future War*. Gloucester, MA: Peter Smith.

Martin, David. 1991. "The Secularization Issue: Prospect and Retrospect." *British Journal of Sociology* 42:465–74.

———. 1990. *Tongues of Fire: The Explosion of Protestantism in Latin America*. Oxford: Basil Blackwell.

———. 1989. "Speaking in Latin Tongues." *National Review*, September 29, 30–35.

———. 1978. *A General Theory of Secularization*. New York: Harper & Row.

Marty, Martin E. 1958. *The New Shape of American Religion*. New York: Harper & Brothers.

Marx, Karl. [1843] 1960. *A World without Jews*. 4th enlarged ed. New York: Philosophical Library.

Marx, Karl (with Friedrich Engels). [1845] 1998. *The German Ideology*. Amherst, NY: Prometheus Books.

———. [1867–1894] 1954. *Capital*. Moscow: Foreign Languages Publishing House.

Marx, Karl, and Friedrich Engels. 1964. *On Religion*. New York: Schocken Books.

Mathew, C. V. 1987. *Neo-Hinduism: A Missionary Religion*. Kilpauk, Madras: Church Growth Research Centre.

Mathews, Shailer. 1921. *A History of New Testament Times in Palestine*. New York: The Macmillan Co.

Mauss, Armand L. 1981. "The Fading of the Pharaoh's Curse: The Decline and Fall of the Priesthood Ban against Blacks in the Mormon Church." *Dialogue* 41:10–45.

Mayer, Hans Eberhard. 1972. *The Crusades*. London: Oxford University Press.

Mayer, Henry. 1998. *All on Fire: William Lloyd Garrison and the Abolition of Slavery*. New York: St. Martin's Press.

Maynard, Theodore. 1941. *The Story of American Catholicism*. New York: Macmillan.

Mayr-Harting, Henry. 1993. "The West: The Age of Conversion (700–1050)." In *The Oxford History of Christianity*, edited by John McManners, 101–29. Oxford: Oxford University Press.

McBrien, Richard P. 1992. *Report on the Church*. San Francisco: HarperSanFrancisco.

McDonnell, Ernest W. 1954. *The Beguines and Beghards in Medieval Culture, with Special Emphasis on the Belgian Scene*. New Brunswick, NJ: Rutgers University Press.

McKnight, Scot. 1991. *A Light among the Gentiles: Jewish Missionary Activity in the Second Temple Period*. Minneapolis: Fortress.

McLellan, David. 1987. *Marxism and Religion*. New York: Harper & Row.

———, ed. 1977. *Karl Marx: Selected Writings*. Oxford: Oxford University Press.

McLoughlin, William G. 1978. *Revivals, Awakenings, and Reform*. Chicago: University of Chicago Press.

McNeill, William H. 1976. *Plagues and Peoples*. Garden City, NY: Doubleday.

Meeks, Wayne. 1993. *The Origins of Christian Morality: The First Two Centuries*. New Haven: Yale University Press.

———. 1983. *The First Urban Christians*. New Haven: Yale University Press.

Melton, J. Gordon. 1989. *The Encyclopedia of American Religions*. 3d ed. Detroit: Gale Research.

Melton, J. Gordon. 1988. "Testing Truisms about the 'Cults': Toward a New Perspective on Nonconventional Religion." Paper presented at the annual meetings of the American Academy of Religion, Chicago.

Mendes-Flohr, Paul, and Jehuda Reinharz. 1995. *The Jew in the Modern World: A Documentary History*. New York: Oxford University Press.

Metford, J.C.J. 1983. *Dictionary of Christian Lore and Legend*. London: Thames and Hudson.

Meyer, John W. 1980. "The World-Polity and the Authority of the Nation-State." In *Studies of a Modern World-System*, edited by Albert Bergesen, 109–37. New York: Academic Press.

Middleton, John, ed. 1967. *Gods and Rituals*. Austin: University of Texas Press.

Milis, Ludo J. R., ed. 1998. *The Pagan Middle Ages*. Rochester, NY: The Boydell Press.

Miller, Alan. 1997. "The Impact of Japanese Social Structure on Japanese Religion and Religious Behavior." Paper presented at the conference "Religion, Politics, and Economics: The New Paradigm," Seattle.

———. 1995. "A Rational Model of Religious Behavior in Japan." *Journal for the Scientific Study of Religion* 34:234–44.

Miller, Geoffrey P. 1994. "The Legal-Economic Approach to Biblical Interpretation." *Journal of Institutional and Theoretical Economics* 150:755–62.

Mills, J. P. 1922. *The Lhota Nagas*. London: Macmillan.

Mol, Hans. 1969. *Christianity in Chains*. Melbourne: Nelson.

Monad, Jacques. 1972. *Chance and Necessity*. London: Collins.

Monsma, Stephen V., and J. Christopher Soper. 1997. *The Challenge of Pluralism: Church and State in Five Democracies*. Lanham, MD: Rowman & Littlefield.

Montalvo, Jose Hinojosa. 1993. *The Jews of the Kingdom of Valencia: From Persecution to Expulsion, 1391–1492*. Jerusalem: The Magnes Press, The Hebrew University.

Mooney, James. 1896. *The Ghost Shirt Religion and the Sioux Outbreak of 1890*. Fourth annual report of the Bureau of Ethnology to the Secretary of the Smithsonian Institution. Washington, DC: U.S. Government Printing Office.

Moore, George Foot. 1927–1930. *Judaism in the First Centuries of the Christian Era*. 3 vols. Cambridge: Harvard University Press.

Moore, R. I. 1985. *The Origins of European Dissent*. Oxford: Basil Blackwell.

———. 1976. *The Birth of Popular Heresy.* New York: St. Martin's Press.

Moran, J. F. 1993. *The Japanese and the Jesuits.* London: Routledge.

Morganthau, Hans J. 1967. "The Tragedy of German-Jewish Liberalism." In *Studies of the Leo Baeck Institute,* edited by Max Kreutzberger, 47–58. New York: Frederick Ungar Publishing Co.

Muller, James Arthur. 1937. *Apostle of China: Samuel Isaac Joseph Schereschewsky 1831–1906.* New York: Morehouse Publishing Co.

Mulligan, Lotte. 1973. "Civil War Politics, Religion and the Royal Society." *Past and Present.* no. 59, reprinted in *The Intellectual Revolution of the Seventeenth Century,* edited by Charles Webster, 317–46. London: Routledge & Kegan Paul, 1974.

Mundy, John Hine. 1985. *The Repression of Catharism and Toulouse.* Toronto: Pontifical Institute of Mediaeval Studies.

Murdock, George Peter. 1981. *Atlas of World Cultures.* Pittsburgh: University of Pittsburgh Press.

———. 1949. *Social Structures.* New York: Macmillan.

Murdock, George Peter, and Douglas R. White. 1969. "The Standard Cross-Cultural Sample." *Ethnology* 8:329–69.

Murphy, Thomas W. 1996. "Re-Inventing Mormonism." *Sunstone* 29:177–92.

Murray, Alexander. 1972. "Piety and Impiety in Thirteenth-Century Italy." *Studies in Church History* 8:83–106.

Murray, John Courtney, S.J. 1960. *We Hold These Truths: Catholic Reflections on the American Proposition.* New York: Sheed and Ward.

———. 1942. "Christian Co-operation." *Theological Studies* 3:27–51.

Needham, Rodney. 1972. *Belief, Language and Experience.* Chicago: University of Chicago Press.

Neel, James V., et al. 1970. "Notes on the Effect of Measles and Measles Vaccine in a Virgin Soil Population of South American Indians." *American Journal of Epidemiology* 91:418–29.

Neill, Stephen. 1986. *A History of Christian Missions.* New York: Penguin Books.

Neitz, Mary Jo. 1987. *Charisma and Community: A Study of Religious Commitment within the Charismatic Renewal.* New Brunswick, NJ: Transaction.

Neitz, Mary Jo, and James V. Spickard. 1990. "Steps Toward a Sociology of Religious Experience: The Theories of Mihal Csikszentmihayi and Alfred Schutz." *Sociological Analysis* 51:15–33.

Nelson, John. 1992. "Shinto Ritual: Managing Chaos in Contemporary Japan." *Ethnos* 57:78–104.

Netanyahu, B. 1999. *The Marranos of Spain*. 3d ed. Ithaca: Cornell University Press.

Neusner, Jacob. 1984. *Judaism in the Beginning of Christianity*. Philadelphia: Fortress Press.

———. 1975. *First Century Judaism in Crisis*. Nashville: Abingdon Press.

Nickerson, Colin. 1999. "In Iceland, Spirits Are in the Material World." *Seattle Post-Intelligencer*, December 25, A12.

Niebuhr, H. Richard. 1929. *The Social Sources of Denominationalism*. New York: Henry Holt.

Niebuhr, Reinhold. 1958. *Pious and Secular America*. New York: Charles Scribner's Sons.

Niehr, Herbert. 1996. "The Rise of YHWH in Judahite and Israelite Religion: Methodological and Religio-Historical Aspects." In *The Triumph of Elohim: From Yahwisms to Judaisms*, edited by Diana Vikander Edelman, 45–72. Grand Rapids, MI: Eerdmans.

Nock, Arthur Darby. 1933. *Conversion: The Old and the New in Religion from Alexander the Great to Augustine of Hippo*. Oxford: Clarendon Press.

Norbeck, Edward. 1961. *Religion in Primitive Society*. New York: Harper.

Oberman, Heiko A. 1992. *Luther: Man between God and the Devil*. New York: Doubleday.

———. 1984. *The Roots of Anti-Semitism: In the Age of Renaissance and Reformation*. Philadelphia: Fortress Press.

———. 1963. *The Harvest of Medieval Theology*. Cambridge: Harvard University Press.

Oldenberg, Zoe. 1961. *Massacre at Montségur: A History of the Albigensian Crusade*. London: Weidenfeld and Nicolson.

Oppenheim, Janet. 1988. *The Other World: Spiritualism and Psychical Research in England, 1850–1914*. Cambridge: Cambridge University Press.

Ostow, Mortimer. 1990. "The Fundamentalist Phenomenon: A Psychological Perspective." In *The Fundamentalist Phenomenon: A View from within, a Response from Without*, edited by Norman J. Cohen, 99–125. Grand Rapids, MI: Eerdmans.

Oxtoby, Willard G. 1996a. "Traditions in Contact." In *World Religions: Western Traditions*, edited by Willard G. Oxtoby, 531–58. Oxford: Oxford University Press.

———. 1996b. "The Zoroastrian Tradition." In *World Religions: Western Traditions*, edited by Willard G. Oxtoby, 152–96. Oxford: Oxford University Press.

Padover, Saul K., ed. 1978. *The Essential Marx: The Non-Economic Writings—A Selection*. New York: New American Library.

Pagels, Elaine. 1995. *The Origin of Satan*. New York: Random House.

———. 1981. "The Orthodox against the Gnostics: Confrontation and Interiority in Early Christianity." In *The Other Side of God*, edited by Peter Berger, 61–73. Garden City, NY: Doubleday.

Parfitt, Tudor, and Emanuela Trevisan Semi, eds. 1999. *The Beta Israel in Ethiopia and Israel*. Surrey: Curzon Press.

Paris, Erna. 1995. *The End of Days: A Story of Tolerance, Tyranny, and the Expulsion of the Jews from Spain*. Amherst, NY: Prometheus Books.

Parker, Joseph I. 1938. *Interpretative Statistical Survey of the World Missions of the Christian Church*. New York: International Missionary Council.

Parkes, James. [1934] 1961. *The Conflict of the Church and the Synagogue: A Study of the Origins of Antisemitism*. Cleveland: World Publishing Company.

Parrinder, Geoffrey. 1983. *World Religions*. New York: Facts on File.

———. 1976. *Mysticism in the World's Religions*. New York: Oxford University Press.

Parsons, Talcott. [1937] 1949. *The Structure of Social Action*. Glencoe, IL: The Free Press.

Pásztor, János. 1995. "The Theology of the Serving Church and the Theology of Diaconia in the Protestant Churches and Their Consequences in Hungary during the Time of Socialism." *Religion in Eastern Europe* 15, no. 6:22–35.

Patai, Raphael. 1986. *The Seed of Abraham: Jews and Arabs in Contact and Conflict*. Salt Lake City: University of Utah Press.

Payne, Robert. 1984. *The Dream and the Tomb: A History of the Crusades*. New York: Stein and Day.

———. 1959. *The History of Islam*. New York: Barnes and Noble.

Pelikan, Jaroslav. 1996. *Mary through the Centuries: Her Place in the History of Culture*. New Haven: Yale University Press.

Peregrine, Peter. 1996. "The Birth of the Gods Revisited: A Partial Replication of Guy Swanson's (1960) Cross-Cultural Study of Religion." *Cross-Cultural Research* 30:84–122.

Perlmann, S. M. 1909. *The Jews in China*. London: Probsthain & Co.

Peters, Edward, ed. 1998. *The First Crusade: The Chronicle of Fulcher of Chartres and Other Source Materials*. 2d ed. Philadelphia: University of Pennsylvania Press.

Peters, F. E. 1994. *Muhammad and the Origins of Islam*. Albany: State University of New York Press.

Pirenne, Henri. [1936] 1958. *A History of Europe from the End of the Roman World in the West to the Beginnings of the Western States*. New York: Doubleday Anchor.

———. [1922] 1955. *Mohammed and Charlemagne*. New York: Barnes and Noble.

Plaks, Andrew H. 1999. "The Confucianization of the Kaifeng Jews: Interpretations of the Kaifeng Stelae Inscriptions." In *The Jews of China*, vol. 1, *Historical and Comparative Perspectives*, edited by Jonathan Goldstein, 36–49. Armonk, NY: M. E. Sharpe.

Poewe, Karla. 1999. "Scientific Neo-Paganism and the Extreme Right Then and Today." *Journal of Contemporary Religion* 14:387–400.

Poliakov, Léon. 1975. *The History of Anti-Semitism: From Voltaire to Wagner*. Vol. 3. London: Routledge & Kegan Paul.

———. 1973. *The History of Anti-Semitism: From Mohammed to the Marranos*. Vol. 2. New York: Vanguard Press.

———. 1965. *The History of Anti-Semitism: From the Time of Christ to the Court Jews*. Vol. 1. New York: Vanguard Press.

Pollak, Michael. 1998. *Mandarins, Jews, and Missionaries: The Jewish Experience in the Chinese Empire*. 3d ed. New York: Weatherhill.

Poloma, Margaret. 1987. *The Charismatic Movement: Is There a New Pentecost?* Boston: Twayne Publishers.

Poloma, Margaret, and George H. Gallup, Jr. 1991. *Varieties of Prayer: A Survey Report*. Philadelphia: Trinity Press International.

Pope, Earl A. 1992. "The Role of Religion in the Romanian Revolution." *Occasional Papers on Religion in Eastern Europe* 12, no. 2:1–18.

———. 1981. "The Romanian Orthodox Church." *Occasional Papers on Religion in Eastern Europe* 1, no. 3:1–17.

Porter, Larry C. 1988. "'The Field Is White Already to Harvest': Earliest Missionary Labors and the Book of Mormon." In *The Prophet Joseph: Essays on the Life and Mission of Joseph Smith*, edited by Larry C. Porter and Susan Easton Black, 73–89. Salt Lake City: Deseret Book Company.

Pospielovsky, Dimitry. 1997. "The 'Best Years' of Stalin's Church Policy (1942–1948) in the Light of Archival Documents." *Religion, State and Society* 25:139–62.

———. 1988. *Soviet Antireligious Campaigns and Persecutions*. New York: St. Martin's Press.

Pratt, Parley P. [1873] 1985. *The Autobiography of Parley P. Pratt.* Salt Lake City: Deseret Books.

Price, S.R.F. 1984. *Rituals and Power: The Roman Imperial Cult in Asia Minor.* Cambridge: Cambridge University Press.

Quinn, D. Michael. 1994. *The Mormon Hierarchy: Origins of Power.* Salt Lake City: Signature Books.

Radcliffe-Brown, A. R. 1952. *Structure and Function in Primitive Society.* Glencoe: The Free Press.

Radin, Paul. 1956. *The Trickster.* London: Routledge and Kegan Paul.

———. 1924. *Monotheism among Primitive Peoples.* London: George Allen & Unwin.

Radnitzsky, Gerard, and Peter Bernholz, eds. 1987. *Economic Imperialism: The Economic Approach Applied outside the Field of Economics.* New York: Paragon.

Rahman, Fazur. 1987. "Islam: An Overview." In *World Religions,* 342–56. New York: Macmillan Reference USA.

Rahner, Karl. 1975. "Theology. I. Nature." In *Encyclopedia of Theology: The Concise Sacramentum Mundi,* edited by Karl Rahner. New York: Seabury.

Raisin, Max. 1949. *A History of the Jews in Modern Times.* New York: Hebrew Publishing Co.

Read, Piers Paul. 1999. *The Templars.* London: Weidenfeld and Nicholson.

Redford, Donald B. 1984. *Akhenaten: The Heretic King.* Princeton, NJ: Princeton Univerity Press.

Reed, James. 1983. *The Missionary Mind and American East Asia Policy, 1911–1915.* Cambridge: Harvard University Press.

Reichard, Gladys A. 1950. *Navajo Religion.* 2 vols. New York: Pantheon Books.

Reuter, Timothy. 1999. "Carolingian and Ottonian Warfare." In *Medieval Warfare: A History,* edited by Maurice Keen, 13–35. Oxford: Oxford University Press.

Rhee, Song Nai. 1973. "Jewish Assimilation: The Case of the Chinese Jews." *Comparative Studies in Society and History* 15:115–26.

Ricklefs, M. C. 1979. "Six Centuries of the Islamization in Java." In *Conversion to Islam,* edited by Nehemia Levtzion, 100–128. New York: Holmes & Meier.

Riff, Michael Anthony. 1981. "Assimilation and Conversion in Bohemia: Secession from the Jewish Community of Prague 1868–1919." *Leo Baeck Institute Yearbook,* 28:73–88. London: Secker & Warburg.

Riley-Smith, Jonathan. 1987. *The Crusades: A Short History*. London: The Athlone Press.

Robbins, Thomas. 1988. *Cults, Converts and Charisma: The Sociology of Religious Movements*. Beverly Hills: Sage.

Roberts, Keith A. 1995. *Religion in Sociological Perspective*. Belmont, CA: Wadsworth.

Robertson, Roland. 1992. *Globalization: Social Theory and Global Culture*. London: Sage.

———. 1985. "The Sacred and the World-System." In *The Sacred in a Secular Age*, edited by Phillip E. Hammond, 347–58. Berkeley and Los Angeles: University of California Press.

Robertson, Roland, and William R. Garrett, eds. 1991. *Religion and the Global Order*. New York: Paragon.

Robinson, Charles Henry. 1923. *History of Christian Missions*. New York: Charles Scribner's Sons.

———. 1917. *The Conversion of Europe*. London: Longmans, Green, and Co.

Robinson, John A. T. 1985. *The Priority of John*. London: SCM Press.

Rodinson, Maxime. 1980. *Muhammad*. New York: Pantheon Books.

Roetzel, Calvin J. *The World That Shaped the New Testament*. Philadelphia: The Westminster Press.

Rohl, David M. 1995. *Pharaohs and Kings: A Biblical Quest*. New York: Crown Publishers.

Ross, Andrew. 1994. *A Vision Betrayed: The Jesuits in Japan and China, 1542–1742*. Maryknoll, NY: Orbis Books.

Ross, Dan. 1982. *Acts of Faith: A Journey to the Fringes of Jewish Identity*. New York: St. Martin's Press.

Ross, Freda. 1995. "The Krishna Movement in Hungary." *Religion, State, and Society* 23:207–12.

Roth, Cecil. 1965. *A History of Jews in England*. Oxford: Clarendon Press.

———. 1963. *World History of the Jewish People*. Vol. 11. New Brunswick, NJ: Rutgers University Press.

———. 1959. *A Short History of the Jewish People*. London: East and West Library.

———. 1930. *The Jews in the Renaissance*. Philadelphia: Jewish Publication Society of America.

Rozenblit, Marsha L. 1983. *The Jews of Vienna, 1867–1914: Assimilation and Identity*. Albany, NY: State University of New York Press.

Ruether, Rosemary. 1974. *Faith and Fratricide: The Theological Roots of Anti-Semitism*. New York: Seabury Press.

Runciman, Sir Steven. 1951. *A History of the Crusades*. 3 vols. Cambridge: Cambridge University Press.

Runes, Dagobart. 1968. *The War against the Jews*. New York: Philosophical Library.

Ruppin, Arthur. 1934. *The Jews in the Modern World*. London: Macmillan.

Russell, J. C. 1958. *Late Ancient and Medieval Population*. Published as vol. 48, pt. 3, of the *Transactions of the American Philosophical Society*. Philadelphia: American Philosophical Society.

Russell, Jeffrey Burton. 1977. *The Devil: Perceptions of Evil from Antiquity to Primitive Christianity*. Ithaca: Cornell University Press.

———. 1971. *Religious Dissent in the Middle Ages*. New York: Wiley.

———. 1965. *Dissent and Reform in the Early Middle Ages*. Berkeley and Los Angeles: University of California Press.

Salahi, M. A. 1995. *Muhammad: Man and Prophet*. Shaftesbury: Element.

Sawyer, P. H. 1982. *Kings and Vikings: Scandinavia and Europe AD 700–1100*. London: Methuen.

Schäfer, Peter. 1997. *Judeophobia: Attitudes toward the Jews in the Ancient World*. Cambridge: Harvard University Press.

Scharfstein, Ben-Ami. 1973. *Mystical Experience*. Indianapolis: Bobbs-Merrill.

Schmidt, Wilhelm. 1931. *The Origin and Growth of Religion*. London: Methuen.

Schneiderman, Leo. 1967. "Psychological Notes on the Nature of Mystical Experience." *Journal for the Scientific Study of Religion* 6:91–100.

Seager, Richard Hughes, ed. 1993. *The Dawn of Religious Pluralism: Voices from the World's Parliament of Religions*. La Salle, IL: Open Court Press.

Seielstad, Mark T., Eric Minch, and L. Luca Cavalli-Sforza. 1998. "Genetic Evidence for a Higher Female Migration Rate in Humans." *Nature Genetics* 20 (November): 278–80.

Selthoffer, Steve. 1997. "German Government Harasses Charismatic Christians." *Charisma*, June, 22–24.

Seznec, Jean. [1953] 1972. *The Survival of the Pagan Gods: The Mythological Tradition and Its Place in Renaissance Humanism and Art*. Princeton, NJ: Princeton University Press.

Shahar, Meir, and Robert P. Weller, eds. 1996. *Unruly Gods: Divinity and Society in China*. Honolulu: University of Hawaii Press.

Sharot, Stephen. 1982. *Messianism, Mysticism, and Magic: A Sociological Analysis of Jewish Religious Movements*. Chapel Hill: University of North Carolina Press.

Sherkat, Darren E. 1997. "Embedding Religious Choices: Integrating Preferences and Social Constraints into Rational Choice Theories of Religious Behavior." In *Rational Choice Theory and Religion*, edited by Lawrence A. Young, 65–85. New York: Routledge.

Sherkat, Darren E., and John Wilson. 1995. "Preferences, Constraints, and Choices in Religious Markets: An Examination of Religious Switching and Apostasy." *Social Forces* 73:993–1026.

Siddiqi, Amir Hasan. 1969. *Non-Muslims under Muslim Rule and Muslims under Non-Muslim Rule*. Karachi: Jamiyatul Falah Publications.

Siewert, John A. 1998. Personal communication.

Siewert, John A., and Edna G. Valdez, eds. for MARC. 1997. *Mission Handbook: USA and Canadian Christian Ministries Overseas*. 17th ed. Grand Rapids, MI: Zondervan.

Simpson, George Eaton. 1978. *Black Religions in the New World*. New York: Columbia University Press.

Simpson, John. H. 1996. "'The Great Reversal': Selves, Communities, and the Global System." *Sociology of Religion* 57:115–25.

———. 1979. "Sovereign Groups, Subsistence Activities, and the Presence of a High God in Primitive Societies." In *The Religious Dimension: New Directions in Quantitative Research*, edited by Robert Wuthnow, 299–310. New York: Academic Press.

Sklare, Marshall. 1971. *America's Jews*. New York: Random House.

Skorecki, Karl, Sara Selig, Shraga Blazer, Robert Bradman, Neil Bradman, P. J. Warburton, Monica Ismajlowicz, and Michael F. Hammer. 1997. "Y Chromosomes of Jewish Priests." *Nature* 385 (June 2): 32.

Smallwood, E. Mary. 1981. *The Jews under Roman Rule: From Pompey to Diocletian*. Reprint with corrections. Leiden: E. J. Brill.

Smart, Ninian. 1984. *The Religious Experience of Mankind*. 3d ed. New York: Charles Scribner's Sons.

Smith, Adam. [1776] 1981. *An Inquiry into the Nature and Causes of the Wealth of Nations*. 2 vols. Indianapolis: Liberty Fund.

———. [1759] 1982. *The Theory of Moral Sentiments*. Indianapolis: Liberty Fund.

Smith, Christian. 1998. *American Evangelicalism: Embattled and Thriving*. Chicago: University of Chicago Press.

Smith, Daniel Scott. 1985. "The Dating of the American Sexual Revolution: Evidence and Interpretation." In *Reply to Myth: Perspectives on Intimacy*, edited by John F. Crosby. New York: John Wiley.

Smith, George. 1885. *The Life of William Carey D.D., Shoemaker and Missionary, Professor of Sanskrit, Bengali, and Marathi in the College of Fort William, Calcutta*. London: J. Murray.

Smith, Huston. 1991. *The World's Religions*. San Francisco: HarperSanFrancisco.

Smith, I. Gregory. 1892. *Christian Monasticism: From the Fourth to the Ninth Centuries of the Christian Era*. London: A. D. Innes and Co.

Smith, Lucy Mack [1853] 1996. *History of Joseph Smith by His Mother*. Edited by Scot Facer Procter and Maurine Jensen Procter. Salt Lake City: Bookcraft.

Smith, Timothy L. 1983. "My Rejection of the Cyclical View of 'Great Awakenings' in American Religious History." *Sociological Analysis* 44:97–101.

Smith, Tom W. 1999. "The Religious Right and Anti-Semitism." *Review of Religious Research* 40:244–58.

Smith, W. Robertson. 1889. *The Religion of the Semites: Fundamental Institutions*. Edinburgh: Adam and Charles Black.

Snow, David A., and Richard Machalek. 1983. "The Convert as a Social Type." In *Sociological Theory, 1983*, edited by Randall Collins. San Francisco: Jossey-Bass.

Snow, David A., and Cynthia L. Phillips. 1980. "The Lofland-Stark Conversion Model: A Critical Reassessment." *Social Problems* 27:430–47.

Southern, R. W. 1970. *Western Society and the Church*. Harmondsworth: Penguin Books.

Spencer, Herbert. 1893. *Principles of Sociology*. Rev. ed. Vol. 2. New York: D. Appleton and Company.

Spong, John Shelby. 1992. *Rescuing the Bible from Fundamentalism: A Bishop Rethinks the Meaning of Scripture*. San Francisco: HarperSanFrancisco.

Spuler, Bertold. 1968. *The Muslim World: A Historical Survey*. Leiden: E. J. Brill.

Stanley, Brian. 1992. *The History of the American Baptist Missionary Society, 1792–1992*. Edinburgh: T & T Clark.

Stark, Rodney. In press. "Gods, Rituals, and the Moral Order." *Journal for the Scientific Study of Religion.*

———. 2000. "Physiology and Faith: Addressing the 'Universal' Gender Difference in Religiousness." Paper presented at the Society for the Scientific Study of Religion. Houston.

———. 1999a. "The Micro Foundations of Religion: A Revised Theory." *Sociological Theory* 17:264–89.

———. 1999b. "Atheism, Faith, and the Social Scientific Study of Religion." *Journal of Contemporary Religion* 14:41–62.

———. 1999c. "Secularization, R.I.P." *Sociology of Religion* 60:249–73.

———. 1999d. "A Theory of Revelations." *Journal for the Scientific Study of Religion* 38:286–307.

———. 1998a. *Sociology.* 7th ed. Belmont, CA: Wadsworth.

———. 1998b. "A Theoretical Assessment of LDS Growth." In *Latter-day Saint Social Life: Social Research on the LDS Church and Its Members,* edited by James T. Duke, 29–70. Provo, Utah: Religious Studies Center, Brigham Young University.

———. 1998c. "Spiegare le Variazioni Della Religiosita: il Modello del Mercato" (Explaining international variations in religiousness: the market model). Translated by Maurizio Pisati. *Polis: Ricerche e studi su società e politica in Italia* 12:11–31.

———. 1998d. "Catholic Contexts: Competition, Commitment, and Innovation." *Review of Religious Research* 39:197–208.

———. 1997. "Holy Families: Network Origins of Revealed Religions." Annual Plenary Address, North American Patristics Society, Chicago.

———. 1996a. *The Rise of Christianity: A Sociologist Reconsiders History.* Princeton, NJ: Princeton University Press.

———. 1996b. "Why Religious Movements Succeed or Fail: A Revised General Model." *Journal of Contemporary Religion* 11:133–46.

———. 1996c. "So Far, So Good: A Brief Assessment of Mormon Membership Projections." *Review of Religious Research* 38:175–78.

———. 1993. "Europe's Receptivity to New Religious Movements: Round Two." *Journal for the Scientific Study of Religion* 32:389–97.

———. 1992. "How Sane People Talk to the Gods: A Rational Theory of Revelations." In *Innovation in Religious Traditions: Essays in the Interpretation of Religious Change,* edited by Michael A. Williams, Collet Cox, and Martin S. Jaffe, 19–34. Berlin: Mouton de Gruyter.

———. 1991. "Normal Revelations: A Rational Model of 'Mystical' Experiences." In *Religion and the Social Order,* edited by David G. Bromley, 1:239–51. Greenwich, CT: JAI Press.

———. 1987. "How New Religions Succeed: A Theoretical Model." In *The Future of New Religious Movements*, edited by David Bromley and Phillip E. Hammond, 11–29. Macon: Mercer University Press.

———. 1985. "Europe's Receptivity to Religious Movements." In *New Religious Movements: Genesis, Exodus, and Numbers*, edited by Rodney Stark, 301–43. New York: Paragon.

———. 1983. "Religious Economies: A New Perspective." Conference on New Directions in Religious Research, University of Lethbridge.

———. 1965a. "A Taxonomy of Religious Experience." *Journal for the Scientific Study of Religion* 5:97–116.

———. 1965b. "Social Contexts and Religious Experience." *Review of Religious Research* 7:17–28.

———. 1965c. "A Sociological Definition of Religion." In Charles Y. Glock and Rodney Stark, *Religion and Society in Tension*, 3–17. Chicago: Rand McNally.

———. 1963. "On the Incompatibility of Religion and Science: A Survey of American Graduate Students." *Journal for the Scientific Study of Religion* 3:3–20.

Stark, Rodney, and William Sims Bainbridge. 1997. *Religion, Deviance, and Social Control*. New York: Routledge.

———. [1987], 1996. *A Theory of Religion*. New Brunswick, NJ: Rutgers University Press.

———. 1985. *The Future of Religion: Secularization, Revival and Cult Formation*. Berkeley and Los Angeles: University of California Press, 1985

———. 1980. "Towards a Theory of Religion: Religious Commitment." *Journal for the Scientific Study of Religion* 19:114–28.

———. 1979. "Of Churches, Sects, and Cults: Preliminary Concepts for a Theory of Religious Movements." *Journal for the Scientific Study of Religion* 18:117–31.

Stark, Rodney, and Roger Finke. 2000. *Acts of Faith: Explaining the Human Side of Religion*. Berkeley and Los Angeles: University of California Press.

Stark, Rodney, Bruce D. Foster, Charles Y. Glock, and Harold E. Quinley. 1971. *Wayward Shepherds: Prejudice and the Protestant Clergy*. New York: Harper and Row.

Stark, Rodney, and Laurence R. Iannaccone. 1997. "Why the Jehovah's Witnesses Grow So Rapidly: A Theoretical Application." *Journal of Contemporary Religion* 12:133–57.

Stark, Rodney, and Laurence R. Iannaccone. 1996. "Recent Religious De-clines in Quebec, Poland, and the Netherlands: A Theory Vindicated." *Journal for the Scientific Study of Religion* 35:265–71.

———. 1994. "A Supply-Side Reinterpretation of the "Secularization" of Europe." *Journal for the Scientific Study of Religion* 33:230–52.

———. 1993. "Rational Choice Propositions about Religious Move-ments." In *Religion and the Social Order*, vol. 3, *Handbook on Cults and Sects in America*, edited by David G. Bromley and Jeffrey K. Had-den, 241–61. Greenwich, CT: JAI Press.

Stark, Rodney, and James C. McCann. 1993. "Market Forces and Catho-lic Commitment: Exploring the New Paradigm." *Journal for the Scien-tific Study of Religion* 32:111–23.

Stark, Rodney, and Lynne Roberts. 2001. *Contemporary Social Research Methods*. 3d ed. Belmont, CA: Wadsworth.

———. 1982. "The Arithmetic of Social Movements: Theoretical Impli-cations." *Sociological Analysis* 43:53–68.

Stark, Werner. 1968. "The Place of Catholicism in Max Weber's Sociol-ogy of Religion." *Sociological Analysis* 29:202–10.

Stillman, Norman A. 1979. *The Jews of Arab Lands: A History and Source Book*. Philadelphia: The Jewish Publication Society of America.

Stoll, David. 1990. *Is Latin America Turning Protestant? The Politics of Evangelical Growth*. Berkeley and Los Angeles: University of Califor-nia Press.

Stoneking, Mark. 1998. "Women on the Move." *Nature Genetics* 20 (November): 219–20.

Stow, Kenneth R. 1992. *Alienated Minority: The Jews of Medieval Latin Europe*. Cambridge: Harvard University Press.

Strom, Yale. 1992. *The Expulsion of the Jews: Five Hundred Years of Exodus*. New York: SPI Books.

Swanson, Guy E. 1960. *The Birth of the Gods: The Origin of Primitive Beliefs*. Ann Arbor: University of Michigan Press.

Swatos, William, Jr., ed. 1998. *Encyclopedia of Religion and Society*. Wal-nut Creek, CA: AltaMira Press.

Swatos, William H., Jr., and Loftur Reimar Gissurarson. 1997. *Icelandic Spiritualism: Mediumship and Modernity in Iceland*. New Brunswick, NJ: Transaction.

Sweet, William Warren. 1964. *Religion on the American Frontier, 1783–1840: The Presbyterians*. New York: Cooper Square Publishers.

Swidler, Ann. 1995. "Cultural Power and Social Movements." In *Social Movements and Culture*, edited by H. Johnson and B. Klandermans, 25–40. Minneapolis: University of Minnesota Press.

———. 1986. "Culture in Action: Symbols and Strategies." *American Sociological Review* 51:273–86.

Sywulka, Stephen R. 1996. "John Paul Woos Straying Flock: Protestants Object to Being Labeled as 'Sects.'" *Christianity Today*, April 8, 94.

Szathmáry, Eörs. 1999. "When the Means Do Not Justify the End." *Nature*, June 24, 745.

Tash, Robert C. 1991. *Dutch Pluralism*. New York: Lang.

Taylor, Marylee C., and Thomas F. Pettigrew. 1992. "Prejudice." In *Encyclopedia of Sociology*, edited by Edgar F. Borgatta and Marie L. Borgatta, 1536–41. New York: Macmillan.

Tcherikover, Victor. 1958. "The Ideology of the Letter of Aristeas." *Harvard Theological Review* 51:59–85.

Thomas, George M. 1989. *Revivalism and Cultural Change*. Chicago: University of Chicago Press.

Thomas, Hugh. 1979. *A History of the World*. New York: Harper and Row.

Thomas, Keith. 1971. *Religion and the Decline of Magic*. New York: Scribner's.

Thomas, Mark G., Karl Skorecki, Haim Ben-Ami, Tudor Parfitt, Neil Bradman, and David B. Goldstein. 1998. "Origins of Old Testament Priests." *Nature* 394 (July 9): 138–40.

Thompson, E. A. 1966. *The Visigoths in the Time of Ulfila*. Oxford: Clarendon Press.

Thompson, Thomas L. 1996. "The Intellectual Matrix of Early Biblical Narrative: Inclusive Monotheism in Persian Period Palestine." In *The Triumph of Elohim: From Yahwisms to Judaisms*, edited by Diana Vikander Edelman, 107–24. Grand Rapids, MI: Eerdmans.

———. 1992. *Early History of the Israelite People: From the Written and Archaeological Sources*. Leiden: Brill.

Thucydides. [ca. 420 B.C.E.] 1954. *The Peloponnesian War*. London: Penguin Books.

Tillich, Paul. 1951. *Systematic Theology*. Vol. 1. Chicago: University of Chicago Press.

Timberlake, Charles. 1995. "Fate of the Russian Orthodox Monasteries and Convents since 1917." *Donald W. Treadgold Papers*, no. 103.

Henry M. Jackson School of International Studies, University of Washington.

Tökés, László. 1990. "The Possible Role of Rumania's Churches on the Social Renewal of the Country." *Occasional Papers on Religion in Eastern Europe* 10, no. 5:29–32.

Townes, Charles H. 1995. *Making Waves*. Woodbury, NY: The American Institute of Physics.

Traboulay, David M. 1994. *Columbus and Las Casas: The Conquest and Christianization of America, 1492–1566*. Lanham, MD: University Press of America.

Troyanovsky, Igor, ed. 1991. *Religion in the Soviet Republics*. San Francisco: HarperSanFrancisco.

Tuchman, Barbara W. 1978. *A Distant Mirror: The Calamitous Fourteenth Century*. New York: Ballantine Books.

Turner, Bryan S. 1991. *Religion and Social Theory*. London: Sage.

Twain, Mark. 1901. "To the Person Sitting in Darkness," and "To My Missionary Critics." *North American Review* 172:160–76, 520–34.

Tylor, Edward Burnett. [1871] 1958. *Religion in Primitive Culture*. New York: Harper and Brothers.

Underhill, Evelyn. 1942. *Mysticism*. 14th ed. London: Methuen and Company.

Underhill, Ralph. 1975. "Economic and Political Antecedents of Monotheism: A Cross-cultural Study." *American Journal of Sociology* 80:841–61.

U.S. Census. 1919. *Religious Bodies*. Washington, DC: U.S. Government Printing Office.

United States Department of State. 1999. *Final Report of the Advisory Committee on Religious Freedom Abroad*. Washington, DC: U.S. Government Printing Office.

Van Wagoner, Richard S. 1994. *Sidney Rigdon: A Portrait of Religious Excess*. Salt Lake City: Signature Books.

Vital, David. 1999. *A People Apart: The Jews in Europe 1789–1939*. Oxford: Oxford University Press.

Voyé, Liliane, and Karel Dobbelaere. 1994. "Roman Catholicism: Universalism at Stake." In *Religions Sans Frontières?*, edited by Roberto Cipriani, 83–113. Rome: Dipartimento per L'Informazione e Editoria.

Wade, Nicholas. 1999. "DNA Backs Tribe's Tradition of Early Descent from the Jews." *New York Times*, May 9, 1, 20.

Waines, David. 1995. *An Introduction to Islam*. Cambridge: Cambridge University Press.

Walker, F. Deaville. 1926. *William Carey, Missionary Pioneer and Statesman*. London: Student Christian Movement.

Wallace, Anthony F. C. 1966. *Religion: An Anthropological View*. New York: Random House.

———. 1956. "Revitalization Movements." *American Anthropologist* 58:264–81.

Wallerstein, Immanuel. 1984. *The Politics of the World Economy*. New York: Cambridge University Press.

———. 1974. *The Modern World System*. New York: Academica Press.

Walter, Tony, and Grace Davie. 1998. "The Religiosity of Women in the Modern West." *British Journal of Sociology* 49:640–60.

Ward, Roy Bowen. 1992. "James of Jerusalem in the First Two Centuries." In *Aufstieg und Niedergana der Römichen Welt*, edited by Hildegard Temporini and Wolfgang Haase, 780–813. Berlin and New York: De Gruyter.

Ware, Bishop Kallistos (Timothy). 1997. *The Orthodox Church*. London: Penguin Books.

———. 1979. *The Orthodox Way*. Crestwood, NY: St. Vladimir's Seminary Press.

Warner, R. Stephen. 1997. "Convergence toward the New Paradigm: A Case of Induction." In *Assessing Rational Choice Theories of Religion*, edited by Lawrence A. Young, 87–101. New York: Routledge.

———. 1993. "Work in Progress towards a New Paradigm for the Sociological Study of Religion in the United States." *American Journal of Sociology* 98:1044–93.

———. 1979. "Theoretical Barriers to the Understanding of Evangelical Christianity." *Sociological Analysis* 40:1–9.

Washington, Peter. 1995. *Madame Blavatsky's Baboon*. New York: Schocken Books.

Waterfield, Robin E. 1973. *Christians in Persia*. London: George Allen & Unwin.

Watt, W. Montgomery. 1961. *Muhammad: Prophet and Statesman*. London: Oxford University Press.

Waxman, Chaim I. 2000. *Jewish Baby Boomers*. Albany: SUNY Press.

Weaver, Mary Jo (with David Brakke and Jason Bivins). 1998. *Introduction to Christianity*. 3d ed. Belmont, CA: Wadsworth.

Weber, Max. [1922] 1993. *The Sociology of Religion*. Boston: Beacon Press.

———. [1917–1919] 1952. *Ancient Judaism*. Glencoe, IL: The Free Press.

Weber, Max. 1946. *From Max Weber: Essays in Sociology.* Edited by H. H. Gerth and C. Wright Mills. New York: Oxford University Press.

Weightman, Simon. 1984. "Hinduism." In *A Handbook of Living Religions*, edited by John R. Hinnells, 191–236. London: Penguin Books.

Weisskopf, Michael. 1993. "'Gospel Grapevine' Displays Strength in Controversy over Military Gay Ban." *Washington Post*, February 1, A1, A10.

Wertheimer, Jack. 1993. *A People Divided: Judaism in Contemporary America.* New York: Basic Books.

Wessels, Anton. 1994. *Europe, Was It Ever Really Christian?* London: SCM Press, 1994.

Whitefield, George. [1747] 1969. *George Whitefield's Journals.* Gainsville, FL: Scholars' Facsimiles and Reprints.

Whittaker, Thomas. 1911. *Priests, Philosophers and Prophets: A Dissertation on Revealed Religion.* London: Adam and Charles Black.

Williams, Michael Allen. 1996. *Rethinking "Gnosticism": An Argument for Dismantling a Dubious Category.* Princeton, NJ: Princeton University Press.

Williams, Robin M., Jr. 1951. *American Society.* New York: Alfred A. Knopf.

Wilson, A. N. 1999. *God's Funeral.* New York: W. W. Norton.

Wilson, Bryan. 1975. *Magic and the Millennium.* Frogmore (England): Paladin.

Winock, Michel. 1998. *Nationalism, Antisemitism, and Fascism in France.* Stanford, CA: Stanford University Press.

Witham, Larry. 1998. "France Determines Jehovah's Witnesses Are Not a Religion." *Washington Times* (National Weekly Edition), July 6–12, 21.

Wolfram, Herwig. 1997. *The Roman Empire and Its Germanic Peoples.* Berkeley and Los Angeles: University of California Press.

Wood, Gordon S. 1993. "Founding a Nation, 986–1787." In *The Almanac of American History*, edited by Arthur M. Schlesinger, Jr., 15–143. New York: Barnes and Noble.

Wurmbrand, Max, in collaboration with Cecil Roth. 1966. *The Jewish People: Four Thousand Years of Survival.* Jerusalem: Massadah-P.E.C Press.

Yamane, David, and Megan Polzer. 1994. "Ways of Seeing Ecstasy in Modern Society: Experiential-Expressive and Cultural-Linguistic Views." *Sociology of Religion* 55:1–25.

Yates, T. E. 1994. *Christian Mission in the Twentieth Century.* Cambridge: Cambridge University Press.

Yearbook of Jehovah's Witnesses. Published annually. Brooklyn: Watchtower Bible and Tract Society of New York.

Yuval, Israel. 1995. "The Haggadah of Passover and Easter." *Tarbiz* 65:5–29.

Zagorska, Anna. 1998. "Sharing the Power: The Growth of Non-Traditional Religions in Poland." *Religion in Eastern Europe* 18, no. 2:1–16.

Zernov, Nicolas. 1959. Christianity: The Eastern Schism and the Eastern Orthodox Church." In *The Concise Encyclopaedia of Living Faiths,* edited by R. C. Zaehner, 86–107. Boston: Beacon Press.

Ziegler, Philip. 1971. *The Black Death.* New York: Harper Torchbooks.

Zinsser, Hans. [1934] 1960. *Rats, Lice and History.* New York: Bantam.

Zürcher, Eric. [1959] 1972. *The Buddhist Conquest of China.* Leiden: E. J. Brill.

Following page references, *i* indicates illustration; *p* indicates photograph; *t* indicates table; and *m* indicates map.